THIS IS MY GOD

Works by Herman Wouk

Aurora Dawn
City Boy
The Caine Mutiny
Marjorie Morningstar
Youngblood Hawke
Don't Stop the Carnival
The Winds of War
War and Remembrance
Inside, Outside
The Hope
The Glory

This Is My God (nonfiction)
The Caine Mutiny Court-Martial (play)

THIS IS MY GOD

The Jewish Way of Life

HERMAN WOUK

This is my God, and I will praise him;
The God of my father, and I will exalt him.

Exodus 15:2, The Song of Moses

BACK BAY BOOKS

LITTLE, BROWN AND COMPANY
BOSTON • NEW YORK • LONDON • TORONTO

ISBN 0-316-95514-0

Library of Congress Cataloging-in-Publication information is available.

10 9 8 7 6 5 4

MV NY

Published simultaneously in Canada
by Little, Brown & Company (Canada) Limited

PRINTED IN THE UNITED STATES OF AMERICA

This book is dedicated to the memory of my grandfather and teacher, Mendel Leib Levine, rabbi in Minsk, New York, and Tel Aviv. His lifetime of ninety-four years stretched from the last days of Abraham Lincoln to the first years of the nuclear era. He served as a Jewish jurist and minister under czarism and communism, in the freedom of America, and in the reborn land of Israel, where his bones lie.

The book with all its earnings belongs to a fund for charity and education established by my wife and myself in 1954, in memory of our first-born son, Abe.

Nobody can be more aware of the deep lacks in *This Is My God* than I am. The theme needs a prophet. The subject needs monumental scholarship. I offer the book, relying on the maxim of Rabbi Tarfon in *Ethics of the Fathers:*

"The work is not yours to finish; but neither are you free to take no part in it."

HERMAN WOUK

Contents

Preface to the New Standard Edition

IN 1959, when *This Is My God* first appeared, the new Jewish State was in its eleventh year of independence. Most Jews in other lands regarded it with sympathy, lent it charitable support, and kept their distance; a few Diaspora Zionists crusaded in vain for a mass return to the homeland; a few anti-Zionists loudly proclaimed that Israel had no claim whatever on their resources or loyalties. Such were the conditions in which this work was composed.

The twenty-second chapter of this book, entitled "Israel," was accurate enough in 1959. Today it mainly shows, dated as it is, how amazingly the country has advanced in three decades. We live in a new Jewish era now. After the Six-Day War, I wrote a postscript to this book, "The Ashes and the Gold," which recorded the way my own ideas were changing under the impact of Israel's struggles and triumphs. For this edition, I have further updated my picture of the Jewish State with an added essay, "Israel at Forty: The Land and the Faith."

On rereading *This Is My God,* I find little else that I would alter. I have become more interested in Hasidism, but I remain essentially an admirer, rather than a participant, of that mystical sect. My knowledge of Yiddish literature has grown, and I am less pessimistic now about its survival. Modern Hebrew literature, too, interests me more. All in all, if I were to write it afresh now, the book would have a more intensely Jewish tone. In 1959 I was preoccupied with proving that an educated Westerner could live a traditional Jewish existence, not only without any intellectual sacrifices, but much to his enrichment. Today I take that for granted.

But *This Is My God* is written already. Its portrayal of what is timeless in the Jewish religion remains as accurate as I could make it. I am glad that I have received, in a large volume of mail from readers in many countries, no substantial correction necessary to the text. I am grateful to my publishers, Little, Brown, for bringing out the work in this handsome new durable format.

The success of *This Is My God* has been a satisfying reward for a labor of love. I planned the work for fellow Jews, perhaps a few thousand of them, who had an impulse to learn about the faith but lacked the time or the Hebraic grasp to study the sources. Instead, the book has found a place as an informal popular guide and reference work, for Jew and Gentile alike. Therefore, I have added a subtitle, *The Jewish Way of Life.*

There are many Jewish ways of life in this day and age. I know that well. In my book I describe them. But the departure point of all of them was and remains our ancient and living faith. The very name for the Mosaic Law in tradition is *Halakha* — the Way.

For those who are looking for that Way, and for those who are merely curious about it; for anyone who wants to know something clear and true about our eternal people, I wrote this plain book.

Herman Wouk

Palm Springs
15 March 1987
Purim 5747

Part 1

✦

THE REMARKABLE SURVIVAL OF THE JEWS

Prologue

A Jewish friend of mine, a skeptic far removed from practice of Judaism or belief in it—I must add, an admirable man with a keen mind—one chill evening in November said to me rather shyly and casually, "This may surprise you, but can you recommend to me any good reading matter on Hanuka? I think my son should know a bit more about his Jewish background than he does." With a sidelong glance of wry humor he added, "Purely for culture, you understand, not for religion!"

It is not often that anyone, even a prolix fellow like a novelist, sits down and writes a book in answer to an offhand question, but I'm afraid that is what I have done here. Obviously the book was waiting to be put on paper; my friend's inquiry only precipitated it. I have wanted for some years to write an account of the Jewish faith.

Judaism has always been a strong interest of mine. It is part of my life and of my family's life. My two sons speak Hebrew, and are familiar with the Scriptures and with rabbinic literature. That is the way we live. With this background, I may be able to sketch the faith so as to give the interested reader information and pleasure, using what writing skill I have learned to keep from boring him with detail, or with my own not very relevant theories.

There are many Jews who do not observe the religion, who yet would like to know a lot more about it. There are non-Jews, too, who now and then grow curious about the old Hebrew faith. But the literature is so vast, it is usually so scholarly in tone, and so much of it is not in English, that such readers are often at a stand, not knowing where to begin. I offer this volume as a beginning.

Of course, one man's minimum information is another man's choke of detail. I have tried to steer a middle course. If scholars choose to glance at this book I hope they will not conclude, seeing all that I have left out, that my ignorance is equal to the omissions. Cutting has been much of my labor. I have had to write a short book about a subject that spans nearly all history, that fills whole libraries, that ranges across the classic problems of human life, and that causes turbulent many-sided controversy to this hour. The undertaking forced appalling compression.

God

There is no use in talking about religion with anybody who is sure that God does not exist. My book will irritate such a person and give him no light. I cannot change his mind, and I am not attempting it. But I suggest that agnosticism, when it becomes an ear-stopping dogma, may be as bad a mental handicap as superstition. There has never been any decisive proof either way about God's existence. Ours would be a decidedly queer world if the Creator of it were as visible as, say, a playwright at his opening night. Here is the universe, a dazzle of orderly wonders, which seems to imply a Maker. Here is human life, full of sadness and disaster and futility, ending always in black death; and it seems to many people to refute any notion that a God could exist. To assert anything about God — that he is there or that he is not, that we can know him or that we cannot — is to jump off into the dark, either way.

Religious people tend to encounter, among those who are not, a cemented certainty that belief in God is a crutch for the weak and the fearful. It would be just as silly to assert that disbelief in God is a crutch for the immoral and the ill-read. I am hard put to it not to smile when a man who has obviously read nothing in the field beyond, say, a pleasing agnostic summary like *Man and His Gods* tells me generously — and as though he were inventing the notion — that it is fine for people to be religious if they get solace out of it.

Now the belief in God may turn out at the last trump to be a mistake. Meantime, let us be quite clear, it is not merely the comfort of the simple — though it is that too, much to its glory — it is a formidable intellectual position with which most of the first-class minds of the human race, century in and century out, have concurred, each in his own way. We live in a time when non-belief is in fashion; it has been for about a hundred years. Hence the regular pulsing of rationalist books from popular book clubs and paperback publishers. But this popularity of one point of view should be enough to make any serious man suspicious. Sheep are sheep, whether they are all leaping over the fence or all huddling in the fold.

Kierkegaard, who dug his heels in a century ago, stands now in the van of new thought. His deeply religious books, neglected for a hundred years, have not changed. The vanguard is changing direction, that is all. It is becoming all too clear that — speaking of crutches — Freud can be a crutch, Marx can be a crutch, rationalism can be a crutch, and atheism can be two canes and a pair of iron braces. We none of us have all the answers, nor are we likely to have. But in the country of the halt, the man who is surest he has no limp may be the worst-crippled.

It will fall on me to tell the views of God in Judaism as well as I can. In a diagrammed kind of book, such a chapter would perhaps come first. I have to hope that the Hebrew idea of the Creator will rise from the whole picture drawn here. I know I can describe the life of our religion, but I suppose my hand will falter when I get into theology. Nevertheless I will do my best. I record at the outset my awareness that questions about God haunt every page of this book. I write for people who have at least an open mind on God, and who would like to know something about the Jewish way to him.

A book on Judaism is almost bound to make out some case. The subject defies impartiality. To write anything at all about it is to take a stand. The reader will soon see that I believe the survival of the Jewish people looks like the hand of Providence in history; and that I also believe in the law of Moses as the key to our survival. Many Jews who feel strongly about their Jewishness will differ from the viewpoint I am taking. If the book attracts attention, there will be controversy. My aim is to waken interest in Judaism. Those who dispute my work will be serving the same cause by their best lights.

There are people — and they are not few, and not stupid — who honestly think that the absorption of the Jews into mankind at large is the only sensible end to the Jewish problem, and one that is long overdue. This book stands at the other pole. I believe it is our lot to live and to serve in our old identity, until the promised day when the Lord will be one and his name one in all the earth. I think the extinction of Jewish learning and Jewish faith would be a measureless tragedy.

Purpose

In the United States today, Jews live as free and equal citizens, a status they have seldom known elsewhere during their long saga. In Israel, they walk their holy soil as free men, a visible miracle that still staggers the thoughtful mind. Behind the iron curtain, they have a formal socialist equality, the price of which is the loss of their culture. Everywhere, because of the huge changes of the past century, there has been an attrition of Jewish learning, with a sharp drop in knowledge.

This kind of thing has happened before, during eras of wide change. The books of Ezra and Nehemiah, rising from the Babylonian exile, describe a Jewish community much closer to ignorance and extinction than ours is. Happily the revival through study is today well under way, in the lands where we are free. My hope is that, in this study, my book will be of some use as an elementary tool.

The reader will find me dwelling on those things in Jewry and Judaism that are attractive and impressive. I think they are the chief things. In every generation the faults of the Jews — and we are as full of faults as other men — have been publicized with exaggerations and lies. The Nazis spent millions to portray us to the world as subhuman, in a prologue to the attempt to destroy our people, man, woman, and child. In this book I intend to speak of my faith and my people as well as I can, and I will tell the truth.

One note on style: if I sometimes write here with a light hand, it is not because I am the less serious in what I say. It is no service to the reader to load him with technical jargon to convince him that my words have weight. I have risked being as clear and pleasant as I could, and I have worked very hard for clarity.

Chapter 1

Who Are We?

THE Jewish people is over three thousand years old. Archaeology has long since verified this startling tradition which our grandfathers took on faith. Many thinkers have tried, and are still trying, to account for this survival of a folk, a religion, and a culture through three millennia of nearly impossible historical conditions. The fact itself is as unique in history as the velocity of light is in physics. It needs explaining.

The Bible, our ancestors' source book of history, says the Jews descend from a Mesopotamian nomad named Abraham, who came with his flocks and his tents in the shadowy dawn of history to Canaan, the place we now call Israel. The line traces through his son Isaac to his grandson Jacob, who migrated to Egypt with his large household to escape a famine. Jacob's family prospered and multiplied in the cattle-raising northern province of Goshen.

Egypt was then the glory of Mediterranean civilization, the Rome or America of its day, brilliant in arts and sciences, formidable in war. Its architecture and sculpture have in some respects never been surpassed. Its government was an unchanging tyranny of Pharaohs, bureaus, and priests. Its religion, like all religion of the day, was a foul tangle of idolatry. The rites were obscene, the myths childish, the gods weird half-human, half-bestial monsters. An obsession with death and magic ruled the land.

Instead of becoming Egyptian cattle barons, the prolific family descended from Jacob retained its separate identity, growing into a sort of nation within the nation. What set these people apart from Egypt was their religion. Abraham had passed to his descendants, the Bible says, a vision of a great invisible Spirit, the Creator of the universe, who had promised them an eventual life in the land of Israel, and a historic destiny as teachers of mankind. The Bible goes on to say that Egypt in time made slaves of the strange folk within its borders. An emancipator arose among them, Moses the Lawgiver, who in a spectacular, in some respects supernatural, triumph freed the slaves and led them through the desert to the border of the promised land. His greatest feat, however, was not this deliverance.

At a mountain in the desert called Horeb or Sinai he experienced — and his people to some extent experienced with him — a mystic occurrence which changed the history of the world. What exactly happened in the revelation at Sinai we are not likely ever to know. The Bible speaks of prodigies of nature that recall a volcano in eruption. No other volcanic eruption has ever resulted in a body of statutes that became the law of civilization. When the Israelites left Horeb to resume their trek to the promised land they were no longer a tribe held together by faith, but a nation living under a statutory law, or *Torah,* given at the hand of Moses as the word of the Creator.

This Torah contained folk history as well as law; and it concluded with an accurate prophecy of the future of the Jews. The prediction was that after a brilliant period of monarchy in the Holy Land they would become calloused by prosperity, would lose their hold on the advanced religion that had made them a nation, and would slide into the idolatry of their Semitic neighbors, with resulting political collapse, military defeat, and national destruction. The Torah prophesied that a remnant of the people would survive in a long agony of exile, undergoing ordeals of wandering and persecution; that they would never die out; and that in the far after time they would return to Israel to live by the law of Moses, and to be a light to the nations.

Of this vast drama, most of the acts have long since passed from prophecy into history. Some Christians indeed hold that the curtain went down on the whole story forever two thousand years ago. We Jews believe — it is cardinal to our faith — that the last acts are still to come.

How True Is All This?

At the low ebb of respect for the Bible in the eighteenth and early nineteenth centuries, when the world's best minds were still laboring to cast off the straitjacket of the dark ages, the view became popular that the Bible's history was a mass of old wives' tales, that Moses was an invention like Apollo, and that neither the Exodus from Egypt nor any of its related events ever occurred. Then the science of archaeology arose. As its discoveries multiplied, respect for the Bible as a source book of ancient events revived. This process is still going on. The extent to which the Hebrew Scriptures stand confirmed by external evidence is not quite general knowledge. Fashionable writers tend to echo the commonplaces of the nineteenth century; such tides reverse themselves slowly, with long slack water. Archaeologists have known for some time that the history of eastern Mediterranean civilization in the Bible is accurate; that we have in hand substantial corroboration of the main points of the Jewish national narrative; that in fact — setting aside the miraculous details which the scientific mind in principle demurs from — it all happened.

The writers of the Bible were of course not cool historians

but passionate prophets. They did not select, organize, and judge facts the way a modern university professor does. Professors bear this in mind when they read the Bible. But they cannot dispense with this all-encompassing document of ancient days. That Moses lived and legislated, that the descendants of Abraham conquered Canaan, that the Hebrew monarchy rose and fell — no serious thinker questions these things anymore.

When we reach the records of Greece and Rome, which in large measure needed no digging out because they have been the continuous possession of learned men, we are — from the Jewish viewpoint — practically in the vicinity of yesterday's newspaper. Greece and Rome knew the Jews and the Mosaic law very well, and reported about them at length. There are chaotic times after the fall of Rome when the Jewish narrative becomes for a while much harder to reconstruct than in the imperial eras. But we know that during those times the Jews went on living and observing their law.

To sum up, then, we are Israelites, descended from the small nation which came out of the Sinai desert into Canaan three thousand years ago, with a tradition of liberation from Egypt, under a lawgiver and deliverer named Moses. We are called Jews, and our heritage Judaism, because in the political decline and fall of our nation the tribe which held out longest and became the surviving remnant in exile predicted by the Torah was named Judah.

Almost all living Jews stem, at a remove of no more than four or five generations at the most, from observant Jews. Historically, Israelites who have discontinued the practice of the law of Moses have faded into the environment and lost their identity within a century or two. The attrition over the centuries has of course been enormous. The Jews who are left are mainly the sons and grandsons of those who have kept the faith, preserving the chain unbroken through time, from the twentieth century back to the sunrise of the human intelligence.

Before examining this faith, we can surely acknowledge two things: first, that as a feat of gallantry of the spirit of man, the preservation of Judaism ranks high; second, that if ancient lineage be a source of legitimate pride, the Jews have a right to be a proud people.

Proud?

How odd
Of God
To choose
The Jews

runs the old doggerel:* to which many Christians, and not a few Jews, incline to say under their breath "Amen," despite the pressure in our land today against criticism of minorities.

Get two non-Jews confiding in each other, after cautiously finding that they have enough common ground not to mistake each other for the kind of mental defective called an anti-Semite, and they are likely to agree that notwithstanding all this liberal talk Jews tend to be brash, pushing, sharp in business, vulgar in manners, loud in public, and so clannish that they band in a knot against the Christian world. They will also agree that they know Jews who are different, and that they number such Jews among their valued friends. There are, of course, many Christians who will take no part in such an exchange. But the reader will recognize the commonplaces.

*The late Sir Peter Medawar once reminded me of the classic doggerel retort:

Though not as odd as those who choose
A Jewish God and spurn the Jews.

— HW (1987)

There are Jews who think even less of themselves and their background than critical Christians do. They are not so ready to confide these impressions to each other; it is too easy to give offense.

But let us take a well-to-do and fairly cultivated Jew of this mind. To give him a character we will make him a successful minor executive, or perhaps an accountant or a lawyer. He is a graduate of a good eastern college. He lives in a pleasant suburban home. He likes to read serious books, classic and modern, and has almost all of Trollope on his shelves. His state-of-the-art stereo system is rather his pride, and he has a genuine love for Brahms. His golf and tennis are good, and sailing is his chief pleasure. His grandparents were fairly religious, his parents much less so, and he is wholly indifferent. He barbecues pork chops or steaks in his barbecue pit with equal pleasure, with not a trace of bother because pork is pork. Of late he may have joined a temple in the neighborhood, because his children seemed at loose ends without any religious ticketing; or he may have made a point, in an argument with his wife, against joining an institution representing a faith that is quite alien to him. He is a warm, good-hearted, charitable, and exceptionally intelligent American.

Now we see him walking down Fifth Avenue after a hard day at his Rockefeller Center office, taking the pleasant evening air instead of hurrying in a taxi to Grand Central. Two men pass him on the street. They are obvious vestigial survivors of some ghetto destroyed by Hitler. The older one wears a beard and a hat trimmed with fur, and gray earlocks curl down his cheeks; he is dressed in a long rusty black coat, though the day is warm. The younger man is pallid and clean-shaven, and he has ordinary American clothes, yet he looks hardly less alien than his companion. His hat is too big, and he wears it at a clumsy angle, far back on his head. His jacket is double-breasted, in a time when no alert man will be caught dead in a double-breasted suit (unless he is an Englishman wearing the really newest thing, cut in London, and subtly different from the old double-breasted, and this fellow is obviously not such a one). His trousers are not well pressed, and they do not taper as they should, so that they seem to flop about his ankles. He has an odd abstracted look around the eyes. The two men are talking in Yiddish, with sweeping hand gestures. As they pass our man, these two unmistakable Jews, he is filled with resentment. He cries out in his heart — it will not do to shout it in the street — "I am not one of you! If you are Jews, I am not a Jew!" His misery is double because he knows that he could actually shout this through a bullhorn to all the world, and it would make no difference. He is one of them.

And yet why is he? What has he in common with these people from a group of which he knows little and wants to know less? He has dim memories of the atmosphere in his grandparents' home, and these men bring unpleasantly to mind the recollection of the boredom, the peculiarity, the ball-and-chain dragginess of the Judaism he found there. These old people were meshed in a web of taboos which disabled them from living contemporary lives. They went through the motions of bizarre customs without being able to explain them. There was foolishness about not striking matches or turning on lights on holidays; niggling suspicion about the ingredients of packaged foods; obdurate mistrust and disdain, based on no intelligible reasons, for anybody who lived differently or believed differently. He visited the apartment of his grandparents with reluctance, and came into the sunlight of the street with the joy of a man getting out of jail. If there is anything he is sure of in this unstable world, it is that he has not, and never will have, anything in common with this grimy ghost of a dead culture.

These men who pass him on Fifth Avenue offend him not only because they tar him with the brush of the alien; they offend him by being alive today, by keeping up that dead culture and confronting him with it, by insisting with their mere presence in the street that he is burying a part of his background that cannot be buried. They are skeletons out of his closet.

It may be that he has heard of modern individuals who are actually "orthodox": a doctor, or a lawyer, or a businessman here and there. It may even be that he has met such people and found them oddly like himself, so far as tastes in books, music, and clothes go, but clinging to the nonsense of food pickiness and Sabbaths. He finds them incomprehensible, and has dismissed them as neurotics who have somehow plugged up a bad hole in their psyches with this stuff.

Tell such a man that he should be proud of being a Jew, and he will laugh at you. Tell him that he is a member of a chosen people, and he will be ready to take off his coat and fight you, so deeply do you affront everything he believes. It would be a hopeless task for the most eloquent writer that ever lived, I suppose, to get him to think differently, except for one thing.

It is this. Deep in the heart of both critical Christian and alienated Jew, there is a — I cannot say what, a feeling, not even a feeling, a shadow of a notion, nothing more substantial than the pointless but compelling impulse to knock on wood when one talks of the health of children — *something* that says there is more to the Jews than meets the eye. There is a mystery about the Jews. This mystery makes the very word "Jew" a sure shocker on the stage. Because of this mystery many readers will come to this book and read it through, disagreeing, it may be, with every line of it, but pressing forward to find some light on the puzzle. And within this mystery lies the reason for the folk pride of the House of Abraham. This pride exists despite the disabilities that come from many centuries of ostracism, including lack of polish and — in the vanishing extreme — earlocks and fur hats, the defiant proud old answer of Jewry to the yellow badge of the ghetto.

The Mystery

Some time ago there was a great stir in the state of Israel over the question, "Who is a Jew?" One would think that after some thirty-five hundred years of continuous history a people would have worked out a fairly handy definition of itself. But the disputants went at it as though nobody had ever thought of the problem before.

It was an urgent discussion because the matter of Israeli citizenship was at stake. The land having been born as a refuge for oppressed Jewry, its founding law held that any Jew could become a citizen at once by declaring he wanted to. This eventually led to the question, Did *anyone* who would elect to acquire Israeli citizenship by that act declare himself a Jew? Just what was a Jew? The debate died away at last in mutters of hard disagreement, as it always has. I believe the government appointed a commission to look into the matter; the classic political way of dropping a hot potato. Perhaps by the time this book goes to press the commission will have solved the problem to everyone's pleasure. The odds are against it.

In the United States you can start a parlor argument any time on the same question. Various disputants will hold that the Jews are a race, or a nation, or a religion, or a people, or a sect, or a state of mind in non-Jews. Agreement on the topic does not occur (except among the anti-Semites, who know that the Jews are international fiends). I can here describe how Judaism itself defines what a Jew is. But I do so without expecting that my version will settle a question which has so long defied time and wisdom.

Note that our history ascribes several strange things to us that no other people today claims or particularly wants to claim. The first is that we began as a family. A nation of some eleven million souls descends from one man, Abraham, and one tribal house, Israel.

The second thing is that blood is not decisive in this kinship. Faith is. A man or woman who undertakes to worship the God of Abraham, and to follow his law given at the hand of Moses, can become a member of our ancient house. In this way, though we are not a faith that crusades for converts, our numbers have much expanded, and we have gained some of our noted leaders and scholars. Scripture too tells of such adopted kin. By the reverse way, through apostasy, we have lost a great many Jews. So strong, however, is the identifying strain of Hebrew descent, that a Jew who converts to another faith remains in the eyes of the world a converted Jew, no more. Descent, then, or faith, determines who is a Jew. So our tradition holds.

The third thing is that our nation came into existence before it had a land. We received our statutory law from Moses in the desert. Nationhood for other peoples means first of all living together in one place. The Jews are peculiarly a nation in time. They sprang into being not in a certain place, for even their father Abraham was a wanderer, but at a certain time, long before they could call any soil their own. This fact, I believe, lay under their ability to survive so long the loss of their soil. The Holy Land was their historic fulfillment, but not their origin.

The strangest thing of all is the purpose that our tradition ascribes to our history and origin. It is frankly supernatural. Tradition says the Creator gave our folk the task of bearing witness to his moral law on earth. This is what the battered phrase "the chosen people" means. Our history, in the Scriptures and afterward, is in the main a melancholy account of our failure to live up to this high election, and the catastrophes that came from our failure. But the election stands, the mission remains, and we live because these things are so. That is what our faith teaches.

"The Chosen People"

But this is an idea calculated to make any thinking modern person uneasy. We had better take a good look at it.

There are obvious "chosen people" around us, of course, envied by all. There is the elegant and durable British ruling class. There are the international darlings of money and power who race the blooded horses, fly the chartered planes, sail the private yachts, and squire the beautiful actresses. There are the strong dour men who sit on the boards of our giant corporations, and who prefer never to be photographed. There are the tough privilege-cliques of Communist countries. These people, chosen by birth, events, or luck to be the elite, are noted for the general absence of Jews among them.

There are lesser groups of the chosen in the arts, in industry, in sports, in finance, in the fashionable world. One finds them dwelling in the finest city neighborhoods and suburbs, or playing in the luxury hotels and the upper-crust clubs. Here one may find some Jewish people, but they will be a conspicuous minority.

Where then is the "chosen" aspect of the Jews? Is it solely in their own minds? That would make them no different from the in-groups all over the world, the Babbitts of Zenith, Boston, Moscow, Paris, Buenos Aires, and every smaller community, blissfully sure that theirs is the best way of life, and that they are the best people. It is an old joke that the provincial worships himself for his own provincialism. If "the chosen people" meant no more than that, it would be part of the common folly of men, and not worth discussing.

But it is the Holy Bible that so describes the Jews. The quotations run into the thousands. The theme rules Scripture. Here are verses at random from the book which most of the Western world takes in one sense or another as the oracles of God:

> Genesis 12:
>
> . . . God said to Abram, Go from your country, your birthplace, your father's house, to the land that I will show you. And I will make of you a great nation . . . and in you shall all families of the earth be blessed. . . .
>
> Exodus 19:
>
> . . . Now therefore if you will truly obey my voice, and keep my covenant, then you will be a peculiar treasure to me of all the peoples, for all the earth is mine. And you shall be for me a nation of priests, and a holy people. . . .
>
> Isaiah 49:
>
> . . . And I will give you as a light to the nations, that my salvation may reach to the end of the earth. . . .

Christianity accepts this view of Jewish destiny and rests on it. An important Christian doctrine (as I understand it) is that Jesus broadened this chosen communion to include all those who believed in his divinity and followed his teachings. For this reason an accepted Christian name for the church is "The New Israel." Christianity added one vital point: those who did not enter the new communion risked, or in some views actually incurred, eternal damnation.

But this idea of salvation limited to one group never had

any place in the Jewish faith and has no place in it today. In Judaism right conduct is the path to God. This path lies open to Jews and non-Jews.

The Jewish faith does not even claim that the Jews originated the worship of one God. The Book of Genesis teaches that this worship existed in Abraham's time. It was, and it is, the universal ethical religion of right-thinking men. Our tradition calls it the law of the sons of Noah, resting on seven grand precepts:

The worship of God
The ban on murder
The ban on theft
The ban on incest and sex aberrations
The ban on eating "the limb of the living" — cruelty to animals
The ban on blasphemy
Justice — the establishment of courts, judges, and a system of equity.

Nations and persons that live by these precepts are, in the Talmud's phrase, the righteous of the world. Our faith recognizes that men outside Judaism have risen to heights of Godliness that few mortals can reach. To question their salvation is for us impossible. Our tradition has it that Job, the supreme figure of the man of faith in agony, was of the righteous of the world, and not a Jew.

What then becomes of the choice of Israel? It remains as the Bible puts it, an election of Abraham's family to special disciplines and duties in the service of God. The disciplines are the laws of the Torah, meant to forge Israel into a lasting folk. The duties merge in the task of living by God's law and keeping alight in history, with national dedication, the knowledge and love of the Lord.

Through the generations, beginning with the Exodus, non-Jews have taken on this yoke and become converts; the Bible speaks of the mixed multitude that went up from Egypt with Israel, awed and inspired by Moses. Judaism has never tried to save souls by converting them. It teaches that salvation lies in people's conduct before God, not in their taking on the special commands that bind the House of Abraham. The difficulties of being Jewish are well enough known so that few people in any age seriously seek out this destiny, though any man or woman can.

This then is the mystery of the Jews. Their tradition teaches, and Western religion does too, that they are the remnant of an old great House, with a historic purpose that is from God. Of course convinced rationalists find this impossible to swallow; and they are numerous today, and count many highly intelligent Jews among their ranks. They are left with the problem, How is it that the Jews have lasted so long, and still last?

Because one cannot dismiss the idea of the House by pointing to the very ordinary Jewish people one sees everywhere, and the less than noble ones on display at some resorts. The armed forces of the United States have the mission of preserving the existence of our land, the highest purpose we know. Drunken sailors, embezzling colonels, stuffed-shirt generals, do not alter the high nature of the mission; they are instances of the gap between human nature and human ideals. Jewry's failure to measure up to its mission is the burden of Jeremiah and Isaiah, as well as of country-club chatter.

To those who believe, the Jews are a mystery because such an intervention of God in the tale of mankind cannot be reasonably accounted for. To those who do not believe, the Jews are a mystery because by the ordinary laws of national organisms they should have vanished many centuries ago; yet here they are.

Survival, Yes; Miracle, No

Secular thinkers are far from helpless in the face of this odd fact, which is all they will grant it to be.

Historians and social scientists, speculating on the staying power of our people, all converge on the one element of our life that marks us off from other nations: the Mosaic law. In the religious legislation by which we have lived so long, the modern mind finds an institutional system, a web of habits of thought and conduct, remarkably calculated to enable a small nation, even when fragmentized among other nations, to go on existing against all odds, under all possible adversity, from millennium to millennium.

The traditional view starts at the other end, as it were. It holds that the survival system is the law of God, the law is to be obeyed because it is the will of God, and the eternal people survives by the grace of God. All the lore of our folk, exploring and defining Judaism, begins with this concept, ends with it, and burns steadily with it.

The rational man prefers to construct his theory of Judaism out of the plain visible facts: the strange durability of the Jews, the stature and power of the Bible, the important Hebrew strain in Western culture. He leaves out God as a fact, but is willing to admit him as a work of human imagination, an element in the Jewish problem like other elements. He traces in Hebrew law certain resemblances to ancient Semitic legislation which indicate that the general time and place of its origins are what the tradition says they are. He concedes differences in the Jewish law: its literary grandeur, its charge of moral light, and its striking survival scheme. He concedes no more.

The traditional view has lasted thirty centuries. It has the heaped-up knowledge and natural authority of an old community wisdom. To hear a learned rabbi expound the Torah, and then to read a rationalist appraisal of Judaism, is a little like the descent from hearing a Mozart opera to reading the next day's criticisms. The chief claim of the skeptical view is that it is up-to-date, scientific, nearer the truth. It holds the religious view, for all its accumulated resources and majestic structure, to be naïve; a dream, albeit a charming, durable, well-wrought dream. The religious thinker regards this as the lifeless estimate of an uninformed outsider. And there the matter stands.

And there, for the moment, can we let it stand? It is an old stable dilemma; we are not likely to resolve it with more words on one side or the other. Perhaps we can take our lead from the mental heroes of our time, the physicists. They tell us that light acts in some ways that make sense only as a kind of wave action, while other effects prove light is a stream of particles. This could be a paralyzing dilemma. But the physicists, with the cheerful horse sense that distinguishes the modern mind, use combinations of the wave and particle theories to work their experiments as they labor toward a clearer idea of the truth; reserving final judgment, and pursuing their tasks with the best knowledge in hand.

That is what we can do here. I am sketching Judaism for those who want to know about it, whatever the source of their curiosity. We will not part company over our theories about the mystery. The light of this faith has burned longer than any other. It is the oldest living religious light, the source of Western religion, and even of the ethical humanism which proposes to discard religion. This light challenges our study. We can study it together, whether you call it waves or particles — or an odd mixing of both.

Chapter 2

✦

The Prevalence of Symbols

What Symbol Does

WE are going to spend a lot of time on symbols and ceremonies. These comprise the substance — you might say the technical tools — of the survival system that is so striking in Jewish life. Agreed, this system is but a means to an end, the historic mission of Jewry — if one comes to believe in the mission; otherwise it is only an interesting piece of sociology. Either way, a study of Judaism starts with these things. In the end it must penetrate as far as it can into the religious vision of Moses.

Of course the Jews did not invent the idea of symbolic tools. They belong to all cultures. Human life is so brief, so various, so complex, that it would grind to a standstill — it would never have come to exist at all — without the shorthand invented by Adam's unique intelligence when he separated himself from the brutes: symbol and rite. Any activity that concerns human existence, any serious business, is controlled in this shorthand. The transfer of ownership of a New York skyscraper today is a ceremony as long and complex, and as filled with curious props and tokens, as the coronation of a Roman emperor. Such symbolism varies from activity to activity, from land to land, from culture to culture, from age to age; but there is no activity, no land, no culture, no age, without its shorthand.

The rites and symbols of Egyptian religion, of Babylonian finance, of Byzantine jurisprudence, are extinct, though men still study them for curiosity, or for the light they may shed on living practice.

The symbol language of Judaism is alive now, as it was ages ago, still ruling the behavior of millions of people. It is the hieroglyph of the master ideas of the Bible carved on daily life. A Jew can hardly live Judaism without his ancient sacred shorthand any more than a financier can conduct modern finance without its symbols. True symbol is not make-believe or mummery; it is reality distilled.

The Source of Jewish Symbol

The Torah set forth the symbols as well as the civil and criminal law of Judaism. The codes in agriculture, damages, crime, property, were suspended by conquest and exile. The religious code survived, and survives to this day.

There have been times in Jewish history, both in Biblical days and thereafter, when the survival of the religious legislation seemed in doubt. We live in such a period today, though broad masses of Jews still observe the law. Our period resembles that of the Hellenistic anarchy, when Palestine was under Greek rule. For a time the sophisticated and lovely culture of Greece seemed to render Judaism dated, naïve, and incapable of further survival. Nearly all the wealthy Jews and many of the most intelligent ones dropped the old symbols. They spoke Greek; they wore Greek clothing, ate like the Greeks, built Greek stadia and ran races naked in them, called Greek philosophy and science the only truth, and in the end worshipped like Greeks. But the masses, remaining true to Judaism, produced new political, financial, and intellectual leaders; and Jesus of Nazareth and his apostles as well. The Hellenizers vanished. They may have led very pleasant existences, surely many of them did, but we have no way of knowing. They left no literature and no tradition, and there is no trace of them.*

The symbols of the Sinai legislation have some parallels in other cultures of ancient Semitic lands. This is what one would expect, of course, given the origin of the Mosaic law in place and time. The people of Israel from the start had to live in given terms. They could no more have undertaken a wholly queer new culture pattern dropped from the sky than they could all suddenly have begun talking English. The Mosaic law took existing elements of Semitic life and organized and ennobled them into a scheme of survival for an eternal people; as the American Revolution took the ideas of Locke and his contemporary philosophers, and some parts of British law, and made of them the bedrock of a new nation.

Here, since we have referred to both Hebrew and American law, a point of importance arises, and we may as well meet it. Those who find use or pleasure in baiting the Jews have asked in every generation, How can they be loyal both to their religious law and to the law of the land in which they live? Which loyalty is overriding?

The answer is that in Jewish doctrine both laws are one law. The loyalty is single. When the Jewish commonwealth fell two thousand years ago and its civil legislation ceased to

*I am trying to avoid footnotes — my few amplifying comments are in a section of notes at the back of the book — but here I should pause. The scholarly reader, if he has come along so far in an obviously non-technical book, will think of Philo, Josephus, and the authors of the Apocrypha. I mean by Hellenizers the Jews of that day who discarded Judaism, not those who mastered both cultures and remained faithful to the tradition. Philo and Josephus were both observant Jews.

be a reality, the Talmud sages laid down the rule for Jews in all the ages of exile: *dino d'malkuto dino,* "the law of the land is our law." Into the vacuum left by the fall of the state, steps the state which is the home of a Jew, and which gives him a civic identity. Therefore the traditional Jew, beyond his civic sense, is obliged by his religion to be a law abider; a Frenchman, if born in France; an Israeli, if in Israel; an American, if in America. If a state decrees that Jews may not worship their God, they fight such decrees, and they have often died fighting them. That is the one point in which a conflict could exist. It could exist equally, I believe, for Christians or Moslems put under such a decree.

The Force of Symbol

Consider, for a minute, a game of bridge. To pass an evening in a trial of wits, four people agree to pretend that cards have value. They put rewards and punishments of money on the outcome. They groan at the unexpected appearance of an ace, laugh with delight when a finesse works. Then the game ends, and the cards become mere colored paper again. Even in such fleeting symbolism some authority is needed to keep the symbols stably in force. There are rule books, bridge associations, and unwritten laws of etiquette. A man may signal to his partner what cards he holds — in certain approved ways. If he is caught signalling in a way that is frowned upon, he may never play bridge again in this company, and even his reputation in real life may be hurt. He gave his consent to the bridge ceremony; he violates honor by behaving unceremoniously.

The symbols of money are more serious. They are in fact iron-rigid. A bank check is but a piece of paper. It is a simple matter to get such a piece of paper and duplicate the signature of a rich man on it. If you are caught doing so you are called a forger, your good name is gone, and your bodily freedom is forfeit for years. All you were trying to do was to get some money, which is what everybody tries to do all the time. But you did it in an unceremonious way. Your crime was not that you tried to get money by manipulating paper symbols. Financiers grow very rich manipulating paper symbols. Some people will argue that their manipulations are mere sharp shortcuts to money-getting, like your forgery. But at no point in their symbolic manipulation is there a punishable lack of right ceremony. The symbols and rites of finance are backed by the state. The consent of people to take them for what they represent is automatic and universal. The aspect of ceremony quite vanishes from dollar bills, bank checks, stock certificates, and insurance policies. They seem as real, as solid, as true, as trees or children. Indeed they are, while the authority that created them and the consent that sustains them continue to exist.

Now the laws of our religion, though no policeman enforces them, form an organic whole, a living pattern of behavior for a community and for each individual in it. The symbols and rites of the faith are stamped on every important part of life: on food, on clothing, on shelter, on time, on sex, on speech. To a Jew of the old school, these laws and ceremonies were as familiar as American ways are to an American. For him they had acquired the same invisibility, so to speak; had merged with everyday reality, and seemed natural. To eat matzo and avoid leaven during Passover was as real a matter and as much taken for granted as banking or voting (two very curious rites) are for us today. Rationalization and analysis were for a few scholars. A man did these things because he was a cultivated Jew, and this was how Jews behaved themselves.

Such a natural Judaism exists among few Jews today in the United States, or indeed anywhere in the free communities of the Western world. We live tensed between two cultures, that of our faith and that of our environment. In this we resemble the Jewish communities in other periods of comparative freedom: in Babylon, under liberal regimes of Greece and Rome, and during part of the Mohammedan rule of the Mediterranean. The tension may be less comfortable than quiet living under the shelter of the law; but most of the great post-Biblical figures and writings of Judaism have emerged out of these tense periods. The challenge of the environment stimulates and fertilizes the old faith. So it has been; so we have every reason to hope it will be.

Meantime our generation has the heavy task of meeting the challenge of the twentieth-century West. All too many of us must start by finding out what our faith is, where authority lies, and what we are asked to consent to. Our fathers, Jews of the old school, tried to tell us that these strange complex laws and rituals were natural everyday behavior. They were hurt and baffled when we refused to believe them, and communication broke down.

Conformity

Not long ago, in a fashionable suburban home, I fell into a parlor discussion of religion. I try to avoid these because they almost always end with my sitting silent while my interlocutors enthusiastically explain to me what is wrong with Judaism. The usual gist of the explanations is that pork is unhealthy only in hot countries, that religion is a matter of ethics and not of ceremonies, and so forth. This particular argument was pleasanter than most, because the person setting me straight was a pretty seventeen-year-old girl, a college sophomore, and it was no strain to smile at her with good humor as she went about her work.

She had been reading sociology and was full of terms like

anomy, other-directedness, acculturation, and similar jaw-breakers, which she got off with athletic ease. The burden of her tale was that Judaism meant ritualism, and ritualism meant conformity, which was a great evil. I had been hearing a lot about conformity just then; the girl convinced me that it has at last ousted insecurity as the final hurled curse of parlor talk. I for one am glad of this development. The drift to conformity is a very real evil in American culture, discerned by Tocqueville a century ago, and now far advanced. It is much the greatest threat to the survival of the Jews in the United States. I shall have more to say on that later. Parlor talk seems to me on much more promising ground worrying over conformity than gnawing the bones of Freud.

The interesting thing was that my charming enlightener, while she delivered her philippic against conformity, was dressed in garb as ceremonious as a bishop's, from the correct wrinkles in her sweater sleeves to the prescribed smudge on her saddle shoes. She spoke her piece for autonomy in a vocabulary of the teens as rigid, as circumscribed, as repetitious, as marked in intonation, as a litany. Her gestures, her haircut, her paint, were wholly stylized. Her mother and father, who listened with beaming pride as she spoke, were good-hearted people, both encased beyond release in steel-hard suburban manners and dress, ruled by unbreakable social ritual from sunrise to sunrise.

Is this shooting fish in a barrel? But the case is no different in intellectual circles. I have heard sophisticated littérateurs, men of a sharply critical turn of mind, explain that the conformity of religion made it unacceptable to them. Their dress has been as markedly literary as the girl's was adolescent; their haircuts and their vocabularies have been no less special and predictable. To drink with them, and talk with them, and go to their homes, has been to observe gestures, and hear ideas, and note books on shelves, and hear music played, and see food eaten and wine drunk, as generically uniform as one finds among the Hasidim. To see the really rabid, hidebound, obsessive ritualists of the day, one must go to the young non-conformists of Greenwich Village, whose identical tonsures, and talk, and dress, and convulsive dancing mark them as a sort of secular dervishes.

But this is all inevitable. There is nothing whatever wrong with it. Human life cannot be formless. The only true non-conformists are in the asylums; the only radically free spirits are in the death house awaiting the chair. We live by patterns. We move in comradeships. We cannot move hand or foot without high signs and passwords, no matter what our work or our station may be; and while life lasts, we all wear uniforms. Conformity is evil when it distorts, flattens, and erases fruitful ways, strong ideas, natural identities; it is evil when it is a steamroller. But a man cannot escape being part of a milieu — and a recognizable part — unless he flees naked to a cave, never to return.

The sensible thing is to use hard thinking to find the right way to live and then to live that way, whether many other people do or few do. If a Jew concludes to enter upon his heritage and make it part of his life, he does an obviously reasonable thing. The chances are that — at least today — he will seem a mighty freakish non-conformist in some neighborhoods; but that is changing too, and anyway, what does it matter? What matters is living with dignity, with decency, and without fear, in the way that best honors one's intelligence and one's birth.

Part 2

THE FAITH

Chapter 3

✦

We Cannot Study All of It

THE nearest thing to an encyclopedia of Judaism is the Babylon Talmud, a work in twenty immense tomes touching on almost every human activity. Law codes extracted from the Talmud, like the *Mishna Torah* of Maimonides and *The Ready Table* of Caro, run to many huge volumes. Mastery of them is a lifetime job for specialists. We cannot hope, of course, to deal with the subject on such a scale.

But we can sensibly undertake a more limited job. When the commonwealth fell and the Temple was destroyed, many sections of the law became inoperative, including the criminal, agricultural, and priestly codes. This does not mean that Jews stopped studying those sections. You can hear close reasoning today in any yeshiva in the United States or Israel on the rules for proclaiming a new moon at the Temple, or the four classes of damage in Talmud law. The spirit and sense of Judaism are so woven through the entire Talmud that serious students of Judaism try to learn all of it. But most laymen encounter little of this theoretical part of the faith. We can study here the things that affect daily action.

By tradition Judaism has six hundred and thirteen commands. This formidable figure is fairly well known. It is less well known that most of those commands are in the dormant codes of farm, temple, and criminal law. A meticulous pietist can perhaps find a hundred precepts that touch life today. The Jew who holds to a couple of dozen key observances will probably be called orthodox. Quite a drop: twenty-four instead of the frightening six hundred and thirteen. This is the kind of fact that I think one needs in reaching an adult estimate of Judaism.

I am not saying, and let nobody take me as saying, that by keeping up a few formal practices one can meet in full the call of the law of Moses, and for the rest go about a busy modern existence with an easy mind. I say that to have Judaism in one's life the price is not total withdrawal from existing manners, thoughts, and activity; nor is it the taking on of a way so tangled and strange as to be paralyzing; nor is it self-isolation from the common human destiny. These are popular misconceptions.

The Vilna Gaon's Weakness

They tell a story of the Dubno Maggid, the famous preacher of the East European ghettos. Once he was asked by the mighty scholar called the Vilna Gaon to tell him his faults. The maggid at first declined. When the Gaon pressed him, he at last spoke somewhat like this: "Very well. You are the most pious man of our age. You study night and day, retired from the world, surrounded by the rows of your books, the Holy Ark, the faces of devout scholars. You have reached high holiness. How have you achieved it? Go down in the market place, Gaon, with the rest of the Jews. Endure their work, their strains, their distractions. Mingle in the world, hear the skepticism and irreligion they hear, take the blows they take. Submit to the ordinary trials of the ordinary Jew. Let us see then if you will remain the Vilna Gaon!" They say the Gaon broke down and wept.

The clear intent of our law is to enable a man to live in the world and yet hold his faith close to his daily thoughts. The lama and the monk withdraw from society to keep a religious vision bright. Our faith teaches us to stay in the world, but to stamp our hours with seals of commitment. The result is, in a way, a troubled life. It can never be wholly of the moment, wholly fashionable. One's secular pursuits come under the constant review of the Law, in a slant light. The winds of doctrine blow and shift, fads come and go, and one watches all this with a resistant irony, even when one is swept up. But, on the other hand, one's religious ideas face the daily scouring of commerce and of common sense. To survive they must have substance.

The Core of Judaism

I have on my desk a letter from an agnostic friend, part of a running correspondence many years old. Says he, "What is the *core* of being a Jew: to be different in living habits, or to practice a moral way of life based on behavior toward other people? To imply that in some significant measure the terrible problems of social existence on a crowded planet are solved by refusing to eat lobsters seems irretrievably petty to me."

The pious reader may not agree, but I think this is excellently put. Once I think I made a similar point, though much more crudely, about naval service. I had been a midshipman for a couple of weeks, and I was nailed with a demerit for incorrect use of words. I growled to my roommate as the tyrannical ensign walked off, "How will it help beat the Japanese if I call a staircase a ladder?"

I eventually learned to do so. It is not my impression that I thereby advanced the surrender ceremonies in Tokyo Bay, say from September fifth to September second. But I am pretty sure that I became a useful naval officer in part by learning the lingo; and whatever minute service I gave toward that surrender, I gave it as a naval officer.

Possibly because the navy meant so much in my life, I have always thought that the Jewish place among mankind somewhat resembles the position of navy men among other Americans. Are the sailors and officers less American because they are in the navy? They have special commitments and disciplines, odd ways of dress, sharp limits on their freedom. They have, at least in their own minds, compensations of glory, or of vital service performed. The Jews are not cut off from mankind by their faith, though they are marked different. They have their special disciplines, and — at least in their own minds — their rewards.

I remember being looked up to as a naval officer in wartime; then when peace came and I travelled to take my Reserve cruises, people in trains and planes tended to regard me as an unfortunate misfit. One or two actually said, "How come you're still in?" I think that is essentially the question that agnostics address to observant Jews.

We are still in, I suppose, because we take it on faith that the law of Moses is from God, and our observation tells us that the patterns of the law help keep our tiny folk in life, in the grand sweep of history. We share the hope of our fathers that out of our tiny folk, in some way none of us can foresee, the light of lasting peace will someday come. I cannot produce the Messiah. But in my sons, as Providence allows, I can produce two informed Jews who will keep alive that hope beyond my life.

My friend's question, then, answers itself. The core of Judaism is right conduct to other people. The Talmud (if I am not growing too anecdotal here) tells that a Gentile came to the Rabbi Hillel and asked to be taught all Judaism while standing on one foot. Hillel's colleague, Shammai, had driven the man from his door, taking the question for a baiting impertinence. Hillel amiably replied, "What is offensive to you do not do to others. That is the core of Judaism. The rest is commentary. Now carry on your studies." The man became a convert.

The core of a nuclear reactor, or of an apple, or of a religion, is not all of it. We make few core-decisions day by day. Life is too packed with running trivialities, with mechanical repetition. Judaism does not let that part of life go. It weaves commitment, and therefore at least formal significance, all through one's day. It is perfectly true that Gentile and Jew alike have sometimes taken the forms for the core. Hence on one hand the agnostic disapproval of the faith because of its "petty concern with ceremony." Hence on the other hand the ultra-orthodox who will not recognize the state of Israel because its government members are not all pious. But if a way of life be judged by its misinterpreters, which way will stand?

Self-Isolation

How can we sensibly isolate ourselves? The world around us is where we live. The peoples of the world are our brothers under God. Our Scripture teaches that God made all men, not just Israel, in his image. Sacrifices brought by Jew and non-Jew burned on the altars of the two Temples. "Are you not like the Ethiopians to me," cried the prophet Amos in the name of the Lord, "and did I not deliver the Philistines from the land of Caphtor?"

Our own eyes tell us what Moses told us: that but for the Torah we are the most insignificant of the nations. What else can we show against the wisdom and the genius God has given to the world? Did we produce Socrates or Aristotle, Shakespeare or Cervantes, Newton or Galileo, Bach or Beethoven, Michelangelo or Rembrandt, Dickens or Tolstoy, Gandhi or Lincoln? Are we to stay out of planes because the Wrights were not Jews, or keep our hands from electricity because we have no share in Faraday, Maxwell, and Edison? Does this absurd misconstruction of Judaism not collapse into powder at a touch?

Our place in the world, I believe, depends on what we contribute to mankind. We have contributed the Torah, the Mosaic vision of right conduct and of first and last things. It is our life, and the length of our days. As we keep that flame burning, it seems to me, we earn our right to survive as a people before God and men.

Understanding this, we approach the vision as our fathers did, through a structure of symbol and discipline. To the newcomer, this structure is a maze. But enter it we must. To get to the heart of the matter, we have to study the seals that Judaism has stamped on life; the commentaries, as Hillel put it, on the core of the Torah.

The first set of seals is on Time.

Chapter 4

✦

The Sabbath

LOGIC compels us therefore to start with one of the most involved and ramified symbols of Judaism; one moreover that goes much against the grain of current manners and habits of thought. Perhaps it is just as well for the climb to begin steeply.

Sabbath law comprises one of the largest tractates of the Talmud. There are uncounted millions of words on the subject in Hebrew literature. Yet the reader certainly knows the few words that are decisive: the first chapter of Genesis, and the Fourth Commandment.

The opening pages of Genesis were, of course, the ground of the nineteenth-century war between theologians and scientists. Now the guns are still, rusting broken here and there in tall grass; the dead are buried; the smoke of battle has long since cleared away. We see a quiet green plain, which has a new look to our eyes because of the struggle that was fought out there. The scientists won. The theologians went down crying that their infamous victory would mean the extinction of the Bible. That extinction has not come to pass, nor is it visibly closer. But the world certainly understands Genesis differently.

The Real Point of Genesis

The first chapter of Genesis cut through the murk of ancient mythology with a shaft of light — light that the whole world lives by now, so that we can scarcely picture its effect when it first shone forth. The universe was proclaimed a natural order created and unfolded by one Force and set going like a vast machine to proceed under its own power. There were no manlike gods. Nor were the animals gods, nor were the gods animals. There was no sun god, or moon god, or love god, or sea god, or war god. The world and mankind were not the product of titanic incest and sodomy among monsters in the skies. Sun, moon, wind, seas, mountains, stars, stones, trees, plants, beasts were all part of nature, without any magic of their own. Mumbo-jumbo was a mistake. The gods and priesthoods which demanded burnt children, or hearts cut from living men, or ghastly obscenities, or endlessly draining gifts, were useless, silly, doomed libels on the universe. The childhood nightmares of mankind were over. It was day.

The Genesis account of creation cut the cancer of idolatry out of human discourse. It took a long time to prevail; but at last even the charming Greek and Roman gods withered under the stroke. Genesis is the dividing line between contemporary intelligence and primitive muddle in the realm of first and last things. As such, I do not see how it will ever be superseded.

The fundamentalist theologians maintained that either Moses had been using literal arithmetic in the imagery he used or else everything he wrote had to be dismissed as the words of a Stone Age ignoramus. The scientists gladly accepted this formulation of the issue. They won, but the dire consequences did not follow, because the theologians had posed a false choice. Men still prize Genesis. Modern thinkers now take it for granted — as the rabbis long ago suggested — that Genesis is a mystic vision of the origin of things, put in the purest and strongest words, intelligible to the child, inspiring to adult genius, clear enough to survive in primitive eras, and deep enough to challenge sophisticated cultures.

The Sabbath in Genesis

All this is by the way. One can hardly bring up Genesis without mentioning the imposing war monuments on the field. Our main purpose here is to trace the Sabbath to its source, the Jewish account of creation.

The whole world knows what the Sabbath is. One day in every seven, work stops, in honor of the Creator. This Jewish ordinance permeates civilization. It is the law of the land almost everywhere. The production schedule in the United States exactly follows this rule. The worst rigors of wartime scarcely invade it. Habit is a persuasive thing, and maybe that is why there seems to be a fitness, an exact estimate of human rhythms, in the proportion of six days of work to one of rest. Though a five-day work week has become standard in our extravagantly productive land, we are well aware that the extra day or half day of rest is a luxury, a dividend of enterprise, energy, and science, and not in the nature of things.

Rest is only half the ordinance, the negative part, one might say. The seventh day is holy: set off by changes in dress, manners, diet, and occupations, and by special worship of the Creator. This Jewish way too has its counterpart in general culture. We all know about Sunday best, Sunday manners, Sunday dinner, Sunday quiet, and churchgoing. If we did not live in a Christian land we would know of these customs from British and American novels, which portray the Christian Sabbath vividly.

It is not all idyllic. Travellers in the South or visitors in Boston who find they cannot get a drink of whiskey on Sunday are not inclined — at least at the moment of discovery — to laud their Creator for his marvelous works.*

*I'm told things are easing up in Boston nowadays. — HW (1987)

Urbane Londoners have complained for generations at the suspension of theatre on Sunday. The blue laws surviving in Anglo-American society from the once-general Puritan code cause inconvenience, a lessening of ordinary amusements, and a sense of irksome restraint for many people. But so strong is the hold of the Sabbath idea on the Christian spirit that these laws change slowly, and in some places hold their ground without a prospect or even a popular urge for change.

Compared to the Jewish Sabbath, however, the most stringent Sunday laws are mild. Anti-Sabbatarians among the Christians have always objected that the restrictive laws are a form of Judaizing, and that it makes no sense to submit Christians to these Old Testament disciplines. The Puritans took the Old Testament, they say, far too seriously.

The pious Jew on the Sabbath does not travel, or cook, or use motors or electric appliances, or spend money, or smoke, or write. The industrial world stops dead for him. Nearly all the mechanical advantages of civilization drop away. The voice of the radio is still; the television screen is blank. The movies, the baseball and football games, the golf courses, the theatres, the nightclubs, the highways, the card tables, the barbecue pits — indeed most of the things that make up the busy pleasures of conventional leisure — are not for him. The Jewish Sabbath is a ceremony that makes steep demands to achieve a decisive effect. A Jew who undertakes to observe it is, from sundown on Friday to the end of twilight on Saturday, in a world cut off. We had better make no bones about this.

But it can be a very pleasant world. Having, I trust, sufficiently appalled the reader with the hard part of the Sabbath, I can now fairly tell him that this day is the fulcrum of a practicing Jew's existence and generally a source of strength, refreshment, and cheer. To assert this is easy, but uncommunicative. Let me try to explain it.

The great difference between the Puritan Sabbath and the even more restrictive Jewish *Shabbat* is an impalpable but overwhelming one of spirit. Our Sabbath opens with blessings over light and wine. Light and wine are the keys to the day. Our observance has its solemnities, but the main effect is release, peace, gaiety, and lifted spirits.

A Personal Digression

The Sabbath has cut most sharply athwart my own life when one of my plays has been in rehearsal or in tryout. The crisis atmosphere of an attempt at Broadway is a legend of our time, and a true one; I have felt under less pressure going into battle at sea. Friday afternoon, during these rehearsals, inevitably seems to come when the project is tottering on the edge of ruin. I have sometimes felt guilty of treason, holding to the Sabbath in such a desperate situation. But then, experience has taught me that a theatre enterprise almost always is in such a case. Sometimes it does totter to ruin, and sometimes it totters to great prosperity, but tottering is its normal gait, and cries of anguish are its normal tone of voice. So I have reluctantly taken leave of my colleagues on Friday afternoon, and rejoined them on Saturday night. The play has never yet collapsed in the meantime. When I return I find it tottering as before, and the anguished cries as normally despairing as ever. My plays have encountered in the end both success and failure, but I cannot honestly ascribe either result to my observing the Sabbath.

Leaving the gloomy theatre, the littered coffee cups, the jumbled scarred-up scripts, the haggard actors, the shouting stagehands, the bedevilled director, the knuckle-gnawing producer, the clattering typewriter, and the dense tobacco smoke and backstage dust, I have come home. It has been a startling change, very like a brief return from the wars. My wife and my boys, whose existence I have almost forgotten in the anxious shoring up of the tottering ruin, are waiting for me, gay, dressed in holiday clothes, and looking to me marvellously attractive. We have sat down to a splendid dinner, at a table graced with flowers and the old Sabbath symbols: the burning candles, the twisted loaves, the stuffed fish, and my grandfather's silver goblet brimming with wine. I have blessed my boys with the ancient blessing; we have sung the pleasantly syncopated Sabbath table hymns. The talk has had little to do with tottering ruins. My wife and I have caught up with our week's conversation. The boys, knowing that the Sabbath is the occasion for asking questions, have asked them. The Bible, the encyclopedia, the atlas, have piled up on the table. We talk of Judaism, and there are the usual impossible boys' queries about God, which my wife and I field clumsily but as well as we can. For me it is a retreat into restorative magic.

Saturday has passed in much the same manner. The boys are at home in the synagogue, and they like it. They like even more the assured presence of their parents. In the weekday press of schooling, household chores, and work — and especially in a play-producing time — it often happens that they see little of us. On the Sabbath we are always there, and they know it. They know too that I am not working, and that my wife is at her ease. It is their day.

It is my day, too. The telephone is silent. I can think, read, study, walk, or do nothing. It is an oasis of quiet. When night falls, I go back to the wonderful nerve-racking Broadway game. Often I make my best contribution of the week then and there to the grisly literary surgery that goes on and on until opening night. My producer one Saturday night said to me, "I don't envy you your religion, but I envy you your Sabbath."

I mention this experience because I think it comes closest to reproducing in my own life what the Sabbath must have been to our forefathers. In a lucky group like the American Jewish community, which has its full share of life's good things, and which lives at peace, the change from the weekday to the Sabbath is not quite the old dramatic plunge from gloom, trouble, penury, and crisis to peaceful and graceful pleasure. Our fathers saved all new clothes, all luxurious food, for the day that honored the Creator. No man was so poor that he did not have the wine, the lights, the twisted loaves, and the bit of meat and fish. The synagogue gave him these things if he could not buy them. The restrictions of the Sabbath again, which seem to tug at every turn of American life, were second nature to our fathers, and had vanished into ordinary reality. One did not do a large number of acts on the seventh day as a modern gentleman does not do a large number of acts on any day. Of course the Sabbath rules were laws of religion, not of convention. But they were so familiar that they were the very air of life rather than self-consciously executed disciplines. There was no grain for them to go against. They were the grain.

The American Jew, by taking thought and pains, by keeping the Sabbath over the years, by accepting its difficulties for the sake of the results, can have what the Sabbath offers. He has to work at it more than his fathers did, with a lower charge of religious energy. It is a hard case. That the Sabbath should be the usual breaking-off point from tradition is perhaps inevitable. It is also the point at which many Jews rejoin Judaism. Probably it is the natural and the best point.

Because, for one thing, the Sabbath is the only Jewish symbol you will find in the Ten Commandments.

The Fourth Commandment

The two tables contain the seven great prohibitions that establish civilization: against idolatry, perjury, murder, adultery, theft, false witness, and covetousness. And they contain three positive commands: worship of the One God, honoring of parents (which makes tradition possible), and keeping the Sabbath. That is all. I have sometimes wondered at Jews who take the Day of Atonement and even the festivals — perhaps Hanuka too — more seriously than the Sabbath, when every time they enter a synagogue or temple the Sabbath law confronts them, blazoned on the tablets over the Holy Ark. But I guess it is natural enough not to see what it would be highly troubling to see.

What is this symbol — out of so many that make up the structure of Judaism — doing in the tables of the law, exalted in dramatic emphasis above all other rites and ceremonies? There are two wordings, one in Exodus and one in Deuteronomy. They give the two bases for the Sabbath, which are really the bases for all the rest of the Torah's commands. The Sabbath takes the leading place, I suppose, because it most clearly carries these two charges of meaning. It is the whole Torah in miniature.

Here is Exodus:

> Remember the Sabbath day, to keep it holy. Six days you shall labor, and do all your work; and the seventh day is the Sabbath of the Lord your God. You shall not do any work; you, nor your son, nor your daughter, your manservant nor your maidservant, nor your stranger within your gates. For in six days the Lord made heaven, the earth, the sea, and all that is in them; therefore the Lord blessed the seventh day and made it holy.

And this is Deuteronomy:

> Keep the Sabbath day, to make it holy, as the Lord your God has commanded you. Six days you shall labor, and do all your work. But the seventh day is the Sabbath of

the Lord your God. You shall not do any work, nor your son, nor your daughter, your manservant, nor your maidservant, nor any of your herd, nor your donkey, nor your beasts, nor the stranger within your gates, so that your manservant and maidservant may rest as well as you.

And remember that you were a servant in the land of Egypt, and that the Lord your God brought you out of there with a strong hand and an outstretched arm. Therefore the Lord your God commanded you to keep the Sabbath day.

The Sabbath, then, is first of all a dramatic gesture of the community, the immemorial collective gesture of stopping work and celebrating. All nations celebrate the day of their coming into being with a work stoppage and ceremonies. The Jews, who believe that God created the universe, celebrate its coming into being, and give thanks to its Maker, once a week. That the proportion is proper is perhaps indicated by mankind's general adoption of the custom.

In the second place the Sabbath marks the founding of the Jewish nation in the Exodus from Egypt. Jews worship not only the God of creation, but the God who cares about human history. This is for us the meaning of the Exodus from the Goshen slave camps. Slaves have no choice in the matter of work or rest; they are talking beasts, subject to the master's will. The creation is not in their hands. Time is not theirs to apportion. Freedom is the condition of Adam, the possession of choice, and the mastery of time. The Sabbath carries special national meaning for the people of Israel, who came into their nationhood by passing from slavery to freedom.

This doubled thread of meaning runs through the symbols of the Jewish religion: grateful worship of the universal God and celebration of Israel's peculiar destiny as his witness in history.

What the Sabbath Achieves

But we are not dealing here with an ordinary work stoppage. That is only the beginning of Sabbath observance. Its essence is a ceremonious abstaining from all acts, even the most effortless, that contain an element of innovation, of process, or of workmanship.

The Torah mentions gathering sticks and lighting fires, two easy and (one would think) harmlessly necessary labors that a cripple, a child of five, or an old woman of ninety can do, as forbidden. Tradition stemming back to Mosaic time lists thirty-nine banned labors. They fall into a few groups covering the basic pursuits of men: bread, clothing, shelter, meat and leather, manufacture, and commerce. Exploration of these thirty-nine in the Talmud throws a web of withdrawal over all the common productive acts. The usual objection to (say) the ban on striking a match — that a flick of the wrist is not hard work — quite misses the point. Anybody will avoid hard work if he can, any day of the week. Avoiding slight efforts is ceremony. The Jewish Sabbath may be too hard for some people, or they may not subscribe to its ideas; but within its own terms it is a dramatic ceremony penetrating all of life. It is not simply a day off. This demanding rite turns twenty-four hours of every week into a separated time, apart in mood, texture, acts, and events from daily existence.

Religious symbol and ceremony aim, like art, at the shock of truth. Perhaps this similarity of aim led Santayana to conclude that religion really was a variety of esthetic invention, the best of man's creative dreams; which is not quite so, I imagine, unless we are prepared to put Moses and Dickens in the same line of work. It is true, all the same, that religion and art both fight, on different fronts, against the dull rust that habit puts on the wonder of things. A tree is a surpassingly beautiful creation; but most of us need Cézanne or Corot to remind us how beautiful trees are. The Sabbath is a recurring sign and reminder of creation, and of Israel's beginning. As such, it works.

One should not exaggerate the claims for its effect. Perhaps a few Jewish geniuses have on the Sabbath day achieved regularly something like the exalted Mosaic visions of creation, and of the destiny of Israel. For plain people, the Sabbath mainly keeps fresh their awareness that those visions exist. The seven-day cycle is a seal that cuts very deep into Jewish life. All planning relates to the creation day: plans of work, of travel, of leisure, even of a place to live. Bulking so large in life, coming so often, the Sabbath has a lifetime in which to imprint its meanings on the spirit and the brain. Those who keep the day inevitably have the ideas of creation and the Creator, of the Exodus and of Jewish identity, strongly in mind.

I am not attempting here even to suggest the philosophy and imagery that irradiate the Sabbath in Jewish thought and lore. The literature is vast, the mystic pictures are copious . . . The Sabbath is a bride, and nightfall the wedding hour, so that every Friday at dusk pious Jews read the sparkling love poetry of the Song of Songs . . . The Sabbath is the seal of partnership between God and man in the rule of creation . . . The Sabbath is the beginning of man's imitation of God . . . The Sabbath is a day in our time of the Messianic era, a foretaste of the coming peace between man and God, man and nature, man and man . . . Such themes throng the writings on Sabbath, and the Sabbath liturgy and customs. The reader will take up the trail if he wishes. If I have conveyed three ideas — that the Jewish Sabbath is on the far side of its tough disciplines, a day of ennobled pleasure; that it is hard to achieve but worth all the effort it calls for; and that in our religion it is the keystone of the arch of symbol through which we pass to seek the great truths — I have done all I can. Two footnotes to this spare sketch of a tremendous subject, and I must go on.

All the restrictive laws of Sabbath vanish in the presence of emergency: illness, disaster, urgent rescue, and the like. Common sense is the second layer of Judaism's bedrock, if faith in One God is the first. The definition of emergency is an austere but realistic one. Peril to life or limb is an emergency. Peril to a deal which might net many thousands of dollars is not. There are, I know, people who will take anxious exception to such a view, but so it is written.

The Sabbath seemed in philosophic trouble in the nineteenth century when the best scientists thought that the existing evidence showed an eternal universe, without a beginning in time. The Jewish idea of creation had opposed for millennia the Greek idea of time without beginning, but the dispute, for lack of observed facts, had stayed in the realm of words. Today the informed verdict is swinging the other way. The accumulating evidence, we are told, now increasingly shows a universe finite in extent and in duration. You and I of course want to know, "But what happened before creation? And what lies outside the boundaries of the universe?" The scientists answer us with wise smiles and change the subject, very much the way my grandfather used to when I pressed him with a question he knew was absurd, but even the absurdity of which he could not explain to me, such was the gulf between us. As I recall, the puzzler I threw at him most often was, "Who made God?"

Chapter 5

✦

The Nature Festivals

TIME on earth is a pattern of wheels within wheels — the day, the week, the seasons, the year — and on each of the wheels Judaism has set its stamp.

The festivals that mark the turns of the calendar are three: *Pesakh* in the spring, *Shavuos* in the summer, *Sukos* in the fall. Agriculture was the life of the Jewish people in its first thousand years. These holy days are marked with symbols and mementos of farming. Long exile, mostly in urban Europe, did not erase these tokens of life on the soil, nor the prayers for favorable weather in the Holy Land.

The three feasts are then celebrations of the plenty of nature; and like the Sabbath, each is also a historic holiday. Pesakh is of course the feast of the Exodus. Shavuos, falling on the anniversary of the Sinai revelation, is the Day of the Lawgiving. Sukos betokens the forty years of wandering in the desert, with the symbolic hut called a *suko,* or tabernacle.

The liturgy for all three festivals is almost the same. Minor changes in wording, and some late medieval poetry, mark the different seasons and anniversaries. But the ceremonials vary widely and give each feast an intense and special color.

These holy days, ancient as the Jewish people, are part of the law of Moses, and count as work stoppages like the Sabbath. Their legislation is similar, though somewhat more lenient to allow for the merrymaking in a thanksgiving fete.

A Digression on the Hebrew Calendar

The Bible says the Jews left Egypt at midnight by the light of the full moon, the moon of the spring equinox, on the fourteenth night of the month Nisan, about thirty-two hundred years ago. This, then, is the night for observing Pesakh, the Passover.

An immediate timing difficulty arises. The Jewish year, like the Mohammedan, has twelve moon months of twenty-nine or thirty days. The year of the sun, which governs the seasons, is about eleven days longer. A moon calendar drifts backward at a rate of about a month every three years. Mohammedans successively observe Ramadan in winter, fall, summer, and spring. But the Mosaic law specifies that Passover is a spring holiday; the freedom feast must come in blossom time. The old Jewish solution of this problem was a leap month every few years, proclaimed by the Sanhedrin. When the dispersion destroyed the nation, and communication between the centers of learning in exile began to break down, the rabbis worked out a perpetual calendar on a nineteen-year cycle, with seven leap months so arranged as to keep Passover for ever at the equinox. This calendar has the respect of modern astronomers. In nearly two thousand years Passover has not drifted out of the springtime, and in the foreseeable future it will not.

In ancient days each new month was proclaimed by the central court in Jerusalem when the crescent moon appeared. The only doubt, of course, was whether it would show up twenty-nine or thirty days after the last new moon. As soon as the month was announced, runners went out all over the Mideast to advise the Jewish communities of the date of their holy days. Those settlements that were more than fourteen days' journey from Jerusalem had no way of knowing the exact day of Passover. To be sure of keeping the festival properly, they observed both possible dates. The custom became general in time to double up the observance of festival days outside the land of Israel. Today, when the Jews have possessed an exact calendar for nearly a score of centuries, when you can telephone Jerusalem from New York or from Tokyo, when the only doubt left about the moon is whether the U.S.A. or the U.S.S.R. will land on it first (and by the time this book sees the light that doubt too may be over),* Jews outside Israel still double up the festival days. In such things we tend to be a bit conservative.

Passover

The central and most picturesque rite of Passover, the eating of the Paschal lamb, no longer exists. With the fall of the Temple this symbol, like so much of Judaism, went dark.

The lamb had to be killed in the court of the Temple, and then roasted whole and eaten at night at a large family feast. Hordes of gay pilgrims converged on Jerusalem for the Passover celebration. In the Temple the priests had a remarkable hand-to-hand conveying system to provide all of Jerusalem and all the pilgrims with Paschal lambs in the one afternoon allowed for the rite.

Polite writers on Judaism sometimes prefer to pass over the fact that the Holy Temple was in part a slaughterhouse, but it was. The taking of animal life was not a matter of course in our faith, but a grant from God, strongly limited by humane laws which we will come to later. At the Temple the meat of the priests and Levites was prepared with much precaution as to purity. The laity brought thank offerings and atonement offerings, dividing the meat with the Temple personnel, and burning some pieces on the great altar. Moses and the

*The U.S.A. beat them. They still haven't done it. Three cheers for the Red, White, and Blue. — HW (1982)

prophets continually pointed out that God was not interested in the sacrifices, except as symbols of dedication and purification for men. Maimonides went so far as to suggest that the sacrifice system was a concession to primitive civilization. A Talmud saying implies that in Messianic times the sacrifices will not be resumed in the restored Temple, except for the thank offerings.

The pilgrims ate the lamb, as the Torah prescribes, with unleavened bread and bitter herbs. Though the lamb rite has long since vanished, the large family feast, the unleavened bread, the bitter herbs, remain a part of living Judaism. The law requires that the elders at the feast tell the children the story of the Exodus, so as to keep the memory of the great deliverance green. This ordinance has worked for over three thousand years. Very few Jewish children reach the age of eight without knowing all about the departure from Egypt and feeling that it is an intimate part of their own history.

The Talmud in its systematic way set up an order — the Hebrew word is *seder* — for the Passover ceremonies. In time "seder" became the popular name for the feast. The seder is a retelling of the Exodus story in a dramatic pageant, enacted by a family and its guests around a festive table. There are spoken parts for children and adults, chorus recitations and songs, and a variety of colorful food symbols, all of which become properties in the telling of the freedom story. The script of this pageant (called the *Hagada,* or Story) is a short vivid book in simple Hebrew, telling the Exodus tale with some Talmudic embellishment and analysis.

Probably the best-loved single piece of Hebrew liturgy, the Hagada has gone through countless printings. Most Jewish artists of note have illustrated it. You can get free Hagadas from firms that manufacture Passover foods, small Hagadas for a few cents, or gorgeously illuminated Hagadas costing over a hundred dollars. Well-meaning modernists now and then try to abridge and revise the Hagada. But the old form endures, far and away the most popular one with the mass of Jews. The people evidently sense that an occasional archaism has its place, and even special value, in a work that has spanned twenty centuries.

The Talmud tractate *Pesakhim* opens with the rules for destroying leaven: that is, yeast. The home is cleared of all leaven and leavened foods before Passover starts. The rabbinic regulations for carrying out this law recall the stringency of hospital antisepsis. Jewish housewives, following the rules in all generations with great strictness, have evolved a sort of sacred spring cleaning in the week before the holiday, meticulous to the last cranny, to the pockets of clothes, to the dark corners of cellars and closets. The housewife cleans her metalware by boiling it in water, locks away the dishes and plates used all year, and takes out china and crockery reserved for the festival.

The destruction of the leaven and the eating of matzo — unleavened bread — are key symbols of Passover. They make a great mark on family life. The children who go around with their father the evening before Passover by candlelight, searching out the last scraps of leaven for burning (these scraps are carefully placed here and there by the mother, who has long since cleaned the house up), never forget the experience. The appearance of the strange dry wafers on the table, the disappearance of bread, are dramatic signs of change. The avoidance of so many customary foods through the week keeps a sense of occasion alive.

If its meaning can be neatly exposed like the parts of a machine or the solution of a detective novel, then a symbol lacks the poetry by which symbols live. But there is nothing wrong with making a partial guess at possible meanings. There is an instantly visible accuracy in marking the passage from slavery to freedom with a change in the kind of bread we eat. Jews give up during Passover the soft breads that leavening makes possible, and subsist for a week on flat hard cakes baked of nothing but flour and water. The Hagada calls matzo "the poor bread that our fathers ate in Egypt," at the first Passover feast, on the night of the Exodus.

The bread of freedom is a hard bread. The contrast between bread and matzo possibly points the contrast between the lush Nile civilization that the Jews left behind them on the first Passover and the gray rubbled desert in which they came into their identity. The Bible tells how they complained to Moses that they could not forget the meat, the cucumbers, the onions that their taskmasters had fed them on the ramparts of Rameses. The whiplash from time to time had been unpleasant, of course. But that memory had faded rapidly as the scars healed in the dry desert air. The memory of the lost security remained.

Economists know that, contrary to the popular impression, slaves do not work hard. A slave civilization is slow moving and easygoing; we still have traces of one in the American South. Take away a man's rights in himself, and he becomes dull and sluggish, wily and evasive, a master of the arts of avoiding responsibility and expending little energy. The whip is no answer to this universal human reaction. There is no answer to it. The lash stings a slave who has halted dumbly, out of indifference and inertia, into resuming the slothful pace of his fellow slaves. It can do no more. The slave's life is a dog's life, degraded, but not wearying, and — for a broken spirit — not unpleasant. The generation of Jews that Moses led into the desert collapsed into despair and panic over and over in moments of crisis. Broken by slavery, they could not shake free of improvidence, cowardice, and idol-worship. All the men who had been slaves in Egypt had to die in the desert, and a new generation had to take up their arms and their religion, before the Jews could cross the Jordan.

Leavening, then, would represent in this image the corruption of slave life. But the symbol has ramifications. The rabbis called the passions of man "the yeast in the dough." Leaven is a strange and pervasive substance. It is alive; it is immortal; it is impalpably everywhere in the air; it ferments grain into bread, and grapes into wine; it is the sour whitish paradigm of the stuff of life itself. For one week in the springtime, in the time of seeding and growth, when the Jews celebrate their independence, they cut all trace of leaven from their lives. No one has ever wholly accounted for this vibrant symbol.* That it has had power over the imagination of Israel through all time, everyone knows.

In recent years, observance of the laws of Passover in the United States has become easier and much more popular. A major industry of Passover products exists. Nearly all the accustomed foods of the year which have, or conceivably could have, traces of leaven are on sale in unleavened preparations. When Passover is confined to a first-night seder with matzos and singing, it becomes a reminiscent gesture toward an old folkway, no more. The power of Passover — and I daresay the real good of it, whether you call that good serving the Lord or maintaining the life of a great people, or both — lies in observing the laws of leaven from dusk of the fourteenth day of Nisan to darkness of the twenty-second. The first and last days of Passover are full holidays. In the interval, called the week of the festival, most work proceeds as usual.

*The Bible of course mentions that the hasty departure of the Hebrews from Egypt left no time for leavened bread to rise. In the uniquely stern laws for total eradication of leaven lies the enigma of the symbol. — HW (1985)

Pentecost: Shavuos

On the morning of the second day of Passover, in olden times, the community brought a measure — called an *omer* — of barley into the Temple for a ceremony hailing the earth's awakening fertility. Barley is an early-maturing crop. With this omer the annual harvest actually began; new produce was never eaten in Palestine until after the barley rite. The wheat crop, in the farming of Palestine, started to mature about seven weeks later. Judaism made of this span one of its major time symbols, the Counting of the Omer. From the day the measure of barley came to the Temple, seven full weeks were told off. On the fiftieth day the nation celebrated the summer festival, Shavuos. A second mass pilgrimage poured into Jerusalem, this time bearing first fruits of field and orchard for Temple offerings.

These facts explain the names of the festival. Shavuos is the Hebrew word for weeks. Pentecost is Greek for the fiftieth day.

The summer festival lasts only one day, two outside Israel. In Temple times it was rich in harvest rituals. Today, beyond the general Sabbath and holy day observances, it has no concrete symbols. The Talmud calls it *Atzeres,* or Last Assembly Day, implying that the holiday is the end of a single religious observance that starts with Passover. Leaving Egypt was the beginning of the event; the climax was Sinai.

The rabbis found, analyzing the narrative texts of Exodus, that the revelation at Sinai occurred fifty days after the second day of Passover, the date of Shavuos. The summer festival therefore became also the feast of the Sinai revelation; and with the disappearance of the harvest pageant, the anniversary of the Giving of the Law has tended to take the central place. By contrast with the other festivals, the day receives scant attention in Jewish law and lore. There is no separate tractate in the Talmud for it. References to its observance are scattered through the agriculture and temple laws.

An old tradition is the serving of dairy foods for the main festive meal. The custom caused the invention of several exquisite Jewish dishes, prized by people who prize little else connected with the faith of their fathers. An echo of the pilgrimage which once heaped greenery, grains, and fruits in the Temple and the streets of Jerusalem is the custom of filling synagogues and homes on Shavuos with flowers and branches.

The period of Counting, or *Sefira,* between Passover and Pentecost, became after the exile a time of national mourning. Tradition connects the sadness with a plague that killed thousands of students of Rabbi Akiba. The symbol of counting and of waiting, full of melancholy overtones for Jews in exile, probably helped make this a semi-mourning time. Religious Jews avoid celebration during Sefira. They schedule weddings for the thirty-third day, *Lag B'Omer,* when by tradition the plague ceased. The thirty-third day is a customary holiday for Jewish schools, and pupils usually mark it with outdoor frolics and picnics.

Sukos or Tabernacles: The Autumn Feast

We are back in the light of the full moon, the moon of the autumnal equinox, the fifteenth of Tishri. Everything that the earth will yield this year lies heaped in the storehouses: the fruit, the grain, the wine, the oil: piles of yellow and green and red, vats brimming purple and gold. The farmers of ancient Israel, like farmers in all lands and times, gather for the autumn thanksgiving.

The full moon sheds its light on every man, woman, and child in Palestine. Nobody is indoors. The law of Moses requires that for seven days and nights all Jews live in huts partially roofed by green boughs, palm branches, or piles of reeds. In these frail structures the families feast, and sing, and visit, and sleep. At the mercy of the weather, they live as their ancestors did in the desert, in the first forty years of independence, before they conquered Canaan.

Sukos is so preeminently a gay and rollicking time that its Talmudic name is simply *The Festival.* For a folk settled in a rich farm country, contemplating their heaping harvests, the suko custom may have helped to limit the smugness of prosperity. In the suko under the night sky, wind and rain could at any moment make life dismal. The moon shone through the loose ceiling of boughs, the old warning of the way fortune changes. The stars — the law suggests that the stars be visible through the roof — may have been reminders that life at its richest is a brief spark in a black mystery. Or so you can interpret the ordinance, if you will. Moses wrote that by dwelling in huts once a year Israel would remember that they had once lived in sukos in the desert, and he went no further.

With the dispersion of the Jews to colder climates, the customs surrounding the sukos have changed. There are pious Jews who still sleep in the hut when the weather permits it, but most of them today confine their observance to eating meals and praying there.

In American Jewish life, especially with the rise of suburban communities, Sukos is recovering much of its old charm and excitement. For the harvest-time hut (the archaic word is "tabernacle") is a perfect instrument for delighting and instructing the children. Those who mourn the absence of something like a Christmas tree in our customs have never given the suko a thought, or more likely have not heard of it.

You can construct the hut in your own yard. There are portable ready-made sukos which take most of the work out of the job. What is wanted is nothing more than three or four walls, some slats of wood at the top, and the covering for the roof — branches, boughs, grass, reeds. There has to be room in the suko for a table and chairs. Decorating the suko becomes a pleasant game of improvising patterns with fruits, vegetables, flowers, and anything else that adds color and gaiety. The small children dart in and out of the booth, playing some version of cops-and-robbers, as the children doubtless did in the hills of Judah thirty centuries ago when the suko was going up. Older children help in decorating the suko or they take over the job entirely, and find enormous fun in doing it. The heaps of fruit, flowers, corn, squash dwindle on the table. The bare walls of the suko disappear under living patterns of yellow, scarlet, and green.

Night falls. The family dines by candlelight and moonlight in the open air, in the curious hut filled with harvest fragrance. The old holiday melodies and chants sound strangely new outdoors. Maybe it is so cool that they dine in coats. Maybe the weather holds, and they have an idyllic dinner alfresco, in the scented gloom of the suko. Sometimes it rains, and a half-annoyed, half-hilarious scramble indoors ensues. The charm of broken routine, of a new colorful way of doing familiar things, makes Sukos a seven-day picnic — one that is dedicated and charged with symbol, as well as delightful.

In the city, these pleasures of Sukos are hard to come by. Community meals in a hut on the roof or in the yard of a synagogue are the best that many people can manage. Even that much is a vivid reminder of what Sukos can be.

The law of Sukos reads, "And you shall take the fruit of a pleasant tree, and palm branches, and thick leafy boughs, and willows of the brook, and rejoice before your Lord God."

This is not a suggestion of improvised decoration, but the basis of one of Judaism's spectacular symbols, the rite of the palm branch.

The *esrog* is a fragrant yellow fruit native to the Holy Land, much like a lemon but larger, with a curious brownish button at the tip, the withered blossom which never wholly drops off. The worshipper takes in one hand a green palm branch wreathed at the base with fresh willow and myrtle, and the yellow esrog in the other; and he marches with these tokens of the ancient Israelite harvest in formal synagogue processions, and waves them in the Hallelujah chants. It is not hard to get willow twigs and myrtle in almost any country. But palm branches do not grow in Copenhagen, nor do esrogs in Quebec. International shipment of these articles begins long before Sukos. By the time the holiday comes, any Jew who wants to perform the rite of the palm branch is usually able to do so.

Distant in time and place as we are from the Holy Land of David and Solomon, the sight of palm branches waving to a Hebrew chant in an American synagogue stirs echoes of a great past. So does the Hosannah procession, a parade led by the cantor carrying the Scroll of the Law, followed by all who have the branch and fruit. In the old country it was often only the rich man of the town who could own a *lulav* (palm branch) and esrog. The congregation bought a set out of its treasury, and all the worshippers took turns reciting the benediction and waving the branch. In the United States today — and more so in Israel — a mass of swaying palm branches in the synagogue, and the perfume of esrogs diffused through the air, make this one of the loveliest of Jewish rites. The impression on children is deep.

Like Passover, Sukos runs all week long, but only the first and the last days are full festival observances.

Sh'mini Atzeres: The Eighth Day

At the end of Sukos there is an eighth day, called Atzeres in the Bible, a separate feast without the symbols of hut, palm branch, and fruit.

This day has become one of the merriest in the Jewish

calendar. The reading of the Torah comes to an end with the last chapter of Deuteronomy and begins again with Genesis; for this reason the holiday has acquired another name, the Celebration of the Law: *Simkhas Torah*. Outside Israel this fete takes place on the added ninth day.

Nobody who has been in a synagogue during the Celebration of the Law needs to be told what it is like. For one who has never seen it, description will be pale. The manner varies from the exalted frenzy of the Hasidic congregations to the decorous dancing and singing in the elegant Manhattan synagogues. The essence everywhere is the same: excitement, music, joking, joy within the usually solemn precincts of worship. Seven times, chanting processions circle the synagogue with all the Holy Scrolls. Flag-waving children march behind in cheery disorder. Hoary jests sprung year after year draw the same laughter always. The honors of the day, grand prizes of congregation life, go to members distinguished in learning, philanthropy, or hard work for the synagogue. The man who speaks the benediction over the last verses of the Torah is Bridegroom of the Law. He is immediately followed by the Bridegroom of Genesis, saying the blessing over the first chapter of the Bible, "In the beginning . . . ," which the sexton chants forthwith. A powerful jubilation irradiates the synagogue. The time comes when the rabbi is himself drawn into the rejoicing and solemnly dances with a Holy Scroll in his arms. My grandfather, patriarchal and reserved all year long, was still performing this dance in his nineties, a few shuffling, tottering steps, his face alight with pleasure as he clasped the Torah in his old arms.

The Cycle of Nature Festivals: Summary

The nature festivals today, even in Israel, are but a remembrance, a token, of what they once were. The gorgeous pilgrim processions along the highways of Jerusalem, the crowded and brilliantly decorated holy city, the great Temple of the Lord, its ranks of white-robed priests, its silver clarions, its golden gateways, its vast musical chants, its awesome solemnities — all these things are words in old books.

But the Torah of Moses, which ordained the festivals, the processions, the priesthood, and the Temple solemnities, prophesied that the glories would be temporary, that the people in their prosperity would lose their hold on the law and on their land, and would scatter into exile; and it ordained that the nation should go on observing the festivals wherever they dwelt, to all time. And so we do. Our people has lived for thousands of years in the faith that in God's good time he will restore the nation to its soil, and that the festivals will take on, in the latter days, their ancient force and beauty.

Meantime — and it has been a long meantime! — these holy days, diminished as they are in substance and in pomp, are bulwarks of Judaism in exile. In Israel, even among the non-religious, they have speedily become major national celebrations. To neglect them is to neglect the dikes that hold back the sea of oblivion, and to cheat oneself of pleasant and informing experiences. Words are dry and tenuous compared to vivid acts like clearing the home of leaven and marching with the palm branch. You can listen to a hundred lectures and read forty books on what Judaism is, and learn less than you can by carrying out in a single year the duties and the pleasures of the festivals.

NOTE: This book transliterates Hebrew in the Eastern European pronunciation I learned from my father and grandfather. Now that I am conversant in modern Israeli Hebrew, I would naturally say Sukot, Shavuot, etrog, and so on. But let the words stand as written in 1958. — HW (1985)

Chapter 6

The High Holy Days

JEWS who never enter a synagogue or temple at any other time, Jews of all shades of thought — Conservative, Reform, orthodox, unaffiliated, atheistic — somehow manage to crowd their way into a congregation for at least an hour or two on Yom Kippur. They will pay high, even the membership fee for the whole year, in order to do so.

This mass behavior has affected synagogue and temple architecture. Designers keep inventing different shapes and compartmentations to allow for a flood of people one day of the year, while trying to avoid the glum spectacle at other times of a handful of worshippers confronting a forlorn rabbi in an almost empty hall. No wholly satisfying solution has yet been found to this puzzle. It has the fascination of an enduring mathematical riddle, like squaring the circle.

So certain is the American Jew of this one fact about Judaism — the importance of Yom Kippur — that he has won recognition of the day from civic authorities. In cities with a large Jewish population Yom Kippur is virtually a legal holiday. Ordinary business calendars note the day. Everywhere schools and employers accept as a matter of course the absence of Jewish pupils and workers. To a certain extent Yom Kippur has carried along with it in popular esteem the Jewish New Year, Rosh Hashana. Together the two observances constitute a major religious event, the

High Holy Days, or Days of Awe. The Talmud calls the period from Rosh Hashana to Yom Kippur *The Ten Days of Repentance*.

What is this hypnotic observance which still binds Jews to their identity when all other links have rusted through or snapped?

Legal Description of Days of Awe

The statute governing the days is bare and brief. It is in Leviticus, Chapter 23, verses 24–29:

> In the seventh month, on the first day of the month, you shall have a rest-day, a day of remembrance, horn-blowing, and holy assembly. You shall not do any servile work, and you shall bring an offering to the Lord.
>
> The tenth day of this seventh month is the Day of Atonement. It shall be a holy assembly for you. You shall afflict your souls, and bring an offering to the Lord. You shall do no work on this same day, for it is a day of atonement, to atone for you before the Lord your God. Every soul that is not afflicted on this day shall be cut off from its people. Every soul that does any kind of work on this day, I shall cause to be lost from among its people.
>
> You shall do no work. It is an everlasting law, for all your generations wherever you shall live. It is a sabbath, a rest-day for you, and you shall afflict your souls. Beginning on the ninth of the month in the evening, from evening to evening, you shall keep your sabbath.

The seventh Hebrew month, *Tishri,* is in harvest time, usually in September and October. The Days of Awe precede the Sukos feast, which starts at the full moon. There is no explanation in the Torah for the rite of horn-blowing on the first of Tishri, and the day is called the start of the seventh month, not of the New Year. We must look to other sources to understand the ceremonial as it now exists.

Yom Kippur, on the other hand, is today exactly what it is called in the Torah: a day of atonement and of ascetic discipline, a day of "afflicting the soul."

An account of the Atonement ceremony takes up the whole of Chapter 16 of the Book of Leviticus. This was the one day of the year when Aaron entered the dread silent space, sealed off by a curtain, in the western end of the sanctuary in the desert: the holy of holies, the place of the Presence, the place where the stone tables of the law, and the broken fragments of the first tables, lay in the golden Holy Ark, under a massive gold lid ornamented with two cherubim. The Talmud describes how the high priest went about this same awesome rite in the last days of the Second Temple.

What the high priest did on this day, in the desert sanctuary and in the two temples, was to seek forgiveness for himself, the priesthood, and all Israel, for transgressions of God's law. When the ceremonies, lasting nearly all day, came to an end without mishap, the news sped from the Temple throughout Jerusalem, touching off jubilation everywhere. Yom Kippur in Temple times was therefore a two-sided day, filled with solemnity and dread, but marked also by exciting pageantry and, in its closing hours, by an outburst of public gaiety.

What has come down to us today is only the solemnity, the asceticism, the sense of confronting one's Maker face to face in judgment, the awareness of time passing and of life's sands running out. The law codes tell us that Atonement Day should have gladness in it. They suggest white vestments for the worshippers, to symbolize confidence in a renewal of purity through the mercy of God. But since the fall of Jerusalem any gaiety that was in Yom Kippur has faded. Our Atonement Day is a time of mordant grieving melodies, of bowed heads and wrung hearts. No one who has heard the

Kol Nidre chanted at sunset when the holy day begins can doubt that the worshippers are carrying out literally a law many thousands of years old, and afflicting their souls.

"Afflicting one's soul" traditionally means five abstentions: from eating and drinking, from sex, from bathing, from anointing the body with oil (the Oriental hygienic practice), and from the wearing of leather shoes. The last four are the abstinences of a newly bereaved mourner, and the rabbis enacted them on Yom Kippur to add to the awe of the day. Fasting is a law of the Torah. Today almost every Jew who has any religious impulse abstains from eating and drinking for the twenty-four hours of Yom Kippur.

The community spends the whole day in the synagogue. The Yom Kippur liturgy is by far the longest in the Hebrew religion. All the prayers turn on the theme of repentance before judgment, of release from sin and error, as do the Rosh Hashana prayers; for the day of horn-blowing is part of the Judgment and Atonement drama. Together the two prayer books picture the Days of Awe in one grand metaphor, which runs through dozens of prose-poems, dithyrambs, litanies, confessional tables, and soliloquies.

The Metaphor of the High Holy Days

A horn blast reverberates through the dark reaches of the universe. The angelic hosts, drawn up in array before the throne of God, shudder at the sound. It is Rosh Hashana, the day of judgment. The scrolls of fate roll open before the Lord. In these scrolls every man's hand has written his deeds of the year past. God reads the entries and pronounces judgment, fixing the destinies of every human being for the year to come: who shall die, who shall live, who shall be rich, who shall be poor, who shall rise in the world, who shall fall, who shall live in peace, and who shall stumble in misery.

This decree on the day of horn-blowing is not final. Men have ten days in which to search their acts, repent of misdeeds, perform good works to alter the balance as it stands, pledge themselves to better conduct, and throw themselves on the Judge's mercy in prayer. Yom Kippur, the last of these days of grace, is a crisis of confession and repentance. As the sun sinks to the horizon, the scrolls of fate roll shut. The destinies of all men for the coming year are sealed. The annual judgment ends at sundown with a last blast of the horn.

This is the burden of a central poem of the High Holy Day, *Unessana Tokef* (Let Us Acknowledge the Power). It comes during the Musaf service, near noon, when synagogues and temples are full. The worshippers stand in massed ranks and chant the poem together. In congregations which have cantors and choirs, this is the moment for an outburst of High Holy Day music on a grand scale.

In this one image, all the rites and themes of Rosh Hashana and Yom Kippur merge. The blowing of the shofar, the ram's horn, is an alarm, as it was for the tribes of Israel in the desert when the enemy approached, and for the armies of David and Solomon in the Holy Land; an alarm waking the soul to Judgment. The enigmatic words, "a day of remembrance," with which the Torah describes the first of Tishri, become clear; God reviews the deeds of the year, and men recall with dread that all acts come at last to an accounting.

So runs the liturgic metaphor. Metaphysical speculation in Judaism is informal; there are few doctrines, dogmas, or philosophic certainties. Our religion assumes that God exists, and that the Torah is his law for us. The Talmud is full of contradictory statements of sages on questions of theology. The statements are preserved and studied side by side, and no official position emerges. Where contradictions touch action, there is always a *halakha,* a decision, so that we know what to do. But in theological abstractions, as well as in natural science, Judaism is inveterately open-minded. This trait has served our faith well.

Does time exist as an unrolling scroll for God? Nobody knows these things. Men live by the clock and the calendar; that we do know. We have only one way of shaping the future — by taking to heart what the past teaches. "The Torah speaks in the tongue of men," the Talmud says. Judaism from the start understood the Torah statutes of the first ten days of Tishri as establishing an annual reckoning of the soul, a judgment and atonement, and so the days stand in the religion today.

The Machinery of Penitence

It goes without saying — though the rabbis were careful to spell it out anyway — that postponement of self-discipline to the saving power of the Atonement Day is ineffectual and absurd, in Jewish law and in common sense. A man who sins away happily, counting on Yom Kippur to get him off, is a fool.

Atonement on this day is a process between a man and his Creator. The atonement for any ill one man has done another, the Talmud says, begins with repairing the injury in full; then one seeks God's absolution. A prayer on Atonement Day does nothing, before God or man, to absolve a hit-and-run driver, or an adulterer who holds to his mistress. Our fathers in the ten days of repentance used to seek out every person they could possibly have injured, and beg forgiveness; they used to go to great lengths to pay all outstanding debts. Devout Jews do so still.

Repentance in our faith looks to the future. The word in Hebrew, *t'shuva,* means returning. The dread promotion jacket of the armed services, where a man's mistakes pile up without hope of erasure, does not exist. The past can be cancelled by a true cry from the heart to God and a return to his law. This holds not only for the annual reckoning, but to the last hour a man lives; so my grandfather taught me.

He had in his Bronx apartment a lodger less learned than himself, and much fiercer in piety. One day when we were studying the laws of repentance together, the lodger burst from his room. "What!" he said. "The atheist guzzles whiskey and eats pork and wallows with his women all his life long, and then repents the day before he dies and stands guiltless? While I spend a lifetime trying to please God?" My grandfather pointed to the book. "So it is written," he said gently. — "Written!" the lodger roared. "There are books and there are books." And he slammed back into his room.

The lodger's outrage seemed highly logical. My grandfather pointed out afterward that cancelling the past does not turn it into a record of achievement. It leaves it blank, a waste of spilled years. A man had better return, he said, while time remains to write a life worth scanning. And since no man knows his death day, the time to get a grip on his life is the first hour when the impulse strikes him.

One can speculate about these puzzles of judgment and atonement. There is little room for argument about the dramatic power and moral force of the High Holy Days. The first shrieking blast of the ram's horn in the crowded synagogue chills the spine. The repeated blasts, the weird alterations from long to short, from wailing to straight, shake the nerves. The voice of alarm has not altered in thousands of years. The ram's horn and the air-raid siren describe the same sound patterns and do the same thing to the human heart. With the alarm comes the remembrance of things past and the confession of failure.

There is no machinery in Judaism for confession to a human being or for release from sin through an agency on earth. Confession in Judaism is a whisper of the entire congregation at once. It is confession in formal unison, not outpouring of one's own misdeeds. An alphabetical table of offenses, two for each letter, with a summary by categories of all religious failures, is a central prayer of the Atonement liturgy, recurring many times. This is all the confessing anybody does. The confession table seems almost to be a mask to keep a man's wrongdoings a final secret between himself and his Maker.

That the confession is drawn up as a prayer en masse is unmistakable. The wording throughout is plural: we . . . us . . . our . . . Such usage in a piece of liturgy at the heart of a holy day cannot be an accident of rhetoric. It means something. A man can acknowledge his own past sins in his heart when he speaks the words that do describe things he has done; but he utters no testimony against himself to any ear on earth. The whole autonomy rests with the individual conscience.

But in a sweeping paradox, this same confession that seals the individual in his privacy with God draws him into an ancient communal bond. All the prophecy of Israel turns on one simple but extremely difficult idea: namely, that *all Israel, living and dead, from Sinai to the present hour, stands in its relation to God as a single immortal individual.* The mass confession stamps that idea at the heart of Yom Kippur.

I shall not attempt to justify this extraordinary concept, but only to describe it.

The Immortal Individual

In itself the idea is not so strange as it at first seems. We have around us immortal compound individuals. General Motors is one. Denmark is another. In principle, General Motors does not die; it enters into contracts; it can commit crimes; it can be punished. Denmark can owe debts though all the Danes who borrowed and spent the money are dead. Were this not so, there would be no selling of Danish bonds. Denmark can be injured and can sue the offending party in court. It treats with other hypothetical super-individuals: Britain, Soviet Russia, France.

Immortal Israel, however, is something more. The Torah laws do establish corporate Israel across space and time. In this they resemble other national legislation, uniting many people under a legal system. But the national idea undergoes a startling extension at the outset, at Sinai. Parallels break down.

The reader remembers the story. Moses ascends and descends the mountain several times, acting as an intermediary between the Lord and the elders of the people, renewing God's old covenant (or testament) with Abraham. The terms of the testament — the word in the Bible means a contract — were these: God undertook to make of Abraham's seed an eternal people, a light to the nations, provided they would hold to the patriarch's monotheism and his obedience of God's law. Now that the descendants of Abraham exist as a small new nation, God inquires whether they want to ratify this covenant. The elders, speaking for themselves and their posterity — as founding fathers do — solemnly declare themselves ready to undertake observance of the Torah. The compact thus sealed, God reveals the Ten Commandments and proceeds to unfold the rest of the law.

This compact is, of course, "the old testament," the one subject of the Hebrew Bible. The name is Christian, setting off the Jewish Scriptures from the gospels which establish a new religion. For the descendants of Abraham, the followers of Moses, this is the one testament they hold from their fathers. In the traditional view neither party has abrogated it, and it is in force.

The party that ratified it at Sinai established an immortal corporate individual — a new nation — like none on earth; a peculiar people bound to observe not only civil and criminal legislation but a moral code. No other nation ever undertook as a matter of law to love God, to observe his commandments, to love their neighbors as themselves, to protect widows and orphans, to feed and clothe the poor, and to preserve the symbols and rites of their fathers. In the practice of the world, these things are the domain of ethics and religion. Israel has them in its statutory law. Perhaps it was an inhumanly difficult undertaking, but our forefathers went into it.

We Americans pay debts that dead Congressmen contracted. We honor treaties that dead presidents signed, sometimes at the cost of our lives. We submit ourselves to a constitution written by long-dead hands. It is the way of the world. But it is startling, for one not used to the color of Hebrew thought, to accept morality and worship of God as commitments of the same force.

We read that the sound of the ram's horn rang out from Mount Sinai continually during the utterance of the Ten Commandments. There is no explanation for this, or for any other occurrences that went with the event. The bold imagery that Jewish prophecy uses so freely, here blazes up into a blinding picture. What happened at Sinai was in its nature indescribable. Something happened there that the world has been unable either to fathom or to forget. The covenant that was proclaimed with blasts of the shofar still exists. The immortal individual who entered the covenant still lives. On days of annual judgment and atonement, this individual strikes the balance of his performance under the covenant and confesses his failures to blasts of the shofar. And so the compact between God and Israel carries forward into a new year, as it has already done several thousand times.

The Season for Hope

"Repentance, prayer, and good works," the liturgy says, "can dissolve the evil decree."

Old Omar put the opposite view on this subject once for all, and FitzGerald clothed it in perfect English:

> The Moving Finger writes; and, having writ,
> Moves on: nor all your Piety nor Wit
> Shall lure it back to cancel half a Line
> Nor all your Tears wash out a Word of it.

Pessimism is certainly the literary vogue at the moment. But a certain inconsistency in fashionable pessimism itself—perhaps its unbecoming energy and wit; perhaps the literary prizes that its proponents gather, and their far from despondent expressions in the photographs after the prize announcements—*something* weakens the crape-hung message. Men who take the trouble to be so brilliantly hopeless at such laboring length do not think quite so little of the universe as they say.

On the visible facts of life, Judaism can be as pessimistic as the happiest of the prize winners. Job, Ecclesiastes, and some passages in the Talmud express despair with black eloquence not bettered in modern literature. What changes the whole picture and throws the verdict the other way is the Jewish conviction that an invisible God exists. As the world grinds on through good times and bad the Jews act in the belief that God is there, that events do not rise out of the chance play of eyeless forces, that men can make themselves and the world better by abandoning past mistakes, resolving on new good works, and looking to God for guidance and long justice. The whole notion of an improvable and improving world, of fate being in men's hands, of a universe that holds steady, of the absence of whimsical gods, of possible progress toward a kinder and healthier day, is Hebrew. It is the chief gift of Israel to civilization after the idea of the God of Abraham; of which, indeed, it is a first corollary.

The Hebrew people draws its optimism from its idea of the universe. Disaster, protracted poverty, mass murder, have never dissuaded the Jews from the vision caught at Sinai of an unseen God. They believe not only that he exists, but that he is interested in men; that he wants them to become better than they are; and that he gave them a law that points the way to a better world. This is solid ground underfoot for those who find it. If he is indeed in the universe, there is hope. Blind forces balanced precariously can churn into final chaos. A seeing force can control its tools. The Jew orders all his acts on the hypothesis that God is there, so he is a hopeful man. Acting on that hypothesis, he has lasted a very long time.

Call it luck if you will. But since hope is the spring of survival on our planet, perhaps the American Jew shows an old race wisdom in clinging to the High Holy Days, no matter how his hold slips for the moment on the rest of Judaism. The spirit of Yom Kippur is a spore out of which the structure of our old religion can grow again; for it is the germ of the whole, and it does not die.

Chapter 7

✦

The Minor Holy Days

WE call certain observances minor which rise not from the law of Moses but from events at the close of Bible times or afterward.

It is a curious fact that out of the spectacular seven hundred years from the conquest of Canaan to the Persian exile — the golden age of Hebrew history, the era of the Judges, the Kings, and the Prophets, of true nationhood, of the First Temple, of great wars and victories, of towering figures like Samuel, David, Elijah, and Solomon — out of such a politically decisive era, which in any other nation would have created all the important legal holidays, the Jewish people celebrate not one event. The holiday calendar leaps from the desert wanderings to the fall of Jerusalem, with no memorial day for anything that happened in the intervening centuries.

The three post-Mosaic holy days are the Ninth of Av, Purim, and Hanuka. Their laws of observance are less stringent than those of the major festivals.

The Ninth of Av: Tisha B'av

You might call this day the Pearl Harbor of Jewry. The Babylonians on the Ninth of Av, 586 B.C., broke into the Temple of Solomon and sacked it. Six hundred and fifty-five years later, on the same date, the Romans destroyed the

Second Temple. This fatal coincidence linking the nation's two greatest disasters has left an ineradicable scar on the memory of the Jews.

They mark the Ninth of Av by a fast and by all the Yom Kippur abstinences, though there is no work stoppage. Some eat no meat during the first nine days of this month. The very pious observe mourning customs: letting beard and hair grow and avoiding festive events in the three weeks between the seventeenth of Tammuz (when the army of Nebuchadnezzar breached the walls of Jerusalem) and this day. There are other minor fasts in the calendar on days of national calamity, but none has the extensive customs and liturgy of the Av rite.

In the last meal before the fast, one dish is eaten sprinkled with ashes; often an egg, symbol of dumb grief and of the rolling changes of fortune. The congregation assembles after sundown in a darkened synagogue, shuffling on slippered feet, talking in the hushed tones of people in a house of death. There are no greetings, no handshakings, no smiles. After evening prayers, the congregants sit on low stools or on the floor, touch ashes to their foreheads, and with candles or flashlights follow the chanting of the dirge over Jerusalem, the Book of Lamentations. They sing medieval mourning songs, the *Keenos,* with funereal melodies. They leave the synagogue as silently as they came and disperse to their homes without farewells.

In the morning service the men pray without phylacteries and shawls, as men do who have not yet buried their dead. They wear these at the afternoon service, the one day in the year when this occurs. Like the other minor holy days, the Ninth of Av carries no Mosaic restrictions on labor or travel. Most people go about their business after worship, though the devout meditate through the fast day on Scriptures like Jeremiah and Job.

The Ninth of Av falls in July or August. Urban congregations are decimated. Many have shut down until Labor Day for want of a quorum of worshippers. For this reason the rite has been until recently at an ebb in American Jewry. With the rise of suburban communities which stay reasonably intact in vacation time, the observance has revived. There is extensive reprinting of its liturgy.

Some have argued that, with the birth of modern Israel, mourning for the fall of Zion has become an anachronism. But the Jewish national memory is long. It is not likely that the grim date of the capture of Jerusalem and the ruin of two temples will be forgotten.

Purim: The Feast of Esther

Purim is the nearest thing Judaism has to a carnival. It is another full-moon celebration, falling on the fourteenth of Adar, usually in February or March. The origin of the holy day is in the Book of Esther. The occasion is, of course, the famous deliverance of the Persian Jews from their Hitler-like oppressor, Haman.

The keynote of Purim is riotous rejoicing. The Talmud gives leave to a worshipper to drink on this day until he cannot tell the difference between "Blessed be Mordecai" and "Cursed be Haman." To the credit of many otherwise non-observant Jews, they often do their best to comply. The most staid synagogue-goer will drink a formal little glass of whiskey. In Israel a public street festival not unlike Mardi Gras has sprung up, with the name *Ad'lo Yoda,* the Talmud words for "until he cannot tell the difference."

The day before Purim is the Fast of Esther, a sunrise-to-sundown abstention. At sundown the synagogues fill up. The marked difference between this and all other occasions of the Jewish year is the number of children on hand. Purim is

Children's Night in the house of the Lord. It always has been, and the children sense their rights and exercise them. They carry flags and noisemakers, the traditional whirling rattles called "groggers," which can make a staggering racket. After the evening prayers the reading of the Book of Esther begins, solemnly enough, with the customary blessing over a scroll and the chanting of the opening verses in a special musical mode heard only on this holiday. The children are poised, waiting. The Reader chants through the first and second chapters and comes at last to the long-awaited sentence, "After these things, the king raised to power Haman the Agagite" — but nobody hears the last two words. The name "Haman" triggers off stamping, pounding, and a hurricane of groggers. The Reader waits patiently. The din dies. He chants on, and soon strikes another "Haman." Bedlam breaks loose again. This continues, and since Haman is now a chief figure in the story, the noisy outbursts come rather frequently. The children, far from getting tired or bored, warm to the work. They do it with sure mob instinct: poised silence during the reading, explosions on each "Haman." Passages occur where Haman's name crops up several times in a very short space. The children's assaults come like pistol shots. The Reader's patience wears thin and finally breaks. It is impossible to read with so many interruptions. He gestures angrily at the children through the grogger storm and shoots a glance of appeal to the rabbi. This, of course, is what the children have been waiting for. The stag is down. Thereafter to the end it is a merciless battle between the Reader and the children. He tries to slur over the thick-falling "Hamans," they trip him every time with raucous salvos. He stumbles on to the final verse, exhausted, beaten, furious, and all is disordered hilarity in the synagogue. It is perhaps not quite fair to make the Reader stand in for Haman on this evening, but that is approximately what happens.

I have described an old-fashioned Purim. The custom has immense vitality, and most American congregations, even Conservative and Reform, are familiar with it to some extent. Those that are not are the poorer. All vital religions have such an interlude given to the comic spirit. Purim is ours.

On Purim Day the burlesque merrymaking continues. There is a very old tradition of mummery. Strolling players in former times acted the surefire drama year after year in the villages of Poland and Russia. Nowadays children dress up and enact the Purim Play at school. The note of parody invades the study halls of the pious. "Purim Torah" is a form of elaborate nonsense-learning carried on to this day, a tangle of wild jokes proving absurd laws by strict Talmudic method. The satire on sacred forms of Talmud study is extremely biting. In the modern yeshivas the Purim Play has evolved into a freewheeling lampoon in music, rhymes, and skits. No personages, no institutions are safe. The deans and rabbis themselves come in for burlesque which draws blood. Purim is a sort of safety valve which lets loose in humor and roistering all the pent irritations and pressures of the year. It is a wonderful time.

Beyond this gaiety, it carries four religious obligations: to hear the *Megillah* (the Scroll of Esther) read, to distribute largesse to the poor, to make a feast, and to exchange presents with neighbors and friends. This last institution is *Shalakh Manos,* the Sending of Gifts: things that can be eaten and drunk the same day.

Our forefathers made a great point of sending food on plates wrapped in cloths from house to house. Children ran the Shalakh Manos through the streets, collecting tips in sweets or wine. The custom was a source of excitement and nerve strain for housewives. The wrong amount or the wrong kind of Shalakh Manos sent to a touchy relative could give undying offense. The Purim feast, the *Suda,* began at noon and continued through the day. Families with crowds of guests ate huge repasts, and then ate the Shalakh Manos as it arrived. There was universal open house. Guests roved from one feast to the next. There was no poor Jew who was not everywhere welcome; no Jew rich or powerful enough to close his doors. The custom survives today in enclaves of the pious. Perhaps it is not wholly restorable in the United States, more is the pity. It is a long way from the Lower East Side in New York to the fashionable suburbs. Nor have we the overpowering sense of community that existed in the ghetto stockade. We are not a sealed-off settlement of inferior citizens, for which we can only thank Heaven. But we have lost some of the levelling camaraderie that prevails in a state of seige.

Hanuka: The Feast of Lights

A casual question about Hanuka occasioned the writing of this book. Yet there is nothing really accidental, in the United States today, in starting an inquiry into Judaism with a question about Hanuka, the last and least of the minor holidays: last in time of origin, least in prescribed observances.

It is the one holy day not rooted in Bible narrative; the one day that celebrates a military event; the day, in short, that comes closest to being a bridge between ancient Judaism and our modern world, and that lies farthest from the Mosaic revelation. Adventuring back in time toward Sinai, we encounter Hanuka first among the calendar milestones. The observance is nearest to us not only in time, but in the nature of the crisis that gave rise to it.

Hanuka celebrates the successful revolt of the Jews, in the days of the Second Temple, against the Seleucid Greeks, inheritors of the Syrian chunk of Alexander the Great's collapsed empire. The eighth in the line of Seleucid kings, Antiochus Epiphanes, undertook to force the Greek religion on Judea, on the old but evergreen theory that religious non-conformists were a threat to the state. He so far succeeded that in 168 B.C. his armed forces installed an idol in the Temple in Jerusalem and appointed Jewish apostate priests to sacrifice swine to the Greek god in the courts of Solomon.

Antiochus made it a capital crime throughout Judea to teach the Bible or to circumcise boys. His army went through the country, installing idols and apostate priests in every village, unopposed at first by the stunned and cowed populace. The break came when one old man, Mattathias of the priestly Hasmonean family, refused to sacrifice to the fetish set up in his town of Modin, and killed with his own hand the man who stepped up to slaughter the swine in his place. His five sons rescued him from the army, took to the hills, and organized a rebellion which in three years swept the Greeks from all Judea. Thus the act of one resolute old man changed an evil tide of events. The entire future of Judaism may well have turned on the blow Mattathias struck.

On the twenty-fifth of Kislev, 165 B.C., the loyalists, led by Judah Maccabee, the warrior son of Mattathias, recaptured the Temple and began eight days of purifying and rededicating ceremonies. Hanuka means Dedication. The festival marks these eight days when the Temple was restored to the worship of God. The service continued thereafter for over two centuries, until the Romans overthrew Jerusalem in the year 70 and destroyed the House of the Lord, which has yet to be rebuilt.

Hanuka Today

I have here summarized the Hanuka story because it is not, like the Bible narratives, part of common Western culture. In a thousand years of national existence on the soil of the Holy Land the Jews over and over drove out oppressors and regained independence, but the Maccabean war, a battle for religious liberty, alone found a place in the rites of our faith. It stood out. It was the Jews' first full-scale encounter with the question that was to haunt them in the next two thousand years: namely, can a small people, dwelling in a triumphant major culture, take part in the general life and yet hold to its identity, or must it be absorbed into the ranks and the ways of the majority? In the two great worlds of current affairs — the Communist empire, which so much resembles an ancient military dictatorship, and the tolerant, skeptical free West — they face the question again.

The Communist position on the Jews is generally, though with less crudity, that of Antiochus. Our religion the Soviets consider a barbarous relic, superseded in wisdom and soundness by Marxism. The training of children in this exploded Semitic superstition goes against good sense and the interest of the state. So the police discourage such teaching, in ways sometimes oblique and sometimes forcible. For Greek religion substitute Marxism, and the Russian Jews are back where their fathers were in 168 B.C. — with whatever differences one may find in the relative truth and beauty of the Greek and Communist cultures.

The challenge of the West is different, though just as serious. The proposition is the old one: that the Jews are confronted with a better way of life and should give up their religion for it. Forces that are not coercive, and therefore do not call forth the human impulse to fight them, urge Jews along this path. The position of the government, and indeed the deep conviction of most American leaders, is that the Jewish community has the right to hold fast to the faith of its fathers and ought to do so. What contradicts them is the tidal force that Tocqueville long ago marked as the great weakness of a democracy in his unforgettable phrase, "the tyranny of the majority." The pressure to emulate neighbors, the urge to conform to popular views and manners, the deep fear of being different — these, in the United States, are the forces of Antiochus. Where the power of the sword long ago failed, the power of suggestion has recently been doing rather better.

It would be pleasant to believe that the stabbing relevance of Hanuka to Jewish life in America has occasioned the swell of interest in the holiday. But a different and perfectly obvious cause is at work. By a total accident of timing, this minor Hebrew celebration falls close in the calendar year to a great holy day of the Christian faith. This coincidence has all but created a new Hanuka.

The old Hanuka was a shadowy half-holiday of midwinter, a time of early night and late morning, of snow and slush, of days filled with blue-gray gloom only half dispersed by feeble yellow street lamps. It hardly seemed a holiday at all. Fathers left for business in the morning in work clothes. Children trudged off to school by day and scrawled homework at night. There was no celebration in the synagogue, no scroll to read, no colorful customs, no Bible story. For eight nights running one's father, when he came home from work, gathered the family, chanted a melody heard only at this time — so that it came for ever to recall the sadness of winter twilight, the feel of cold wet wind on chapped hands, the hiss of steam radiators, and the smell of falling snow — and he lit candles in an eight-branched menorah on the window sill: one the first night, two the second, and so forth, until on the last night eight candles flared in a row. But even then the menorah made but a quiet little blaze. The candles, like the holiday, were slender and unpretentious; pale orange, inclined to bend and wilt, and quickly burned out; not at all like the stout Sabbath candles that flamed half the night.

The first evening of Hanuka had the most life, because then

the parents and grandparents gave the children Hanuka money, a quarter or a half dollar; riches indeed, if a careful mother did not at once produce the steel savings bank and force the children to feed the coins into that horrible thin black maw which consumed half the joy of childhood. And on that night there was the novelty of the *latkas,* the cakes of potato batter fried in deep fat, which only the calorie-thirsty engine of a child could properly digest and be thankful for.

At Hebrew school there was a sort of temperate quasi-Purim; perhaps the acting out of battles between Jews and Greeks, with cardboard helmets, shields, and swords. The teachers told the Maccabean tale and added a legend of a lamp miraculously burning eight days in the Temple. It all seemed of small account because it wasn't in the Bible and because nothing was made of it in the synagogue beyond a few added prayers. Sometimes the children were given nuts, raisins, and hard candies; and also strange little gambling tops, *dreidls,* with which one could quickly triple one's hoard of sweets or lose it all. That, more or less, was the old Hanuka; vivid and recognizable enough, from year to year, but frail compared to Sukos and Passover or the weekly Sabbath. The colossal jamboree of the department-store Christmas of course overwhelmed it like a tidal wave.

It was entirely natural for a new Jewish generation growing up in the United States to feel each December like children in the dark outside a house where there was a gay party, pressing their noses wistfully against the windows. That Judaism had its own rich and varied occasions of gaiety (as perhaps we have seen) was beside the point. Most second-generation Jews were but poorly trained in their own faith; and anyway the Christians had a brilliant midwinter feast, and the Jews did not. Some families solved the problem in the simplest way by introducing Christmas trees, Christmas presents, and Christmas carols into their homes. They argued that it was harmful for their children to feel underprivileged, and that the Christmas tree was a mere pleasant ornament of the season without religious content.

Meantime in schools where there were large numbers of Jewish children a dual celebration of Christmas and Hanuka sprang up, as an official symbol of mutual courtesy and tolerance. This in turn generated a new Jewish interest in Hanuka. Even those Jews who were celebrating Christmas in their homes — tree, holly, "Born is the King of Israel," and all — began to find it seemly to add an electric menorah for their windows and perhaps even to light the candles. This apparently solved the problem by giving the children the best of both worlds.

Of course all rabbis, even of the most extreme Reform tendency, inveighed against this institutional hodge-podge, on the grounds that it could do nothing in the long run but muddle the children. But pulpit words in such a situation are handfuls of sand against a rising river. I once knew a gifted and most liberal-minded Reform rabbi in the suburbs who preached against Christmas trees in Jewish homes. He was called on the carpet by his board of trustees and sternly warned to confine his remarks to religion and leave people's private lives alone.

The interesting point here, and the only one worth making, is the way the pressure of the majority can persuade one that its demands are one's own spontaneous desires. A Jew who feels large chunks of his heritage slipping away from him, and observes himself behaving more and more like the massive majority, should make very sure that this is a result he truly wants, and that he is not being stamped willy-nilly by the die-press into a standard exchangeable part.

The aggrandizement of Hanuka itself is a fortunate accident. The level of knowledge of all Judaism must rise when any part of it happens, for whatever reason, to gain attention. The son of my skeptical friend is not likely to stop after learning about Hanuka. A lack of clear and satisfying religious identity hurts American Jews most in December. That is why the apparently trifling issue of the Christmas tree generates such obduracy and such resentment. It rasps an exposed nerve. It is a good thing that Hanuka is then at hand. If the old custom of Hanuka money has become the new custom of Hanuka gifts, that is a minor shift in manners. The tale of the Feast of Lights, with its all-too-sharp comment on our life nowadays, is very colorful. It is of the greatest use in giving the young a quick grasp of the Jewish historic situation. The gifts win their attention. The little candles stimulate their questions. The observance seems tooled to the needs of self-discovery.

The Hanuka candles by law burn in the window so that the passer-by can see them. The sages called this "proclaiming the miracle." The legend runs that the Maccabees found in the recaptured Temple only one flask of oil still intact under the high priest's seal, and therefore usable in the golden candelabra. It was a single day's supply. They knew that it would require at least eight days to get more ritually pure oil, but they went ahead anyway and lit the great Temple menorah. The oil burned, the legend says, for eight days.

This Midrash is an epitome of the story of the Jews. Our whole history is a fantastic legend of a single day's supply of oil lasting eight days; of a flaming bush that is not consumed; of a national life that in the logic of events should have flickered and gone out long ago, still burning on. That is the tale we tell our children in the long nights of December when we kindle the little lights, while the great Christian feast blazes around us with its jewelled trees and familiar music.

The two festivals have one real point of contact. Had Antiochus succeeded in obliterating Jewry a century and a half before the birth of Jesus, there would have been no Christmas. The feast of the Nativity rests on the victory of Hanuka.

Chapter 8

✦

The Prayers, the Synagogue, and the Worshippers

GOD cannot be much of an Almighty, it has long since been observed, if anything we say in prayer is new to him, or useful, or capable of having an effect. If God exists, he is omniscient. If he knows everything, he knows the future, including any future prayers that we may utter. If he knows the future, it is for practical purposes fixed; and if the future is fixed, prayer is waste motion, the moving of pieces after the game is over. I figured out this neat dead end, or read it somewhere, at the age of twelve or thirteen, and maybe I stopped praying for a while; I cannot remember.

But if I did I started again pretty soon. Dead end or no, a man wants to praise God for the marvels of life, and to ask to be spared its terrors if possible, and to give thanks for what he has in hand, in health, family, and work. He wants to, that is, if a sense will not leave him that God is there. In Judaism praying for benefits is a very small part of the liturgy. Most of it is commitment of one's fortunes to God, and meditation on sacred writings which put in clear words the few great points of our religion. Its daily aim is a renewal of religious energy through an act which declares one's Jewish identity and one's hope in the Lord.

As to whether any material difference in this life results from prayer, who can say? How does one set up the controls of the experiment? One can spin paradoxes about God in action by the hour; they prove nothing at all, and since the eighteenth century they have mainly interested sophomores. Huckleberry Finn prayed for a fishing pole, and got a pole and no hooks, whereupon he gave up religion as an economic recourse. It is a perfect parable. Nevertheless Moses prayed and Miriam was cured of her leprosy. Whether she would have been cured without the prayer, there is no earthly way of knowing. If you believe in fatality, prayer is nothing. If you believe in God, the prayer of a man is an event; not necessarily a decisive event, or we would all have our fishing poles with hooks when we wanted them, but a new element in a situation, like a birth.

No doubt there is much sanctimoniousness in the world, and a lot of empty mumbling is passed off as devotion. A man of urbanity may feel embarrassed at taking part in ceremonies where that sort of thing can occur. I am not sure my urbanity is quite up to the mark. Sometimes, all too often, my own praying has been depressingly mechanical. But sometimes I have felt a sense of communication with the Force that took the trouble to give me life. The uncommitted reader will overlook this as auto-suggestion or mental ailment. Something too much about the author here; but it seemed less than honest to proceed on this subject without a certain clearing of the ground.

The traditional Jew prays three times a day — morning, afternoon, and night. These services vary with the time of day and with the season. Some central prayers never vary; but on holy days the liturgy changes and expands.

A Visit to the Synagogue

Even the most convinced unbeliever is likely to have an occasional religious mood or fancy, no matter how much he may disapprove of it; as the most devoted husband feels an unwanted stir of pleasure now and then when a pretty girl passes by. Nature will out. The human impulse — if the secularist prefers, the human weakness — that has created and perpetuated religion is not absent from any breast. In such a passing religious moment, the Jewish skeptic may go so far as to wander into a synagogue to see what the faith of his fathers has to offer him.

He is handed a prayer book that strikes him as a jumble, with English translations that for long stretches make little sense. He is apt to observe preoccupied and inattentive worshippers reeling off Hebrew with few external symptoms of devotion, or whispering together while a reader chants a long singsong. Now and then everybody stands, he cannot say why, and there is a mass chant, he cannot say what; or if he dimly recalls it from childhood, he cannot find it in the prayer book. The time comes when the Holy Scroll is taken from the Ark for a parade to the reading desk, the bells tinkling on its silver crown. The reading in a strange Oriental mode seems endless, and he observes that it seems endless to some other worshippers too, who slump in an unfocussed torpor, or chat, or even sleep. If there is a sermon, especially from a young rabbi, the chances are that it is a digest of articles from the past week's liberal newspapers and magazines, with a few references to the Bible. The skeptic leaves — early, if he can — well satisfied that his views are sound, that his religious fancy was a temporary touch of melancholia, and that if the Jewish God exists, there is no reaching him through the synagogue.

The experience will be somewhat different, probably, if he happens into a synagogue so old-fashioned that its rabbi is a bearded ancient who speaks Yiddish. In that case the worshippers may seem more fervid in their devotions, though no less apt to chat now and then. The sermon — if the visitor remembers his Yiddish — is likely to strike at least a momentary response from him with vivid racy imagery, with insights into life that are curiously phrased but dig deep. He may leave with a wisp of regret for days and ways that are done; for of course there is no reviving Yiddish as a community tongue or teaching it to his children, who probably attend a progressive private school.

All this presumes a visit to a traditional synagogue. Conservative and Reform temples, with some differences in manner and custom, offer parts of the same substance. When the whole has no good effect on him, we can assume that parts probably will not either.

A Night at the Opera

The reader will perhaps remember, in this connection, his first visit to the opera. The chances are that he went sometime in his late teens or early twenties, urged on by an enthusiastic companion, perhaps female. The chances are, too, that he was skeptical about grand opera and suspected it might all be an elaborate boring fraud, a dead transplanted art form which American snobs and phonies pretended to enjoy because going to the opera was a high-class European habit. For all I know, this is the present opinion of opera that many of my readers hold.

But those who have changed their minds will recall that they did not do so on their first visit. Then, on the contrary, they probably saw confirming evidence of their suspicions. Fat old men slumped asleep in the boxes, their stiff shirts buckling; their wives more interested in the clothes and faces in the other boxes than in the stage performance; soulful creatures needing haircuts standing in the back of the orchestra, or squatting on the floor, in self-conscious poses of rapture; on the stage a fat screechy woman pretending to be a demure little country bride, a little man with a potbelly and short jerking arms impersonating Don Juan, a chorus of aging painted ladies, and men with ridiculous matchstick legs in tight hose, making tired clumsy gestures at acting now and then; while the orchestra tootled and tinkled without cease one monotonous kind of sugary noise; that, in all likelihood, was his first impression of one of the miracles of human inspiration, Mozart's *Don Giovanni*.

Sir Thomas Beecham once said that *Don Giovanni* has never had an adequate performance — that is, a troupe of singers capable of singing it, and an audience equipped to hear it. The run of singing artists does not produce in one generation enough voices to match Mozart's demands. The people who fill an opera house on any night are — people; some wonderful, some ordinary, some stupid, some insufferable, some dragged there by wives, some coming there to prove they are intelligent, some coming out of habit, some to tell the folks back home that they saw a New York opera, and some who love Mozart as they love the sunlight, and who are willing to endure all the coarseness and failure of another performance for the sake of the shafts of lovely light that despite all will break through now and then.

As performers and audience cannot usually rise to Mozart, the rabbi and his congregation cannot usually rise to Moses. That does not mean that the law of Moses is less sublime than world opinion acknowledges it to be, or that the forms of popular worship it has inspired are not capable of carrying its message down the years. The fact is that the synagogue, for all its human weaknesses, has done so. Every synagogue at every service has worshippers to whom the words and the ceremonies are transfusions of strength and intelligence; perhaps a few, perhaps many. The visitor's quick look cannot go inside their heads and hearts; in the good phrase of the jazz addicts, he does not dig what he is seeing.

What the Synagogue Is

The synagogue began as a kind of popular law school well over two thousand years ago. In classic synagogue architecture there are always study tables placed where the light is best. The tables have become vestigial or have disappeared in many American structures, as the synagogue, with the rest of Judaism, has undergone the dislocation of a shift of hemispheres. It is a pretty good guess that where an old rabbi sermonizes in Yiddish the tables will still be found; and the old rabbi will be found at one or another table with his followers, expounding the law.

It is a social axiom of Judaism — like our American doctrine that all men are created equal, which we know to be romantic, but which nevertheless stands as our working ideal — that all Jews are law students, commencing their studies at five. From this course in Torah law nobody graduates. Advanced students become rabbis; that is, literally, teachers. But in the Jewish diction rabbis do not teach; they learn with their students. One says quite literally of a master of the Talmud, "He knows how to learn." The theoretical norm of Jewish conduct includes enough labor in the marketplace to support one's family, the rest of one's time going to the law. Since this norm operates for perhaps one percent of Jewry, it is a somewhat abnormal norm; admirably intellectual, perhaps, but not geared to the distribution curve of human traits. Nevertheless, as a working ideal it deeply stamps our institutions and our manners.

It determines, for instance, the liturgy and the atmosphere of the synagogue; what we do there, and the way we do it. The very heart of synagogue practice is the reading of the Torah, week by week, in fifty-two sections, so that once a year in perpetuity we review and discuss our whole statutory law.

When the First Temple fell and the great daily service in Jerusalem stopped, the vacuum at the core of the religion might have brought on a total collapse. But Jewry, with the regenerative power that is its magic, created a new institution. In the houses of law study that existed everywhere in Judea and Babylon, the Jews took to offering devotions like those that had gone with the priestly ceremonies, adding prayers for an end to the exile and a restoration of the Temple. The house of study evolved into a house of worship. It kept its character as the law school of the masses, but services became fixed in its pattern.

The Second Temple revived Jewish life in the Holy Land, but much of Jewry remained in Babylon. The synagogue held its place as a center of worship as well as of study. When the Romans levelled the Second Temple, the synagogue became the fortress of the faith, the place where Jews gathered, learned the law, and prayed; the intellectual fortress, and in times of attack often the physical fortress.

In this form, the institution successfully traversed twenty centuries.

Naturally, such an immense stretch of time left its marks. The liturgy kept gathering layers of new devotions. A simple structure became overlaid with additions from Bible and Talmud, and with fresh compositions by rabbis of different centuries. Copyists and printers tended to cut nothing that had once been added, for that approached sacrilege. The prayer books became steadily longer, the Hebrew more difficult — pure clear Hebrew is usually ancient — and the forms more complicated. By the nineteenth century a morning festival service contained enough material to take up, if spoken with due attention, six or seven hours. The habit of racing through prayers arose. When I was a boy, I marvelled at the ability of the adults in the synagogue to proceed at such breakneck speed through difficult medieval poetry. I looked forward to the day when I too would have such mastery of Hebrew and such powers of concentration. Now I know that nobody has such powers.

A change in such a state of affairs had to come. The Reform movement tore the liturgy to bits, retained a few fragments translated into German — later into English — and that was that. The Conservatives kept more of the liturgy and more Hebrew, but drastically modified or cut out prayers and ceremonies going back to Temple times. In the traditional synagogue there has been a slow process of bringing the prayer book back to its classic form. More and more we tend to skip the cabalistic acrostics of the Middle Ages, which not one worshipper in a thousand can understand — though those who do maintain that they are deep and lovely — and to give more time and attention to the pure and transparent Hebrew of the prayers that come down from the oldest times, that are the core of the service, and that anyone who knows even a little Hebrew can easily say.

This process is not a smooth one. Old pietists naturally dig in against omission of any prayers they have come to know. Youngsters can hardly be trained to handle the essential liturgy in the time given to Hebrew study. The mere machinery of an American religious center — membership drive, building drive, committee meetings, men's club, sisterhood, youth league, and so forth — tends to overwhelm all. The young rabbi comes out of his ordination with a head full of Talmudic lore and plunges into a vortex where everybody is an authority: the synagogue's president, the chairlady of the sisterhood, or even a novelist who pokes into the Talmud now and then. He is told to comment on the news; not to comment on the news; that he speaks above the people's heads; that he is debasing himself to the popular level; that a modern rabbi must be a social leader, a fund-raiser, an inspirational orator, a jolly good fellow, a passable cardplayer, and a pious figure no less awe-inspiring than his bearded forebears in the old country; and in this whirl of contradictions and impasses he must spend his days and gain his bearings. The wonder is that we still have young rabbis, that the number of synagogues is increasing, and that the outlines of a stable modern service are appearing. The vitality of Judaism is the reason. While controversy waxes over the coming shape of the tree, the old tree slowly and steadily puts out its new branches. And as the French say, the more it changes the more it becomes what it was.

The Creed and the Service

At the heart of all our liturgies — the forty minutes of an ordinary Tuesday morning, as well as the twelve solid hours of the Day of Atonement — lie two devotions. I will call them the Creed and the Service, to indicate their nature. In the synagogue their names are the *Sh'ma* and the *Shmone Esrai* — that is, literally, Hear, and The Eighteen.

Around these two key prayers cluster excerpts from the classics of Jewish literature and law: the Torah, the Prophets, the Psalms, the Talmud: for the synagogue remains, as it always was, a study hall. The worshipper, repeating the day's prayers, traverses the main fields of Judaic learning, fulfilling his formal duty of perpetual study.

The two basic prayers are short. The Creed itself you can say in a few seconds, the Service in a few minutes. A worshipper pressed for time, reciting these two devotions, performs the ritual of Hebrew worship; for the Sh'ma is the essence of our law, and The Eighteen is the link between the synagogue and the ancient Temple. The full texts of both are in a note to this chapter, so the reader who is wholly strange to the prayer book can know what they are.

The Sh'ma contains the one verse of Scripture that probably every Jew in the world knows by heart, or has at least heard often, Deuteronomy 6:4:

Hear, O Israel, the Lord our God, the Lord is One.

The observant Jew says it in the morning and at nightfall every day of his life, with three related passages from the Torah. It is the first Hebrew sentence a child learns, and it is the utterance with which every Jew is supposed to breathe his last.

On this point I will obtrude a short personal anecdote. I used to wonder whether, in the last extremity, a man could really call to mind and recite the Creed. Then once during a typhoon in the Pacific I was almost blown off the deck of a ship, and I remember quite clearly thinking, as I went sliding toward my fate, "Well, if I drown, let me say the Sh'ma as I go." Luckily for me the lifeline I grabbed happened to hold; and so I postponed the utterance, and the world has a few plays and novels it could well have wagged along without, and the patient reader is enduring the present harangue. I believe there are one or two literary critics who may wish I had gotten to say that watery Sh'ma, but I cannot help that, a man hangs on if he can.

The Service is an extremely old litany of eighteen blessings. A nineteenth was added in Talmudic times; and on Sabbaths and festivals there are only seven; but The Eighteen is still what everybody calls the devotion. There are three Eighteens, morning and afternoon and evening, to parallel the Temple rites.

Must Prayer Be in Hebrew?

The first tractate of the Talmud, *Benedictions,* fixes the times and customs of saying the Sh'ma, does the same for The Eighteen, and then develops the blessings for all occasions of life. The antiquity of the Creed and the Service is evident in the matter-of-fact way the Talmud discusses them.

Benedictions lays down the rule that one should bless the Creator for every good in this world; and it even contains a remarkable blessing on evil news. Perhaps the most startling passage in it, for a modern reader, is an open authorization to pray in English, that is, in any language one understands. The popular notion is that English prayer is a shattering heresy. Our common law allowed it two thousand years ago.

Despite that, the Jews have always clung to a Hebrew liturgy. In previous times it might have caused less trouble and disaffection if the prayers had been in Greek, Aramaic, Latin, Egyptian, Arabic, Spanish, French, Turkish, German, Polish, or Russian. But the community, by a continuing mass instinct, has held to the Scripture tongue. That instinct is asserting itself today in the United States, in the Reform and Conservative movements, which year by year bring back more Hebrew into their devotions.

Today we have printed translations. In olden times, when knowledge of Hebrew was sometimes scantier than it is today, there was an important synagogue officer, the *meturgeman* or translator, who called out line by line the vernacular meaning of Torah readings. In certain Sefard prayer books you will still find interlinear Spanish. Our people have put themselves to all this awkwardness and difficulty and persisted in praying in Hebrew. My guess is that they will always do so.

A language has a genius. Some works translate well, others are untranslatable. Molière is effective only in French. Without knowing Arabic nobody has ever understood the Koran. Pushkin remains a possession of the Russian people, though the world has acquired Tolstoy. In general, the higher the charge of peculiarly national identity and emotion, the less translatable a work is.

The Hebrew Bible speaks with power in all the tongues of earth, but it sounds to nobody else as it does to the Jews. The

Second Table of the Ten Commandments reads in Hebrew something like this: "Don't kill; don't be vile; don't steal; don't tell lies about others; don't envy any man his wife or house or animals, or anything he has." This sounds shockingly wrong in English. For the English genius, religion is solemn and stately; Canterbury Cathedral, not a *shul*. The grand slow march of "Thou Shalt Nots" is exactly right. Religion for the Jews is intimate and colloquial, or it is nothing.

Our liturgy, at least the classic part, is as colloquial and easy-flowing as the Torah. No adequate or even approximate translation of the prayer book exists.* The King James Bible serves as a mine for splendid translations of Psalms and other Scripture stretches. Even so the change from Hebrew to English drastically alters the feeling. Translators of other sections use the King James diction — *wouldst* and *thou* and *vouchsafe* and *loving-kindness* and all the rest — and the tone and texture of our prayers nearly evaporate. People complain sometimes that praying in English makes them feel as though they were in a church. It is a just reaction. They experience the English genius, not the Hebrew.

All the same, half a loaf is assuredly better than none. If prayer in the current language resulted in a stronger and better informed Jewry, whatever the watering down of meaning, every man of sense would be for it. But on that head we have twenty centuries of experimental evidence. Translated prayer has been, in the communities that have adopted it, a first step toward general loss of Hebrew. Loss of Hebrew has always been a long step toward loss of law, custom, and knowledge, and toward oblivion by absorption.

The fact is that Judaism always has worked by raising the small cadre of Jews to an extraordinary cultural level. The

* This situation is improving. — HW (1985)

Jews to stay alive have had to know two or three languages. All of them have always had to read and write. It is everlastingly uphill work. Nothing else seems to answer.

During the war I led many services in English, and I have prayed in English. The Talmud surely is right to advise a man to pray in any language that he understands rather than to give up prayer because he does not know Hebrew. For all that, I do not imagine that I can spare my children the old Jewish task of mastering the holy tongue. This was true before the birth of Israel made it an important modern language. Goethe in his day, Edmund Wilson in ours, learned Hebrew to find out what the Bible was driving at. So in all times have many Christian scholars. We learn it to find out what our Torah is telling us and what we truly mean by our prayers. It is work. But any intelligent adult in a year can command the simple Hebrew of our liturgy if he wishes.

One worshipper becomes the prayer leader, or "messenger of the assembly." His special status lasts for one service, then he returns to his place. Anybody who can read Hebrew aloud correctly can take a turn at the reading stand. Most congregations use a prayer leader with a good singing voice — a cantor — on Sabbaths and festivals. The purpose is to add charm to the service and draw crowds. Of course the piety of the cantor, who week after week leads the service, becomes a matter of concern. The mistaken impression thereby arises that a cantor holds some kind of religious office. He is, however, simply a Jew who knows Hebrew and can sing.

Every Jew has the same prayers to say. There is no intercession, no praying by proxy, and the most pious and world-revered rabbi has no different duties or offices to perform in worship than any thirteen-year-old boy.

The prayer leader keeps order by chanting first and last lines of prayers. He repeats aloud the Eighteen Benedictions, with the congregation responding, "Amen." The task is an easy one. Many a neophyte who knows Hebrew goes confidently to the reading stand and leads the prayers, and nobody has anything but praise for him. After some attendance in the synagogue he realizes he is missing all the refinements of *nigun* (melody) and he becomes shaky and self-conscious. But in a lifetime of worship he will always encounter Jews who know nigun better than he does, so there is nothing for it but to plunge in and do his best. Any man who speaks the Hebrew loud and clear performs the office.

A truly necessary office is the *shamas,* or sexton. An expert in nigun, he is the factotum of the synagogue. He cares for the library, prayer books, and shawls, serves as prayer leader when no qualified worshipper appears, ensures a quorum of ten at all times, and reads the Holy Scrolls. A synagogue can get along without a rabbi and a cantor. But there must be a shamas, or some worshipper must do a shamas's work.

Some Major Variations

After the Roman dispersion, the Jews pulled together in two general communities: the Ashkenaz of North and East Europe, and the Sefard of the Mediterranean lands. They came to pronounce Hebrew differently. Their customs and their liturgies branched into distinct forms. This split exists today. Israeli Hebrew, for instance, is Sefard. It takes some relearning for a Jew who has the Ashkenaz education usual in America.

In New York there is an important Sefard congregation more than three hundred years old, founded by the first Spanish-Jewish settlers in the New World. In this charming Spanish-Portuguese Synagogue, at Seventieth Street and Central Park West, the Sefard liturgy lives on, different in rite and melody from the Ashkenaz worship that wholly surrounds it, and to some tastes more evocative and picturesque.

A number of the congregants bear old names of the original Spanish founders, whose families are a roll of honor in American history.

The interesting thing about Jewish worship, considering the long dispersion, the total absence of a governing religious body, and the difficulty of communications until recently, is not the variation in customs and text but the underlying sameness. One finds in the Talmud, written before the nations of Europe even existed, minute discussions of how to say prayers that Jews still recite today in Tokyo, Johannesburg, London, and Los Angeles. An American or British Jew wandering into a Sefard synagogue in Israel full of dark-skinned Yemenites will feel temporarily at sea; but once he is handed a book he can follow the service and say his prayers.

Utter silence during prayer is the rule, and words spoken during the Sh'ma and The Eighteen are especially serious violations. In the old-time East European synagogue this rule suffered partial eclipse.

The poverty of the ghetto forced synagogues to support themselves by auctioning off Sabbath and holy day honors. Calls to the Torah, opening of the Ark, and so forth, all went for a price. The auctions were colorful and exciting enough, but the mood of prayer naturally vanished while they went on. They were often quite long. During the reading of the Torah, moreover, it became the practice for each man, as he was called to his *aliya,* or reading turn, to announce his contributions to the synagogue's many charities. For each announcement he or his family received a public blessing by the shamas. Again this was a process of high economic value, but not attuned to thoughts of the higher world.

These customs came to America with the great waves of Jewish immigrants at the turn of the century. They enabled many tiny congregations to survive and grow into majestic synagogues and fashionable temples. With the prospering of the Jewish community, these devices of desperation have gradually given way to conventional fund-raising. The auction atmosphere of the Torah-reading time, and the exodus of sidewalk gossipers during this part of the service, are only memories now. There has been a fairly effective restoration of the rule of silence.

I would not give up for anything, all the same, my remembrance of the mournful auction chant of the shamas: *Finif tollar um shlishi!* Five dollars for the third reading!" Nor do I want to forget the historic auction one Yom Kippur afternoon nearly forty years ago, in a synagogue in a Bronx cellar, when my father outbid men with far more money (though they were all poor struggling immigrants) for the reading of the Book of Jonah. One by one the competitors dropped out as the bidding went up past a hundred, a hundred twenty-five, to the incredibly magnificent sum of two hundred dollars, bid in one devastating leap by my father. I can still hear the crash of the sexton's palm on the table, and his shaken happy shout, *"Zwei hunderd tollar um maftir Yena!"*

My father made this tremendous and costly beau geste because his own father, a shamas in Minsk, had had the prerogative of reading the Book of Jonah, and he was determined to keep the custom in the family. He did, too. In that synagogue nobody ever seriously bid against him for the honor again. To this day my brother and I read the Book of Jonah at Yom Kippur services wherever we can. We have done so in places as far apart as Chicago, Hawaii, and Okinawa.

The auctions are a thing of the past and it is better so, but they served a purpose. Children in such synagogues learned unmistakably what a precious thing a call to the Torah was.

Some Difficulties

The newcomer in a synagogue will of course feel strange and ill at ease; he will be put off by the matter-of-fact manner of many of the worshippers; he will find the process hard to follow, and he will be an exceptional person not to feel discouragement at first. But persevering attendance, especially linked with any kind of elementary Hebrew training, will in a short time give him back the key to the storehouse of Jewish prayer. Then when he wants to, he will pray in the measured and fine words of the tradition; at the synagogue if he can go there, at home if he cannot.

The difficulties of a newcomer are matched, possibly overshadowed, by the problems that face the pious. If the newcomer is not at home, the novelty at least excites his attention. The synagogue-goer is too much at home. The prayers are too familiar. Years of repetition have grooved the words into his memory. If he is not at pains to concentrate, they slide by like water.

The fact is, prayer is never easy. True prayer is as demanding — at least as demanding — as the carrying on of a business conversation or the writing of a letter. It purports to be a communication with a Listener. The child and the newcomer struggle with their unfamiliarity. Devout worshippers struggle with their overfamiliarity. All men of any training or any faith are put to the greatest mental effort, I imagine, to get at any real sense of talking to God.

That being the case — since so much praying is, by the limits of human nature, doomed to fall short of what it sets out to be — the question arises, Is not prayer three times a day, in forms long fixed, mere empty machinery? It might be so, perhaps, except that the synagogue always remains what it was in origin: a study hall. One learns worship by worshipping or by trying to — there is absolutely no other way. The natural outpouring of the heart in moments of crisis is not, as the romantic would imagine, prayer at its best. Those who have been through such experiences know that they find themselves reduced to incoherent shamefaced stammering. Improvised prayer is honored in Judaism, and some inspired improvisations have entered the liturgy. The fixed prayers are the base for a man to stand on, in everyday devotion and in extremity.

Daily prayer at the very least is a review of one necessary instrument of the good life as Judaism knows it. It is a duty done, a link in the chain going back to Abraham's acknowledgment of One God, a link we add as God adds a new day to time. And there is no such thing as wholly absent, wholly mechanical prayer. A glint of the light in the words and the thoughts of the Jewish liturgy falls at some instant, at several instants, into the mind of the most preoccupied worshipper. At least he is there, praying to God, so that the glints can come.

Perhaps for saints and for truly holy men fully conscious prayer is really an everyday thing. They live, in that case, in clarity that plain people do not know. For the ordinary worshipper, the rewards of a lifetime of faithful praying come at unpredictable times, scattered through the years, when all at once the liturgy glows as with fire. Such an hour may come after a death, or after a birth; it may strike after a miraculous deliverance, or on the brink of evident doom; it may flood the soul at no marked time, for no marked reason. It comes, and he knows why he has prayed all his life.

Chapter 9

✦

Symbols of Food, Clothing, and Shelter

THE Jewish diet discipline cuts sharply across general manners and ideas. It is one of the stress points where observance tends first to break down, and so it is a sore subject. A detached picture is not likely to please anybody. The non-observant dig in their heels at the whole idea. The devout, on the other hand, who have to work pretty hard at keeping up the diet, expect to be praised, and they want to see the non-observant excoriated. The purpose here is only to tell what the dietary laws are. The reader will have to supply the moral judgments; from his emotional bias if he approaches the topic with one, otherwise from his common sense.

We are looking at a detail of a symbol system that stamps all the customary acts of life. This is the stamp on eating: an act that all people perform several times a day, given the choice. People may neglect work, play, prayer, and lovemaking, but they seldom forget to eat. All religions include grace over food. Many religions go further and set a mark on what one eats and how one eats. Often such austerities are reserved for the monk, the nun, the priest, the ascetic, the lama. Judaism's disciplines are relatively mild, but they are for everybody.

The Torah gives only one brief reason for the laws: they will help discipline Israel to holiness. My agnostic friend, you will recall, thought that declining to eat lobsters was no answer to the threat of hydrogen war. I think he has something there; but neither is getting married, or building a home, or having children, or doing a day's work. There is nothing I can think of that does not look pitifully absurd under the threat of a hydrogen holocaust, except possibly the quest for God. If the diet laws have some structural purpose in a major religion, we ought to try to find out what that may be.

We will get into guesswork. The sages of Jewry have offered varying opinions on the laws. The great trap is to notice a visible effect of the diet in one's own time, and to assume that that was the whole cause of the laws when they were given in the Sinai desert. But let us see what the laws are and how they operate.

The Diet

There is no limit on food that grows from the ground; the disciplines deal only with sentient life. The Bible gives us physical tokens of the creatures that may be eaten.

For animals, the two marks are a split hoof and cud-chewing. In effect this admits a small class of beasts that live on grass and leaves, and shuts out the rest of animal life: beasts of prey, rodents, reptiles, swine, horses, pachyderms, and primates, most of which have been eaten at one time or another by various peoples. It is sometimes argued that the ban on pigs was meant only for hot countries in olden days. Obviously the range of excluded animals puts that argument out of court. We cannot eat polar bears either. The pattern has nothing to do with climate. It seems to be formal; in logic it almost has to be. If the diet were only an advanced health notion of the brilliant Moses, the world would have in time caught up with his wisdom, and the Jewish forms would have vanished in universal observance.

Of the creatures in the sea, Jews eat those with fins and scales. This rule eliminates the shellfish so popular in America — shrimps, oysters, and lobsters; also a number of French delicacies — sea urchins, snails, mussels, frogs, octopuses, squids, and the like. I have read attempts to defend this discipline on the ground that octopuses and lobsters are revolting, while fish are not, but I think this resembles the debater's point about pork in hot countries. To anyone who eats octopuses, I am sure that a well-cooked one is an attractive sight, tentacles, suckers, and all. The fact is that within the Hebrew formal diet lie many excellent fish, and outside it — as in the case of animals — lie creatures which some folks esteem as delicacies.

There are no specific marks for birds. The Torah lists a large number of proscribed ones, all birds of prey or carrion eaters. In general Jews and non-Jews eat the same fowl. The difference is in the kosher slaughtering. Insects are wholly out. Few insects show up as food in America, but now and then at a cocktail party one has to forgo such tidbits as chocolate-covered ants.

Kosher Rules

"Kosher means pure" runs the slogan of a major manufacturer of such products.

It is pleasant to see the advertising mind strike such a round blow for Judaism, but as usual it speaks to simple intelligences, at some sacrifice of exactness. The concept is in all truth a hard one to pin down. "Kosher" is a late Hebrew word that does not occur in the books of Moses. Perhaps the nearest English word is "fit," in the sense of proper or suitable. But the fitness, it must be clear, is mostly ceremonial. Kosher preparation of food does result in a high degree of hygienic fitness. But a hog could be raised in an incubator on antibiotics, bathed daily, slaughtered in a hospital operating room, and its carcass sterilized by ultraviolet rays, without rendering kosher the pork chops that it yields. "Unclean" in Leviticus is a ceremonial word. That is why the Torah says of camels and rabbits, "They are unclean *for you,*" limiting the definition and the discipline to Israel. Chickens and goats, which we can eat, are scarcely cleaner by nature than eagles and lions, but the latter are in the class of the unclean.

All this being understood, "kosher means pure" may perhaps stand as a statement of fact. There is a general ban against eating carrion: defined as the flesh of an animal that dies of old age or of disease, or that is torn to death by beasts of prey, or that meets any other violent death. The assurance that no such meat can be sold as kosher is certainly of hygienic value, even today. In less civilized times and places it has given the Jewish diet a vast margin of sanitary excellence. This law supplies a word that Jews extend to all unfit food: *trefe,* or torn.

The Torah has four main rules for preparing meat. Commentators variously take them as humane regulations and as sanitary laws. Without forcing logic, one can perhaps find both aims in the rules. At any rate, breaking any one of the four renders the meat "torn" and inedible under Hebrew law.

The first rule, the only law of diet in the Bible for all mankind, is clearly humane in intent. It bars the eating of flesh cut from a live creature — "the limb of the living." If the reader shrinks with horror at the thought, he is not familiar with ancient killing and cooking practices that still survive in primitive communities, and in some not considered primitive.

The second law forbids the drinking of blood, on the ground that "the blood is the life." The use of blood in sophisticated cookery is common, especially for sauces.

Jewish law not only bans this, but it excludes the meat itself unless most of the circulatory blood is removed. The impression is widespread that for this reason one cannot get a decent kosher steak. Since we barbecue excellent rare steak in my home — sometimes to the stunned surprise of Jewish guests — I can testify otherwise. Enough juice remains in the tissues to make perfect steaks. But in the old country, Jewish housewives fried steaks gray-brown. They brought the style with them. The so-called Jewish steak is therefore done to death by the standards of American cookery, but it need not be. Out West on the farm one usually encounters the Jewish-style steak fried clear through. It is a matter of regional taste, nothing more.

The third rule stems from the bizarre prohibition repeated three times in the Torah in identical words: "You shall not boil a kid in the milk of its mother." The repetition suggested to Maimonides that in Mosaic times this was a common rite of idolatry. However that may be, the strong emphasis led long ago to complete separation of flesh and dairy food in the Hebrew diet. Food from the ground or from the sea is eaten with meat meals or dairy meals. Meat and milk, or their products, never appear together on the table. In observant homes, there are separate utensils and crockery for the two types of meals. In Israeli army kitchens and navy galleys, this dual equipment is standard.

The fourth rule bans suet, the hard fat formed below the diaphragm. The regulations separating suet from edible fat are complex and help make butchery of kosher meat a work for skilled and learned men. Prohibited fats are identical with those specified for the altar in the Book of Leviticus.

The Genesis tale of Jacob's wrestling with a mysterious stranger accounts for another ban in Jewish diets: the sciatic nerve of the hindquarter. Jacob was injured in the nerve of his thigh, we are told, and left the battle with a limp. The story has all the marks of a mystic vision. The encounter occurs the night before he meets his vengeful brother Esau after a separation of twenty years; it goes on till dawn; and Jacob's successful struggle against the stranger results in the change of his name from Jacob to Israel, "because you have contended with God and with men and have prevailed." The Torah adds, at the end of the tale, that in memory of the event the children of Israel do not eat the sciatic nerve.

It seems like a small deprivation. It could be small, but today it is not. The complete removal of the nerve from the hindquarters of an animal is a difficult point of butchery. It is simpler, and evidently less costly, to sell the hindquarters of kosher-slaughtered cattle to the general packers. Observant Jews therefore forgo some excellent cuts of meat. This is a remediable situation, and with a rise in demand it may be remedied.

Slaughter

The bans against drinking blood and against "the limb of the living" determine the rigid, indeed sacred, method of taking animal life under Hebrew law. There is only one way: a single instantaneous severance of the carotid arteries in the neck. The blood pours out; the supply to the brain is at once cut off; the animal's consciousness vanishes. The rest is muscular reflexes, to which the beast is as oblivious as a man in a coma, and swift death. This is what the animal physiologists tell us. Scientific testimony, gathered when this mode of slaughter has been under attack, shows that it is a death as merciful as any that humans can visit on animals, and far more merciful than most.

Stringent conditions to ensure a painless death are part of our law. If one of these precautions is omitted, the meat is called torn, and we cannot eat it. The death stroke must be a single slash. Even one sawing motion disqualifies, let alone a second stroke, a stunning blow, or any other inflicting of pain. The edge of the knife must be ground razor-sharp and smooth; one detectable nick causes rejection of the meat. The animal must be motionless at the instant of the death stroke, so that the knife may cut true. Skilled professional slaughterers, who undergo qualifying examinations for dexterity and technical knowledge, do this work. Equally knowledgeable inspectors watch each move. The guilds of slaughterer and inspector (the Hebrew terms are *shohet* and *mashgiah*) are ancient and strong. Often the office, with the complete training, passes from father to son.

The inspectors study the carcass for certain traces of disease which for thousands of years have rendered meat non-kosher. This part of our procedure is unquestionably sanitary, centuries in advance of its time. Over the generations it has helped create the exceptional health statistics of Jewish communities. As the meat passes to the consumer, there are further procedures for draining the residue of blood. These were once the province of the housewife, and mothers handed the knowledge to their daughters, but more and more today the mass distributor of kosher food performs these last steps and sells meat ready for the pot. He assumes the responsibility for getting a rabbinic opinion on doubtful symptoms.

Degrees of Observance

In former times this was not so. The housewife did most of her own inspection, especially of poultry. She bought a chicken slaughtered before her eyes, took it home, and in cleaning it checked the viscera for signs of disease and internal injury known to her since childhood. In doubtful cases she brought the meat to her rabbi. Friday morning was always the busiest time of the week for my grandfather, in his twenty-three years of ministry in the Bronx. The stream of housewives with *shailas,* religious queries, on bloody new-killed fowl was almost continuous. If he and I were studying together that morning we did not get far.

Nowadays answering shailas on fowl does not loom large in the Jewish ministry; not nearly so large as raising funds, making amusing speeches, writing persuasive brochures, and so forth. New times, new tasks. Old-fashioned people look askance at the change and hint that young rabbis today are mere affable ignoramuses. The fact is that the orthodox seminarists still get an exhaustive training, and have to pass a searching test, in the laws of meat inspection. Nineteen out of twenty seldom use the knowledge. They hardly can, unless they go into the kosher-meat-packing industry. The main task of a rabbi today is elementary education; not for the learned few, naturally, but for the disoriented general community. I for one would like to see the young divines speak, and write, and raise funds, even better than they do, since that is the task in hand. I joined the faculty of Yeshiva University to make available to them my scraps of knowledge about English usage. Once my grandfather said to me, "What do you have to teach them English for? They're American-born. They know English." This comment can stand as a summary of the distance, for better or worse, between the old and the new.

In the old country a pious man either did his own slaughtering or he worshipped side by side with the town shohet and knew his piety, skill, and intelligence at first hand. In the United States we must rely on seals of eminent rabbis, guaranteeing proper slaughter, inspection, and handling. There are devout people who cannot bring themselves to trust the guarantees. Such control of industrial processing seems too loose, too liable to error. To them the most remote risk of eating defiled meat — let alone the flesh of banned creatures or a fragment of their products — is unacceptable. My grandfather during his twenty-three years in the United States did not eat the flesh of cattle. His Sabbath meat was a fowl killed under his own supervision. He did not ask the rest of the family to follow his example. He ate in my mother's home and in mine, but he would not eat our meat. Yet even he had to rely to some extent on seals and signatures. The milk and butter he used bore guarantees of rabbinic supervision. He did not see the milking and the churning himself because he could not.

My grandfather was such a cheerful and jovial man that it never occurred to us that he was an ascetic; as indeed he was, a rather extreme one. Few people are able to forgo beef and lamb for half an adult lifetime as he did, on a point of ritual. The exceptionally pious today eat flesh called *glat kosher,* carrying special guarantees. Some members of Hasidic sects eat only meat which has been canned by other members of their sect under the seal of their own chief rabbi. If they travel, they carry enough of such provisions to last them the journey. If they run out, they subsist on raw vegetables and fruit. They will not use the utensils of public dining places. So the degrees of observance shade upward, or leftward if you will, to strictness, scruples, and self-denial, which some consider extravagant and which others regard as minimum compliance with the law.

An important point in this matter of shades of observance, it seems to me, is to avoid calling one's own practice the only true Judaism; to label anything stricter mere fanaticism, and anything less strict mere pork-eating. One can fall into such an attitude because the old stability and uniformity of practice do not at the moment exist. People who eat ham or shrimps, or steaks from electrocuted or poleaxed cattle, are clearly not following the law of Moses. People who never eat or drink in public restaurants surely run less risk of accidental deviation from the diet than those who do. The exigencies of an active life may make this strictness difficult. The observant follow conscience under guidance of teachers they trust. They all hold to the same disciplines; the variations are in detail.

Why Bother?

There is no blinking the fact that today following the Hebrew diet takes effort for anyone who is not a recluse. The eating habits of the majority confront one everywhere: in restaurants, in trains and planes, at the homes of friends. Holding to the diet calls first of all for clarity of purpose, then some will power, and certainly an elastic sense of humor, to survive and return the venerable comedy on the subject.

It seldom occurred to our forefathers to ask the question which comes at once to the American intelligence, "But why keep all this up?" For them there was far more dislocation, intellectual and physical, in searching out a piece of pork, or a shrimp, and eating it, than in eating the way Jews did. These patterns were a part of the satisfying sense of an old proud identity which a Jew had; and, at rock bottom, there was the instinct that the Mosaic law was the will of historic Providence for the Jewish people. The American community, re-examining its heritage, runs a curious questioning eye across the whole range of Hebrew practice. This causes discomfort and even anguish to parents and teachers, who are not always ready with answers to questions they themselves never asked.

In the West among the more assimilated groups, and in Soviet Russia where Jewish practice is being stamped out by the Communists, large numbers of Jews no longer hold to the diet, whether through choice, indifference, coercion, or lack of knowledge. But the majority of Jews in the world still follow the broad pattern of the laws. A very large group observes them with exact care. In the United States, after what seemed for a while a mass flight that would extinguish the practice in a generation, the laws have taken firm hold, and it appears that observance is increasing.

Part of this is surely due to the fact that keeping up the laws is becoming easier. The production of kosher foods has emerged as a large competitive modern industry. With frozen meats in mass marketing, it is becoming almost as simple to keep a kosher home as not. There also seems to be a slow steady tendency of the Jewish community — under a swirl of many movements — toward its center of gravity, the Mosaic law. Immediately, this trend would seem to contradict the law of increasing conformity to the way of majority. But social laws are not astronomic laws. People can learn things and change their motions, as planets cannot. In the United States ones does not necessarily become most like Jones by eating as he does, but by behaving as he does. Speaking very generally, Jones is a man who practices his religion and respects people who practice theirs.

This is to suggest that in the main the American Jewish revival of religion is so far a social change rather than a religious or intellectual one, just as the original drift from the faith was. But for those who want Judaism to live, a revival on any basis ought to be welcome to begin with. Presumably in time the substance can take the central place.

Nobody can argue that the present state of kosher supply is wholly satisfactory. Conflicting guarantees, lack of sure control by a recognized bureau of standards, contradictory opinions on popular brands of food, rumor and gossip on doubtful points in place of published fact — these are persistent troubles of the churning changeover from old methods to new. People who give up observance like to cite one or another of those snags, but such rationalization is not serious.

In general our ancient Hebrew diet remains as clear-cut as it was when Moses gave it to us. It is not a regime for hermits. It offers us meat and drink in great abundance and variety. The limit of luxury is one's purse and good sense, not the law. If we want to follow the diet in good faith, we can. The further improvement of supply is up to the community, exerting its force on the suppliers.

Foods of marginal hygienic value seem to be the only ones the Torah left out of our diet. Certainly Jews have survived for thirty centuries most healthily without eating snakes, pigs, worms, shrimps, or turtles. The kosher rules are on the side of cleanliness and purity, even if "kosher means pure" is less than the whole story. But the most important thing seems to be that a pattern exists in the daily act of eating, a pattern that Jews have shared since Sinai. It is a community bond and a reminder of personal identity that comes whenever a man gets hungry. It is a daily commitment in action to one's faith, a formal choice, a quiet self-discipline. The Jew who travels undergoes inconvenience, and with it a forcible reminder of who he is and what his home ties are. There is no doubt that the food laws work. They are social instruments for keeping the Jewish nation alive, and psychological instruments for preserving the identity of individuals. The essential question, the only one that the whole discussion tends to, is first whether Judaism is worth preserving; and second, whether any practical means of survival exist for it except its law.

Clothing

The obligations of dress are simple and fall mainly on men. A general maxim of Jewish law frees women from any ritual that must be practiced at a specific time of the day; and the symbols of dress are tied to times of prayer.

During morning prayers, men wear a four-cornered

fringed shawl called a *tallis*. The law of fringes is in the Book of Numbers: "That you may see them, and remember all the commands of God, and do them, and not turn aside after your hearts and your eyes." This is a large order for the fringes to fulfill, but at least they are there before a worshipper's eyes while he prays. The shawl-wrapped Jew is a universal image of man at his devotions. Pious Jews wear, besides the prayer shawl, a four-cornered undershirt with fringes all during the day.

Every morning a man also puts on phylacteries, or *tefillin*, the symbols used so much by painters to depict the Jew. These are a pair of black boxes of leather which tie with leather thongs on forehead and left biceps. They enclose small parchment scrolls containing the Sh'ma and other Bible verses. "Bind these words as a symbol on your arms," the Torah says, "and let them be emblems between your eyes." Critics have complained that it is ridiculously literal to don real boxes containing bits of Scripture. But by now we know that the use of visible act, of concrete imagery, is the essence of Jewish method. We have here a ceremony dedicating arm and brain to God. There is no more certain sign of strong Jewish identity than praying in phylacteries. That is why it has passed into the shorthand of painters. The act does not then and there make a man good, but if the imagery takes hold in his mind, it ought to make him a better man, provided he is improvable.

A custom of dress for at least two thousand years has been covering the head, especially during study and prayer. There is no prescribed form of head covering, though a Talmud passage states that a man should not walk four yards bareheaded. Essentially this is a deep-entrenched part of religious manners. A bareheaded Jew at prayers or study is an anomaly, except in the Reform movement, which discards this custom in principle (together with the tallis, the phylacteries, and many of the main Mosaic symbols and disciplines). The actual type of covering varies with time and place. Jews in Oriental and Arabic countries wear turbans. The Hasidic sects favor broad fur-trimmed hats or black felts. Our forefathers in Europe wore the *yarmulka* indoors, a wide black skullcap covering nearly all the hair. In the United States traditional Jews lean to a dark cap at the back of the head; but the caps on schoolboys are sometimes quite bright. In Israel religious workers sometimes wear a knitted cap clipped in place. Today traditional Jews in places of business, and at public gatherings not religious in nature, often go bareheaded, covering their heads at home and in places of worship. It is customary for women to wear a head covering in the synagogue.

Shelter

Two of the Torah passages that prescribe the binding of words on head and arm also require us to write the words on the doorposts of our houses. We affix in our doorways a small case containing these passages written on parchment. The box is known by the Hebrew word for doorpost, *mezuza*. Its presence in the doorway of a private home or a flat tells that the dwellers are of the Jewish faith, and that the house is dedicated to God's service.

There is no basis in law or custom for the practice, fairly widespread today among American Jewish soldiers and also among unmarried girls, for wearing the mezuza on a chain around the neck. To the soldiers it gives the comfort of an amulet. For the girls it is a quiet clear sign of their religion, probably a useful bit of labelling.

Chapter 10

✦

Birth and Beginnings: Men and Women

Circumcision

VOLTAIRE spoke with scorn of a God who could care whether or not people cut off their children's foreskins; thus summing up in one entertaining image the whole skeptical reaction to religious form. Spinoza, an equally severe skeptic, was not as funny as Voltaire; in fact there was little fun in him; but he was the profounder of the two. "So great importance do I attach to this sign," said he, "I am persuaded that it is sufficient by itself to maintain the separate existence of the nation for ever."

Circumcision has lately become respectable, after serving as a joke about Jews for centuries. It turns out to be sound hygiene. On the recommendation of medical science, informed people everywhere are now cutting off their children's foreskins. If Voltaire were alive he would probably have his own cut off. He might even find himself wishing, the day after the operation, that his parents had had it done for him when he was an infant.

But for Jews circumcision today, as in the past four thousand years, is not a detail of hygiene. It is the old seal of the pledge between Abraham and his Creator, a sign in the flesh, a mark at the source of life. It makes a man look different naked, all his life long, than the natural man looks. The levellers like to say that when you strip off men's clothes, nobody can tell the beggar from the king. But naked or dead, the Jew is recognizable for what he is. True, in the twentieth century this sign turns out to be not a comic mutilation, but wise prophylaxis, and so the critics of Judaism lose their old foreskin jokes. But the disclosure should hardly be a surprise. We expect the symbols of a lasting faith, where they touch the body, to be safe and intelligent in themselves, not to kill the faithful off. The Jews have followed the Mosaic law with a confidence which modern medicine progressively ratifies. The medical endorsement is not, however, the glory of Judaism. It is a footnote.

We circumcise our sons on the eighth day after birth, as Abraham did Isaac, except when a doctor puts off the day for a delicate child. The ordinary infant of eight days passes through the operation easily, sleeping most of the time. Done with skill, the cut causes little pain, and it heals in a couple of days.

The event is what we call a *bris,* the Hebrew word for covenant. When lying-in was a part of home life, a bris always meant a family feast, with crowds of friends and kinfolk, learned discourses, and merrymaking. Each step of the ceremony was an honor, remembered for life, conferred solemnly by the parents on a relative or distinguished guest. Babies arrive today in hushed, coldly tiled hospitals, in the odor of antiseptic, with illness above and death below. Regulations often bar any trace of gaiety. But in large cities, in hospitals where Jewish mothers go in numbers, there is sometimes a remote chamber set aside for the purpose, enigmatically labelled the Bris Room; and from this room now and then there still escape muted echoes of an ancient joy.

The father pronounces this blessing at the ceremony:

Blessed are you, Lord our God, Master of the Universe, who have made us holy with your commands, and have commanded us to bring this boy into the covenant of Abraham our father.

Ideally the father should do the circumcision himself, as Abraham did. In universal practice he appoints a highly skilled *mohel,* or circumciser, to do it. Performing hundreds of such ceremonies every year, the mohel attains experience in this operation which many surgeons will candidly admit they cannot match. Mohels use, of course, all existing medical safeguards and antisepsis.

Some Jewish parents allow a hospital surgeon to circumcise their sons, believing that he can perform the act more safely, or perhaps that it makes no difference who does it. They are in error for several reasons.

First, the mohel's familiarity with the surgical problem and its possible complications makes him the proper man for it. Accidents can occur under the most skilled hands on earth, but the parents can do no more to ensure the infant's safety than to get a qualified mohel.

Second, the circumciser takes the place of the father in a dedication rite going back four millennia. It stands to reason that he should be familiar with our religion and given to it.

Third, and perhaps decisive, Jewish circumcision differs from routine hospital practice. There is no margin of extra safety or painlessness in the hospital way, but it may be incorrectly done.

Bar-Mitzva

Bar-mitzva means "son of the commandment." The ceremony is the next milestone in a Jewish child's days; his entrance into a responsible religious life.

In my novel *Marjorie Morningstar,* I did my best to portray a bar-mitzva with accuracy and with affection. I thought I succeeded pretty well, but for my pains I encountered the most bitter and violent objections from some fellow Jews. I had, they asserted, made a sacred occasion seem comical. There were comic touches in the picture, of course, but I believe these lay in the folkway as it exists, not in the imagination of the writer.

It is a sad people that does not have humorous excess as part of its life on one occasion or another. The Dickensian Christmas is the nearest thing in literature I know to an American bar-mitzva. It has in much the same degree the fantastic preparations, the incredible eating, the enormous wassailing, the swirl of emotions and of family mixups, all superimposed with only partial relevance on a religious solemnity. Christmas in the books of Dickens bursts with extravagant vitality, and so does our bar-mitzva. We Jews are a folk of great natural gusto. In the freedom of the United States, where for the first time in centuries we have known equality of opportunity, we have made of the bar-mitzva a blazing costly jubilee. I do not see that there is anything wrong with that. The American coming-out party is not too different. If the religious occasion really held its own, and retained its meaning, all would be well. My reservation about the American bar-mitzva is much the same as the doubts of some Christian clergymen about the department-store Yuletide. The risk exists that the mere machinery of pleasure can work to obliterate the meaning of the event, leaving the celebration a tuneful and colorful hurricane whirling about an empty center.

The event itself is both moving and important.

Like any other way of life, Judaism requires training, beginning when intelligence appears in the infant. A child does not develop the mind to grasp the concepts, nor the stability to hold to the disciplines, until the age of thirteen.

The father then formally gives up the burden of his son's religious duties. The boy takes them on himself. He begins to pray in phylacteries, and on the Sabbath nearest his birthday he receives an *aliya,* a call to the Torah, to speak the blessing over a part of the weekly reading, a privilege of male adults. This call marks his new status.

The most honorific call in the popular view is the last, the *maftir,* because it includes reading the weekly piece from the Prophets. The custom long ago arose in the European communities to give the maftir to a boy on his bar-mitzva Sabbath. That is what we do still.

But of course this custom took hold in a time of general compulsory Hebrew education. For the ordinary European Jewish boy, chanting a maftir in its special melody was no harder than for an American boy of thirteen to pick up a newspaper and read it aloud. All this changed completely when the main body of Jewry shifted to the United States, with a catastrophic drop in Hebrew culture. The American Jewish boy who could read a page of Hebrew prophecy aloud without stumbling was exceptional. One who could translate it at sight, or could chant it without long painful practice, was almost a freak.

Nevertheless the existing custom was to give the boy a maftir. And so during two generations in the United States countless boys who barely knew the Hebrew alphabet were schooled to parrot foreign words in a strange musical mode, by dint of coaching stretched over a year or more. This uninforming and disagreeable process was, for the majority of them, the sum total of their exposure to Judaism.

The damage was great. The boys could see — and the sages were quite right in turning over religious responsibility to boys of thirteen, for they can perceive and evaluate very sharply — the phoniness of what they were doing. The bored coaches who for pay drove them through dreary chanting sessions every night for a year, the crutches of transliterated Hebrew and recordings, did not escape their satiric eyes. They judged that they were being drilled to palm themselves off as something they were not — properly trained young Hebrew scholars.

And yet how inevitable it all was, and is! Which parents would be the first to admit that their children were unskilled in Hebrew, when the custom was to go through a pretense that they were skilled? Human nature being what it is, the choice for the parents of ill-educated boys was to give them the customary bar-mitzva or none at all. For a long time the American rabbis were overborne by the momentum of the custom. The rationale was, "Better this than nothing." At last the evil results became too evident to ignore. Now a new and long-overdue procedure is gaining ground.

What is happening is that educators are harnessing the custom instead of being stampeded and trampled by it. Since parents and children alike have been regarding the bar-mitzva as a graduation, the rabbis have begun to treat it as such; and to require, as in any graduation, satisfying evidence of knowledge before conferring the diploma. The rote maftir under this rule no longer answers. The lad has to pass serious examinations in Hebrew, in the classics, in the laws of the faith, and in the history of Jewry. If he cannot, the rabbis do not permit the family to take over the synagogue for an empty ceremony. This means serious training has to start, at the latest, by the age of eight or nine. Judaism cannot be crammed into a boy in a year, though a maftir can be.

This policy takes courage in the rabbi and firm backing by his trustees. But since it is the obvious alternative to a continuing disaster in education, it is emerging year by year into more general use. As it takes hold, the Jewish faith stands some chance of being judged by the new generations — even if on the very simplest terms — for what it truly is. Our religion has its hard points, but it is colorful and powerful, and for four thousand years it has been interesting. It is not a chant of gibberish, which is all that the most sublime chapter in Isaiah can be to an insufficiently trained boy.

Some people of late, in a reaction to the extravagance of the American bar-mitzva, have dropped the public gala, appropriating the cost of it either as a gift to charity or as a fund to send the boy in later years on a trip to the Holy Land. This austerity seems commendable, but I wonder if it will become the rule. There is a time for everything. To provide a grand feast at such a turning point in life is an old and strong human impulse. Fireworks in season are always welcome, though they blaze and die at high cost in a short time.

When the overburdened bar-mitzva boy used to say in his memorized speech (a vestigial gesture at a scholarly discourse, now on the wane), "Today I am a man," he was of course speaking metaphorically, as his small stature, pink smooth cheeks, and breaking voice usually indicated. The manhood conferred by this event is ceremonial. The father does not expect him to start earning a living, or go to sleep at night without being ordered to, or do his schoolwork with enthusiasm, or begin reading the *Wall Street Journal*. Judaism simply holds that the boy is bright enough and advanced enough now to start operating as a Jew. He is out of his intellectual infancy. As soon as he is, the traditional masculine duties fall on him.

Bas-Mitzva

As sometimes happens with hurricanes, the whirling tempest of the American bar-mitzva has spun off a minor whirlwind called a bas-mitzva. The rationale is that girls no less than boys enter into religious obligations when they reach early adolescence, and that therefore there is no real reason why a fuss should not mark the event for girls as well as for boys.

It is easy enough to understand why there was no "bas-mitzva" for thousands of years and why it has sprung up now. Traditionally girls are exempt from advanced Hebrew studies because they are exempt from most of Jewish ritual. Our faith put the formal structure on the men to uphold, leaving the women free for their family tasks; probably the only way the system could work. The bar-mitzva when it came was a minor synagogue formality, not a family Fourth of July. A girl would have been out of her head to agitate for the burdens of scholarship that engrossed her brothers from the age of five onward for the sake of that formality; and parents would have been fools to impose them on her. But when the intensive training of boys dwindled; when the bar-mitzva became a huge festival, earned at the price of some mechanical drilling which a girl could do as well as a boy; when there were no other visible burdens or consequences; when the boy, after the fun was over, dropped all Hebrew study and most observance, the girls and the parents sensibly saw no reason why they should not have a "bas-mitzva."

The difficulty of course has been to provide the proper synagogue solemnity for girls where none has existed since Judaism began. Since there is no custom, improvisation has come into play. The bas-mitzva is often a sort of graduation from Sunday-school training, or at least the completion of one stage. In traditional synagogues the bas-mitzva does not exist. Among the other denominations it has not taken on the pomp and circumstance of the bar-mitzva. In the nature of things it hardly can.

Men and Women

The bas-mitzva is among the changes in synagogue practice that one finds in the temples of the two major dissenting movements, Conservative and Reform Judaism. Other innovations are the playing of an organ, the seating of men and women side by side, and stretches of the liturgy recited in English. The Reform changes are the more radical of the two; hats and prayer shawls for the men are abandoned, and there is little effort to keep the old service.*

I suppose any normal American would rather sit with his wife in a public place than apart from her, and his wife usually wants to be with him. Those are our manners. The way of a man with his wife in public is no small thing. The dissenting movements have made great headway in the United States by altering old synagogue form to allow for this American taste. The other changes have also been attractive. People unlearned in Hebrew do not enjoy sitting silently through a service. Catholics are trained in attendance at Latin worship conducted by priests, but the old Jewish custom is for everybody to pray at the same time in the same way. The large congregations who know no Hebrew have demanded and evolved a service they can be part of. The organ of course is a sonorous and charming instrument, which fills the temple with reverberations that wake spiritual thoughts. For that matter, it is simple to drive to a Sabbath service in a car, if you live more than four or five blocks away, and it can be a great nuisance to walk, especially in rain and snow. All these things being so, the headway made by the dissenting movements needs little explanation. One has to explain how it is that there are any orthodox people left.

*Since 1958, the bas-mitzva custom has been adopted in some orthodox circles. The dissenters in turn are reintroducing certain traditional practices. — HW (1985)

Orthodoxy remains strong, and lately it is growing stronger. Evidently it has persuasive power for some that overcomes its difficulties.

The orthodox have a general objection to the changes, and beyond that they cite laws and customs that oppose them. The objection is that while the changes do attract followers the price is too high; observance of the law dwindles. Reform they consider impossible, since by doctrine it rejects the Mosaic law; and they believe that Conservatism leads to Reform.

The ban on musical instruments like the organ has been linked to the custom of mourning for the destruction of the Temple. There musical instruments were played; we have hung our harps on the trees, the exiles in Babylon said, never to play them at worship again till we play them in the halls of God, in his rebuilt sanctuary. This decision led to a strong growth of Jewish vocal music.

The custom of separate seating of the sexes at worship goes back to Temple times. The Talmud speaks of it; it was instituted to add to the gravity of the service. It must now be almost two thousand years old. One can hardly imagine natural synagogue form or architecture without it. A variety of arguments has been thrown up on both sides of this touchy point, which — I am almost ashamed to record this, but it is the truth — is the biggest religious issue today in American Jewry. What we have is a head-on clash of American manners and Hebrew forms.

The orthodox tend to argue that one cannot pray with women at hand because of sexual distraction. The dissenters tend to retort that the orthodox are perpetuating an iniquitous inequality of women. As usual with popular debating points, these assertions glance around the main issue. I have no doubt that men are able to pray beside their wives in all solemnity, if the religious impulse is on them. I have seen extremely inattentive worship in pews holding only men. The inequality argument will scarcely wash any better. Anybody who has read the Bible knows that the Semitic common law which preceded the Torah held women as chattels, and that Moses gave them in large measure property rights and independence; Talmud law and subsequent common-law decisions brought women to the status of our mothers and grandmothers, practical equality if not dominance.

In the matter of divine worship, Jewish women hold a privileged place that many young seminarists groan for, in the mornings at chapel call. They are excused. Our common law frees women from all commands that have to be performed at scheduled times. It does not ask the mother to put aside her infant and don phylacteries; nor the woman preparing the holy day feast to leave her work, on religious compulsion, and go to the synagogue. If she has a maid, or if, as our mothers did, she can plan a stretch of clear time, she comes to worship. But in a faith which takes devotion so seriously, and which so loads the days and the years with acts of service, the freedom of women from scheduled prayers seems natural. I cannot imagine that new legislation will ever impose the schedules on them.

The orthodox and the dissenters argue at cross purposes on this matter, and will continue to do so, mainly because for most of the dissenters the great patterns of obligated prayer are weakened or abolished. Men and women alike tend to worship once a week; most of the wheeling symbolisms of Judaism turn outside their lives. The freedom of the women from the schedules is irrelevant and needs no recognition in form; everybody is free of them, more or less. When a family becomes committed to observance, the freedom of the women becomes a matter of moment, and the classic forms of worship spring into sense again. So it is that the new "modern orthodox" synagogues, for all their streamlining, fall naturally into separate worship for the sexes.

Chapter 11

✦

Love and Marriage: and Certain Elegant Variations

Sex

ABOUT one fourth of the vast Talmud consists of the order *Women:* seven long tractates treating the relation between the sexes in all its branches. If the proportion is far smaller in this slight volume — I propose one short chapter — it is not because sex interests me less than it did the ancients, nor because, being a working novelist, I am reluctant to take a busman's holiday. The underlying Jewish ideas on sex and marriage are familiar to cultivated people, needing but a brief review. The Talmud goes into the case law of sex, which is nearly endless; that is why *Women* ranges through so many folios.

From a legal viewpoint sex involves a contract between two parties, perhaps the commonest of all agreements. The contract may be a permanent one like marriage, or a temporary bargain as with mistresses and whores, or even an unspoken agreement, as in amateur fornication, when a deal is struck between two people for an exchange of animal favors. Beasts simply do it; people must agree to do it. If there is absence of agreement on the weaker side, the law calls the event the crime of rape. An act of sex seldom takes place beyond the long nose of the law, though flowery hillsides, deserted beaches, and black hotel rooms often seem refuge enough. What one does may never come up for classification in open court, but it is none the less classified. People are always finding this out in unexpected and uncomfortable legal review of natural pleasures long past. But for this fact, many novelists, newspapers, and lawyers would go out of business. The Talmud in its seven treatises covers a great range of the possibilities in this extremely various legal field.

But of course that is a dusty way of looking at the grand passion, the way of the law. Judaism has its poets and its great lovers. The Bible in its history treats sexual love with realistic understanding, and in its poetry with power and beauty. The enduring bright colors of the Bible's chief figures derive at least in part from their ever-recognizable experiences in love. Each generation has its Jacobs, who love Rachels and have Leahs thrust upon them. Potiphar's bored wife still lives in the elegant homes of the rich, hissing at handsome young Josephs her persistent "Sleep with me." A glimpse of Bathsheba in her bath can tumble a great man, now as then, into sneaking depravity and terrible remorse.

Passion is not a main concern of Scripture, which has mightier matters to tell. But when flares of passion ignite major events, the Bible pictures those flares in swift sure strokes, sparing no details out of delicacy. These are the passages which in school texts of the Bible in my time were left in solid blocks of Hebrew, the helpful side columns of English becoming chastely blank; with the result that we did more honest Hebrew study over those passages, and learned more, than from a hundred translated pages.

In the Song of Songs there is a poetic evocation of sexual love, the dazzling nakedness of which rather troubled some Talmud sages. But Rabbi Akiba called the book a sublime metaphor of the bond between God and Israel, the very peak of prophetic imagery. His view won out. The book entered the sacred canon, there to startle all coming generations with its gorgeous tropes and its sensuous Hebrew word-music, which by a literary miracle can be half discerned in the King James English. The shimmering and shifting pictures, mysterious and ill-defined, of this passion-drenched poem flicker through the Jewish liturgy and haunt the midrashic and cabalistic writings.

Akiba's interpretation may strike the reader as nothing more than a pair of theological tongs for handling such red coals of love poetry. Even if that were the case, the world would owe Akiba enormous gratitude for finding a way to preserve the Song of Songs in the sure immortality of the Bible. But any serious study of the Song brings to light a vein of allegory, or at least of very puzzling allusion, that — in the rabbis' phrase — cries "Interpret me." It becomes hard to believe that the poem is not a rhapsody with many layers of meaning. To pin these meanings down has been a labor of commentators over the ages and will doubtless continue to be.

The major Hebrew prophets used sexual imagery of a totally different kind, lurid as lightning and black as death, developing Akiba's metaphor at the end of the affair. Over and over they picture God as a betrayed husband and Israel as a dimwitted adulteress grinding to her lovers under every green tree. This shocking image so pervades Hosea, Jeremiah, and Ezekiel that Akiba's idea of the Song becomes by poetic contrast almost inevitable. I know of no secular poetry in which the horrible second face of passion appears with more freezing effect. The prophets used sexual jealousy, revulsion, and rage as figures in a grand and terrible argument, the fall of a great people and the coming of a Redeemer. They did not know what it meant to write sky-climbing fireworks of language for entertainment or to create darkly beautiful poetry for its own sake. All their eloquence was utilitarian. They were aiming to make people better. Though they lie in forgotten graves these twenty-five centuries, the tremendous poetry they struck off still works, plucking at the deepest chords of passionate experience in men. The notion that Jewish piety requires goody-goody blandness about sex cannot survive a casual glance through Scripture.

As for the Talmud, it treats sex with candid and sometimes sardonic clarity, not blinking at the overripe variations that Greece, Rome, and Egypt were so fond of (and that enjoy some slight vogue again today). Its handling of such topics indeed might have given Proust himself pause, had he looked so far into his own Jewish background.

Marriage

In view of all the curious arabesques that human invention has woven out of the crimson thread of sex, the Jewish idea of what to do with it probably seems naïve, or, in the current slang, square. Judaism regards sex as the cord that secures the union of two lovers for life: for shared strength, pleasure, and ease, and for the rearing of children.

What is crucial to it — and the point is not easy for a Western-trained mind to absorb — is its acceptance of sex. The marriage of Jewish prophets, saints, and plain people, from Abraham and Moses onward, has had no trace of concession to some supposed frailty or evil of the flesh. Judaism takes the verse in Genesis, "Be fruitful and multiply," as part of its statutory law. Because it is the first law in the Torah it holds a special eminence. The Talmud says that in the world to come the first three questions asked of a man are, "Did you buy and sell in good faith? Did you have a set time for study? Did you raise a family?" The single life is in our faith a misfortune; childless marriage, a disaster; and a good wife, the chief delight a man can hope for.

At the very root, then, Judaism cuts off the haunting Western instinct that sexual intercourse is somehow wrong. That idea is the ghost of crushed paganism rising out of the marble of overthrown temples to Venus in the walls and floors of early Christian churches. The West has enough still of Greece and Rome in it to lean toward worship of sex; but Christianity has subdued the impulse. The residue is a guilty tension nearly two thousand years old. The Jewish view falls between the two. The Jews have not worshipped the body and have not denied it. What in other cultures has been a deed of shame, or of comedy, or of orgy, or of physical necessity, or of high romance, has been in Judaism one of the main things God wants men to do. If it also turns out to be the keenest pleasure in life, that is no surprise to a people eternally sure God is good.

What sex guilt there is, in the Jewish view, is only the guilt of lawbreaking. When one violates the rules, it is as though he steals. His conscience, if he has one, disturbs him. But the sin is individual to him, it is not inherent in sex. That lovemaking does lend itself peculiarly to lawbreaking has long been noted by the minstrels. The urge to copulate is strong and chronic in healthy human beings, as in the apes. The deed can be done in secret without the usual visible traces of crime: the rifled safe, the broken window, the missing purse. Random copulation, moreover (the romance writers tell us), has an excitement that the lawful article lacks, and a parade of sex partners offers more novelty than one lover can. It would be a gayer world, possibly, if people could have true marriage and also sportive mountings with friends, neighbors, and fetching strangers. Much human experience says we cannot. Which road to choose is an equally long-lived matter of dispute. Stendhal reports with admiration a dying father's last words to his son: "Sleep with all the pretty women you possibly can; and four percent is a good return on your money." If the son took the advice he may have had an enjoyable if wearing time and died rich, but he could not have had a real marriage along the way.

Successful marriage calls for good luck as well as good faith. The Talmud puts it that each happy pairing-off is as difficult for the Almighty as the parting of the Red Sea. But even the enemies of the Jews have long recognized the stability of the Jewish family. It comes in part, I am sure, from the fact that the pleasures of sex belong to the interior of married life, not to episodes outside it.

The Marriage Disciplines

Total renunciation of sex is, in some faiths, a major discipline. In his autobiography Gandhi calls this *brahmacharya* and praises its power of spiritual ennoblement. The Roman Catholic and Greek Orthodox churches, as well as some Eastern religions, require celibacy in certain holy orders. For such austerity Judaism has no match. The mild disciplines we do have, in this as in every part of life, apply without distinction to all members of the faith.

Jewish married couples follow an old rule of alternating abstinence and enjoyment. During twelve days after the menses begin — or seven days after they cease, whichever period is longer — wife and husband sleep apart. For this reason twin beds have existed in Jewish homes as long as the religion itself. The main practical result of this is that they rejoin at the time when the wife is most likely to conceive. It is the exact opposite of the rhythm system of birth control. For couples who love each other the separation is a hardship, perhaps the one real hardship in the Hebrew disciplines. Some medical authorities call this alternation good for the health of wife and husband. One marriage manualist said it was "the only answer" to continuing freshness in married love. Whatever the force of such opinions, this self-governance in sex has always been part of marriage in the Jewish faith.

The wife marks the end of the abstinence by immersion in an ocean, river, or lake, or a ritual pool built on an ancient plan. This pool (the Hebrew word is *mikva*) has been the usual place of the rite for many centuries. So crucial to the religion did the Talmud deem this ceremony that it instructed impoverished communities to sell their synagogue building, or even their last Holy Scroll, in order to put up a pool.

The all but general abandonment of the mikva in the United States, followed by its gradual revival, is almost a history of American Judaism in miniature. When the great migration brought crowds of Jews to these shores around 1900, they found no ritual pools, and those that the pious at once put up with scraped-together pennies were necessarily dismal and poor. By contrast, any dwelling above the lowest slum line offered bath plumbing unknown in European experience, or indeed in any previous time or place in the world, excepting the baths of the rich in ancient Rome. It seemed odd to descend to the gloomy squalor of the remote mikva for a rite of purity, when water was at hand in the home, in the private white luxury of a tub.

A rationale arose against observing the rite of the pool, which soon equalled in popularity the argument against the food laws, that they were only for hot countries in the old days — the purpose of the mikva was to make sure that women in the old country bathed once a month. This argument could not survive any true information about the rite, but the level of information had dropped low. Abstinence from baths is in Judaism a sign of mourning. Frequent bathing, daily if possible, is assumed to be normal conduct.

The rite of the pool, which takes a few seconds, is wholly symbolic. In all the great religions, immersion has been a symbol of purity and rebirth. The force of the notion is too clear to need spelling out.

But alas for semantics in a time of transition! The King James English word for a woman in separation was "unclean." In this sense all Israel is "unclean"; we have been since the fall of the Temple. But for these concepts there were no ready New World words. Young American women were annoyed by the term; this, and the poverty of the mikvas, worked up hostility to the ancient practice. Pulpit declarations that children of women who omitted immersion were all bastards did not soothe any unquiet spirits. Tub baths replaced formal pool immersion for more and more couples. Since nearly all the women bathed daily anyway, the gesture had no ceremonial force; and it had no connection with Jewish law. The whole discipline of separation, which turned on the vivid rite at the close, dwindled and was eventually dropped, in most cases.

That it ever came back at all will seem astonishing, except to those who know Jewish history and the power of the river of Judaism to run uphill. In many cities of the United States new ritual pools have recently been built or are going up, handsomely tiled, with something like beauty parlors in their anterooms. The number of women who go to them is so far small compared to those who do not. But the day is past when the mikva was for a fading trickle of foreign ladies. The women who go are mostly young Americans.

As Judaism revives generally — and that it is doing so is unmistakable, from the added Hebrew in Reform and Conservative services to the mushrooming of temples and synagogues all over the land — life and attention, I suppose, flow back to the marriage discipline. Perhaps too the mikva has come to seem less strange as people have realized that the Christian ceremonies of baptism and immersion are evolved wholly out of our ancient Jewish rite. The analogy may offer a bridge to Western-educated minds. At any rate, the hostility of the immigrant generation has dimmed away. There is instead at most indifference, usually based on a lack of information. The information is not, oddly enough, easy to come by. Sex is a great subject for jokes in America, and we have schooled ourselves too in solemn-faced swallowing of graphic lectures on its mechanical side, even in popular magazines. But to talk about it naturally is another matter.

Divorce

Divorces is the name of one of the tractates in the Talmud. Judaism regards divorce as a catastrophe that is bound to occur in a certain number of mistaken marriages. Rather than chain two unsuited and hating partners together for life, our law provides the machinery for dissolving such unions.

The acceptable grounds for divorce are numerous, and the process itself a simple one. The rabbis are under the sternest rule to discourage, postpone, and prevent divorce as long and as far as possible. The law requires mediation, cooling-off periods, and persistent legal efforts at reconciliation. When these means have been exhausted, the husband, in the presence of a rabbinic court, gives his wife an ancient legal document, a bill of divorcement, and the marriage ends.

A civil divorce is not a substitute for this ceremony. A Jewish couple remains bound in religious law until the husband frees his wife according to our practice. The rabbinic court can constrain him to do so if he creates difficulties in bad faith. In a similar case it can force the wife to accept the bill of divorcement. But these are wretched, rare, and complex processes. In practical fact, Jewish divorce should be, and virtually always is, by mutual agreement.

Elegant Variations

So much would have to suffice as a sketch of the huge subject of love and marriage in Judaism were it not that I have written not a word about the most striking sex legislation in the Torah, the list of prohibited unions.

The reader perhaps remembers the Kinsey Report, published some years ago. A respectably opaque scientific study of sex manners in the United States, it became a best-seller, much to the surprise of its sober publishers, who specialized in thick medical tomes selling to a very small trade. People stormed bookstores, waving sheaves of legal tender. The publishers, to their distress, could do nothing but print vast stacks of the report, sell them, and bank the money. Not one purchaser in a thousand, I imagine, read the whole report, or half of it, or one tenth of it. They rooted hopefully through the wadded prose and the puzzling charts, graphs, and tables, sniffing — often in vain — for a few tasty truffles of fact. What they mainly learned was that it took science to make sex uninteresting.

But the newspapers had a carnival. Skilled rewrite men dug out the hidden truffles and served them up hot. The report did disclose, through the seven veils of its style, disturbing things. Fornication, adultery, sodomy, incest, and intercourse with animals it described as widespread, citing statistics from many confidential interviews. A spate of frank novels and plays in recent years had prepared the public for the news that the unmarried girls in the land were not all virgins, and that some married men and women now and then found "outlets," in the report's language, for their copulative energies, other than their proper spouses. But I think that ordinary Americans were really shocked by the disclosures about perversion and bestiality.

While the furor lasted, ministers and rabbis by and large

attacked the report as a libel on the human race and especially on American morality. I cannot quite understand why they did not perceive that a weapon had fallen into their hands. The report proved — so far as modern documentation could — that the Bible's sex code was based on facts of human nature; that the prohibitions against males lying with males, and brothers mounting sisters, and men coupling with pigs and sheep were no obsolete echoes of Bronze Age depravity, but ordinances against felonies bound to occur and to recur down the ages, like theft and arson.

What drew the divines to the wrong side of the controversy was, I imagine, the construction immediately placed on the report by agnostics. The report proved once for all, said they, that the sexual morality of the Old Testament, and therefore of Christianity as well as Judaism, went against nature and ought to be discarded in public thought and law. Dr. Kinsey's insistence that he and his staff had merely reported facts, and had severely refrained from making moral judgments, they dismissed as a sop to the outraged feelings of the yahoos. Substantial minorities of our citizens, they pointed out, enjoyed pederasty. Provided the thing was done discreetly, what then was wrong with pederasty? Fornication before marriage was common; adultery after marriage, almost equally so. Did the real abuse and damage then lie in these obviously natural acts, or in the guilt feelings that stiff Bible morality inspired? And so forth. The eloquence on the theme at the time was tumultuous. So was the eloquence on the other side in pulpits, mainly confined to denouncing Kinsey and questioning his statistics.

I do believe that those who leaped to hail the report as showing up the Mosaic moral law were falling into an old fallacy: nothing wiser or deeper than the romantic notion that in all things nature is the last court of appeal; that whatever comes of a natural impulse must be honest and therefore good. But many natural impulses are very objectionable. We have the word of some mental doctors, for one thing, that nearly all of us have a natural urge to murder our fathers and mothers. It is certainly natural to be lazy, to be idle, to be dirty, to be selfish, to be coarse, to be cruel. Anyone who does not think so has not spent much time observing children at play, or primitive people being themselves. Much of education, most of civilization, and all of urbanity consist in going against nature. So does the greater part of religion and, for that matter, of agnostic humanism.

Law codes of any kind would scarcely exist were it not for natural tendencies in many people to behave contrary to those codes. We have the traffic ordinances because nearly everyone naturally wants to go faster than the speed limit and make pedestrians skip cursing out of the way. We have the laws against robbery because it is natural to want to take money and valuable things wherever they happen to be lying around, instead of drearily drudging for them. I may bore the reader making this very obvious point at any length at all, but it seems to have been almost wholly overlooked in the tumult over the Kinsey Report.

There can be foolish attempts to mold conduct by law. We all know the lasting joke written into the American Constitution in the eighteenth and twenty-first amendments. If the moral code of the Bible were such a folly, human common sense would have dropped it in one generation as it did Prohibition. Instead, civilized men have held to Mosaic morality as the way of right conduct — which is quite a different thing from the way people naturally behave — through the better part of history.

The sex practices uncovered by the Kinsey Report are sometimes defended along another line that is just as old but not quite so short on logic. It sums up in the maxim that what people don't know can't hurt them. By this rule, undetected adultery becomes an enjoyable episode for both parties, that leaves their spouses uninjured. I once knew a highly intelligent man, a fellow novelist and a very successful one, who believed in this as in an axiom of Euclid. Moreover he was certain that everybody else in the world believed it. He argued that there was not a living man who would not sleep with his best friend's wife if he could be absolutely sure that he would escape being found out. (Since we had this discussion he has been married and divorced a couple of times; I do not know whether he still maintains the view.) He extended the rule to sodomy too. Sodomy between two sodomites was their own business, and no concern of policemen. My friend was a non-believer. It may well be that unless one believes there is a God who has forbidden these things in public or in secret the view is unassailable.

If my reader endorses discreet adultery and sodomy, we can leave the topic there. If he recoils from them, I am compelled to ask him what his rational objection may be.

He may argue that adultery damages character; that adulterers can never be sure of getting away with it; that adultery detected is a sure wrecker of the family. All this may be so, but if the adulterers are willing to take their chances, why shouldn't they? He may further say that pederasty is a sterile waste of the reproductive process, and that its practice can spread to corrupt normal people. But if the waste does not trouble the pederasts, why should anyone else care? Moreover they coolly deny there is any corruption in what they do, maintaining rather that it is the highest form of love. They regard any disapproving view of homosexuality as insufferably outdated, silly, and pompous; and for this stance they have fought, and they have won a measure of social tolerance, if not agreement.

Greece and Rome considered the Jewish prohibition of sodomy, and the strict Jewish view of the marriage tie, absurdly narrow prejudices. If we are not to backtrack (or advance, depending on the point of view) to the morality of imperial Rome — if the reader instinctively feels that Jewish and Christian practice is nearer the mark for a sound civilization — I must press him to find a basis for Western morality outside the eye of God; that is, outside the Bible and the faiths built on it. The morality of the West is either, as Nietzsche said, a long mistake based on a long delusion, or it is one of Judaism's great gifts to the human race. If we do not have the religious principle that wrongdoing in sex is wrong in itself, where is the bar to eventual erosion of our Western ways to those of Rome and Byzantium?

Chapter 12

✦

Death

The Enigma

POETS and philosophers sometimes have a go at praising death, and they even strike off beautiful and convincing passages on this theme. But we observe that, like the rest of us, they usually work hard at staying alive. The graybeard author sits wrapped in a shawl to keep off drafts, and writes that he pants for death as for a lover. Anybody who has known very old or very sick people knows the querulous tenacity with which they clutch at the slipping rope. It is all very well to say that death is what gives life its preciousness; that it is the condition on which life exists; that immortality on earth would be a worse horror than death; that one lies down to sleep with kings and with all the great of the earth; that one returns to the bosom of nature, to roll through eternity with stones and rocks and trees. Tell it to a wide-staring gray-faced man in a hospital bed in his last hours.

The Hebrew Bible traverses most of the classic philosophical positions, but I do not recall any passage in it that tries to pretty up death. Moses says, "I have put before you this day life and death; choose therefore life." The Psalmist begs for life. His gratitude flames at a reprieve from the grave. Ecclesiastes sees death as the last injustice in the unjust and futile parade of existence. And Job, whose ironic praise of death marshals all the known arguments for it in a few matchless lines, regards it as a catastrophe which has the sole virtue of ending all catastrophe.

There is in all this not much happy anticipation of Paradise and harps, and equally little fear of hellfire and devils. Death is an evil because it cuts off light and life, and because it is a thick enigma. That is what the common sense of men has always told them. It is pretty much what the Hebrew Bible tells them.

The Hereafter

This starts the great question, naturally, of the existence of such an evil as death in a world created by a good God. Enough ink has flowed in attempts to deal with this question, I believe, to make a blue-black lake the size of the Caspian Sea. It will perhaps relieve the reader if I tell him now that I have no answer of my own to labor, and that I know no truly satisfying answer, though I have read more books in this field than a generally cheerful man should.

The question can be stated so: if there is a good and just God, how can the sum of a man's life result in what clearly seems an unjust balance of deeds and consequences?

Because that is where the worst evil of death lies. It is an arbitrary cutting-off that leaves questions unanswered, things undone, debts unpaid, virtue unrequited, crime unpunished. If death came as the black line at the bottom of an even balance; if the world knew that there was an end, but that the end came when nature, logic, and justice together decreed it, then the problem of evil would either fall away or at least dwindle to a philosophic conundrum instead of being a present agony.

One obvious reply — it was struck on almost as soon as people began to think, and it holds the field to this hour as well as any — is that the time from birth to death is too short an accounting period. The Eastern religions would have it that one lifetime is but part of a long series of lives. Any apparent injustice in this life balances out with the karma, the acts and destinies, of previous incarnations. In effect, we stretch the accounting period into an unknown past before birth, and take it on faith that we arrive at a just balance in this cycle of life or in some future passage. The view holds no place in Judaism, though the cabalists do touch the idea of *gilgul,* of reincarnation.

The basic popular answer of Judaism, and of Christianity and Mohammedanism, is to stretch the accounting period into an unknown future, beyond death. There is a hereafter, another world, the world to come; and in that world deeds and consequences at last balance. The righteous receive the reward for their righteousness. The once-prosperous sinners encounter the punishment they deserve. Islam spells out the nature of this future life in some detail; and we have in Dante a magnificent picture of the hereafter of medieval Christianity.

The Jewish doctrine of the hereafter develops mainly in the Talmud, on a basis of Scriptural interpretation. Since it was one of the main points of battle between the sages and the Sadducees, a sect of the time that departed drastically from traditional law, it took on cardinal standing. What the hereafter was like; what resurrection of the dead actually meant; where and how these things would happen; what one was required to believe; these things, in the characteristic way of Judaism, escaped definition. We find conjectures of individual rabbis in the Talmud, and further guesses by medieval authorities, which differ widely. Judaism is precise where it touches acts. Thought and doctrine remain fluid. I cannot therefore describe the hereafter and the resurrection of Judaism. It is part of the religion that there is a beyond — that God keeps faith with those who sleep in the dust. I can tell the reader little more, without wandering into my own opinions.

Even in the Talmud the idea of the hereafter is shadowed forth only in metaphors and parables. Gehenna, the hell where sinners roast for their misdeeds, is Gai Hinnom, the Valley of Hinnom, a small ravine in Jerusalem where idolaters used to burn their children in sacrifice to Moloch. You can see Gehenna today from your balcony room in the King David Hotel overlooking the old city of Jerusalem. It is clearly too small to accommodate even a small fraction of the sinners of the moment, let alone those of previous generations. Paradise is a Greek word derived from the Persian, meaning park or garden. The Jewish Gan Eden, or Garden of Eden, is the mysterious place where Adam first came to life, the glorious perfect garden where there was no sin, no toil, no poison, no pain, no death, but trees, flowers, and living creatures in their pristine immortal perfection. It is, in short, a parable. We do not know where it is, or what it is like, or what precisely the parable implies.

The Explanation of Evil

The thinkers in all religions have been well aware that, as a whole answer to the problem of evil, the stretching of the accounting period beyond birth and death suffers because the living never see the beyond. We can take it on faith that the hereafter is a fact. But for most people it cannot be the kind of fact that the green of the grass is. The vulgar dismissal of the hereafter hurts: pie in the sky, they call it.

So we have that other broad old vein of religious philosophy, the attempt to account for the existence of evil within the time from birth to death. The arguments are many. Here are eight:

1. Evil is a necessary condition of free will. A world

without possible evil consequences would be a world of clockwork dolls, not of men.

2. If a universe is to exist at all with time and force and change in it, the universe we have is the best balance of all those elements, "the best of possible worlds."

3. Evil properly understood is not an existing thing to be accounted for, but the absence of a possible good. In questioning evil we are really asking for a world statically perfect, whereas we live in a world that moves toward perfection.

4. Life means change, is in fact change. Change is from one condition to another. Comparison of earlier and later conditions causes the contrasts that we call good and evil. But absence of change would mean death or non-existence.

5. The universe, with all it contains, is neither evil nor good. What man makes of it by free choice creates evil. Iron can indifferently be a plow or a sword.

6. The good man is the crown of existence, and in a world without difficulties the good man could not occur.

7. Evil is only what man takes to be evil. It is the shadow cast by desire. Remove desire for the mortal, the fleeting, and the unobtainable, and evil vanishes.

8. Every wicked man has done some good things. Every good man has sinned. In this world each one is requited for the smaller side of his balance. He comes to the hereafter with a clear account of wickedness to be punished or virtue to be rewarded.

I have not tried to exhaust the number of these arguments, but merely to indicate some of the durable lines. Theologians and philosophers, in Judaism and outside it, have developed these ideas and others with persuasiveness that I have neither the gifts nor the space to match here. Perhaps the multiplicity of the answers is enough to suggest that there is no one answer that the world has finally said yes to. Rabbi Yanai in *Ethics of the Fathers* puts the case candidly enough for me:

"The reason for the prosperity of the wicked, and also for the troubles of the good, is not in our hands."

Then there is the old conclusion of the epicureans. Human life is exactly as it appears, an irrational jumble of good and bad. There is nothing before birth or after death. There is no God to whom to appeal for justice or for reasons. All appearance of design in the universe is a delusion generated by the structure of the human senses. The problem of evil disappears, not because there is no evil, but because there is no good Providence who has to give an account of himself. "The only excuse for God," Stendhal put it, "is that he does not exist." There is only the strange accident of brief life on the green earth. The rest is black cold chaos. To cry questions into the darkness is to behave like a child.

And finally there is the Book of Job, which describes the living evil of the human lot with stunning power, opposes to it an even more stunning statement of the evident presence and might of the Lord God, and leaves the matter there. Job the tortured questioner ends firmer in his faith than his narrowly pious friends. They, who offered him partial answers to the problem of evil, stand rebuked by the divine Voice out of the whirlwind. The enigma of existence remains, and back of the enigma, in the depths of the human heart, the sense that the Redeemer lives.

The modern mind is willing to live with such dilemmas and not waste energy groping between the horns. The medieval mind could not rest if there was a single apparent contradiction in its doctrines. It hunted down all the difficulties and found answers, however farfetched. The result gave often the appearance of arguing with a child on the child's terms. Benjamin Franklin relates how he became converted to Deism from hearing it refuted so often in the pulpit; and Saadya Gaon warned a thousand years ago that a main cause of irreligion was weak and ridiculous arguments advanced in defense of a faith. Nevertheless the chewing and re-chewing of the old paradoxes — the existence of evil, free will versus God's omniscience, and so forth — went on until very recently.

I think the new humility of intelligent men rises from the scientific disciplines. Paradoxes abound in nearly all fields of natural research. Two hundred years ago men could still believe that the world was a machine, and that perfected instruments would enable the mind of man to lay bare this machine and discover its workings to the last turns of the small cogs. An educated man can no more believe that today than he can believe that the world rests on the back of a giant turtle. The instruments in some fields have been pushed to the farthest reach. New limits appear, and keep appearing, as the instruments get better. The dilemmas only multiply and deepen with knowledge. To try to resolve all paradoxes and contradictions would bring science to a dead stop. Working principles, working hypotheses, "best guesses," are the bases on which science now acts.

The idea of survival after death poses contradictions and difficulties that have been thoroughly worked over in massive theological controversies and trivial parlor disputes over the centuries. Some of the most pathetic passages in medieval philosophy are the attempts of pious authors to plod through all the challenges, to describe what a resurrected body will look like, to explain which of a man's three successive wives will be his in the world to come, and so forth. The literature of Judaism abounds in warnings that this kind of thing is futile and silly.

The human personality or "soul," says the rationalist, is a sort of exhaust of a chemical machine called the body. The machine stops. No more exhaust. It is that simple.

It is a working principle of Judaism that the dead are not dead to God; that the machine was always something more than a machine; that when the machine stops something remains. My grandfather liked to talk of the poetic hereafter of Jewish fable, the unending Sabbath meal of the righteous, where the fish was leviathan, the meat the legendary ox of the desert, the drink the famous hidden wine made from the grapes of Eden and put away for this very feast. When my mother would beg him to eat beef or lamb and he refused, he would say, "My portion is growing up there, the leviathan and the ox." And he would laugh. He once said to me, "Of course we can never be sure of the hereafter. But *perhaps* . . . remember, *perhaps* . . ."

Is my grandfather eating leviathan and drinking hidden wine in the world beyond? For all anybody can tell me, he is. I think that that is more likely than that his spirit is dead to God.

Kaddish

The Jewish idea of respect for the dead requires the swiftest possible burial, in the most austere possible manner: a shroud and a plain wooden coffin, dust to dust. Accompanying the dead to their last resting place is a commanded act. Formal mourning periods of diminishing intensity follow death. The first seven-day period, *Shiva,* tides the mourners over the first dazing shock. They remain at home, seated on low stools, receiving a continuous stream of condolence calls. Difficult as this is, it works at least to keep their minds active and their attentions engaged. After this comes the *Shloshim,* the thirty days. They resume normal activity, avoiding places of entertainment, and continuing to observe certain forms and prayers. At the end of the thirty days, mourning is over; except for a mother or father, when it goes through an entire year.

Kaddish is a refrain in the synagogue liturgy having no open reference to death or mourning. It is an ancient Aramaic prose-poem sanctifying God's name and praying for the speedy coming of his kingdom. Composed after the destruction of the Temple, it came to be the voice of Job in the Hebrew prayer book — "though he slay me, yet will I trust in him" — hailing God out of the depths of catastrophe. It closed each section of the service, a litany of prayer leader and congregation.

Several hundred years ago the custom started of allowing a newly bereaved mourner in the congregation to speak the last kaddish of the service, as a pledge of his undimmed faith in God despite the disaster in his life. Since there were usually several mourners at every service, questions arose as to who was entitled to the privilege. Rabbinic authorities worked out painstaking lines of precedence. But the lines broke down. It became the custom for all mourners to speak the last kaddish in unison. Traces of precedence remain in choosing a leader for the daily worship from among the mourners.

This narrative of the facts hardly explains the hypnotic power of kaddish as a custom. For one thing, there is the prayer itself. It is a beautiful dithyramb with strong rhythms and stirring sounds. For sheer word-music it is admirable, and though perhaps one mourner out of five knows what the words mean, the utterance itself is moving. There is the emotional impact of speaking it together with others who have recently suffered death in the family. There is the powerful aura of respect for the dead with which long custom has now impregnated the kaddish. The mourner who speaks it feels an instinctive solace and release in the act, as though for the moment he is stretching his hand to the far shore and touching the hand of his departed. I am not saying that this is a rational feeling, but it is a strong one.

But beyond all that, I think the exceptional power of the kaddish may lie in the relation of our generation to the generation that has died or is dying. The overriding feeling is one of guilt. It is a common thing among the living to feel a sense of guilt toward the dead, but it operates with especial intensity among us.

Most American Jewish children, at least until very recently, have been less pious than their parents. Religion dies hard in the heart, even though it can evaporate early from manners. Jewish identity is, I may say, all but ineradicable from the heart. While the parents live, unobservant children obscurely feel that the religion is still being carried on by the old folks, and they go about their secularized lives with relative peace of mind. Then death strikes. The children stare at the broken end of the chain of the generations, swinging free. It is a hard sight. The punctilious reciting of the kaddish, linked so directly with the vanished parents, is a symbolic retrieving of the ancient chain.

And with the observance of kaddish there often comes a partial, and occasionally a general, turn to Judaism. At the very least, the custom brings the mourner to the synagogue, gives him a revived acquaintance with Hebrew and with the liturgy, and isolates a fragment of time each day for meditation. I have heard the kaddish custom criticized for making our faith a religion of the dead. On the contrary, it seems to me that if the dead by their deaths restore our old faith in any degree to the living, they do not quite die in vain. The daily kaddish pilgrimage to the synagogue is one of the most gracious acts the living can perform, and one of the most valuable.

People sometimes object to having to assemble a congregation of ten, a *minyan,* the quorum necessary for community prayer, in order to say kaddish. The above description should make clear how this necessity arises. Kaddish is a community prayer. The words dictate recital before a congregation. It is perfectly acceptable to pray alone, and a great many pious people do so on occasion, but at such times community prayers are left out, and one of them is the kaddish.

On the anniversary or *yahrzeit* (year-time) of a death, the survivors recite kaddish year after year while they live. Then the obligation ceases. There is no mourning duty passed beyond one generation.

Judaism is strict in limiting mourning to the given periods and the customary observances. Excessive grief is taken as want of trust in God. Our faith holds it as natural and desirable that with time the havoc wrought by death should repair itself. Though no man is ever the same after a bereavement as he was before, he is expected, when mourning is over, to take up existence, suppressing for the sake of life itself the remnants of grief. The garment that the pious mourner rends can be sewn and worn again. The mark is there, but life resumes its course.

Part 3

✦

THE LAW

Chapter 13

Where Does Authority Lie?

I HAVE described the way Jews live who believe in God and who follow the Mosaic tradition.

There are many serious Jews of good heart and good conscience who disregard these laws, mainly in the ceremonial part. Some have not been trained in the tradition; some have discarded it. The question arises, Whose laws are they breaking? What authority are they challenging? Who says today that a man born Jewish should perform certain acts and refrain from others, and by what right does anyone say so?

The questions go to the quick of Jewish identity. There is no answer to be had in a sentence or two. A line of law exists. We can trace it to its source. But this law has no policemen to enforce it. Every Jew must himself decide to obey it or to slight it, once he knows what it is, whence it comes and what force it claims.

Our body of law has one name: *torah,* or teaching. The word extends to cover religious law down to last week's decisions and the newest commentary. But the Pentateuch of Moses remains our very Torah, our true law, our constitution and our governing code. So we start where the record of Jewish identity begins: in the books of Moses.

Chapter 14

The Torah

THE survival of the Bible is a miracle. It has weathered down to bare rock, with tremendous waste and loss of essential matter, with marked chasms and faults. It records days so long gone that nothing is left but the words. Everything else of that time is dust under many layers of later dust. Archaeologists, digging under the hot sun in empty deserts, find shards, marked stones, graves, perhaps bits of scrolls, and here and there rubble in a form that suggests a structure. All the rest is translation and guess. If we want to know the tale of Israel we cannot read it in the shards and the graves. We can only read it, for better or worse, in the Bible. Archaeology says, "Yes, this is so; here is a clay tablet that says what the Bible does," or "We find nothing in this mound to substantiate the Bible account," or "This inscription proves the location of the Biblical town it mentions."

Moses

There is as yet no external evidence about Moses. Perhaps we would be the better for it if the diggers turned up next year a cracked Egyptian stone mentioning the Israelite Moshe. What more can we hope for; and what difference, after all, would it make? It may be that scholars will someday construct a second image of him out of debris in Egypt and Mesopotamia. Meantime he lives in the Bible. For an external reconstruction there is one of the great works of art in the world, in a shadowy corner of a small church in Rome, the Moses of Michelangelo.

Not being Michelangelo, I will not try to portray Moses; but it is well to bear in mind a few facts about him when we discuss his Torah. His were the hands that broke the gods of Egypt, Mesopotamia, Greece, and Rome. Islam and Christianity stand on his shoulders; both faiths are unthinkable without him. The faithful believe he talked with God; the record is that he changed history exactly as if he had. He disappeared into darkness on a mountain and came back with a law. First Israel, and then half the world, accepted that law as the word of God. He was a most unlikely kind of folk hero, a man of eighty, a desert dweller with a wife and children. He was called by God to do a hard job, and like a man of sense he tried to beg off. Once he put his hand to the task, however, there was no standing before him. They say a man grows to the stature of his office. Moses grew to the superhuman size of his job, and grew to the last.

The forces of nature seemed to work for him. Other conquerors and master spirits, in the flood tide of their lives, have appeared to have command of favoring events. We call such strange power luck, or destiny, or a star. Whatever power Moses had, wherever it came from, it was enough to wrest the freedom of a slave people from the grand military tyranny of the ancient world.

He described God. There is no God in the West to this hour but the God of Moses. Since the day he brought his vision of God to the earth there have been the most violent objections to his imagery, to his conception, and above all to the laws he said were God's laws: some for Israel as the dedicated keepers of the word, and some for all men. But his laws live today. Challenged more violently than ever, they live.

The Torah of Moses

His law comprises five books of the Bible, the first five: Genesis, Exodus, Leviticus, Numbers, and Deuteronomy. For the Jewish people these five books are one book, the Torah, the heart of Scripture; given to Israel at Sinai, and binding to this hour on the descendants of those who were there.

If one asks who legislated this law, the answer is Moses. If one asks what his authority was, the answer is that we believe he was inspired by Providence and we know he was elected by Israel to write founding statutes that have virtually spanned recorded time. We call art inspired when passing years cannot dim it. It is no proof of Moses' inspiration that his law still lives — nothing can prove this if his words do not — but the rocklike strength of his law at least makes it one of the marvels of history.

The Jewish veneration for the Torah of Moses down the centuries has no parallel. One can say what one pleases about the Jews. But that these people have lived by one book and died for it, and soaked their lives in it — they and their children and their children's children, one generation catching fire from another as though there were no such things as time and change, as though circumstances did not alter cases, as though more than three thousand years made one easily compassed stretch of time — that this thing has happened, nobody can deny.

One cool observer has said that the worship of the Torah is the idolatry of the Jews. It is a sharp half-truth. Denied a visible image to worship, denied any divine messenger or prophet on whom to lavish their affection and heap their burdens and supplications, denied any intercessor at all — for Moses went up on a mountain and died, and no man knows his burial place, and no Jew has ever prayed to Moses or called on him to help bridge the gulf between man and God — denied all but the word of God written in a scroll, the Jews have given to that scroll all the loyalty, love, and honor that men are capable of.

Every civilized person past the age of twelve has read the Torah, in whole or in part, or has had it read to him. The nations do not venerate it as the Jews do, but they venerate it. Much of the law that the Jews regard as the precious life of the book, the nations find hard dull reading and tend to pass by. The two great religions that have sprung from Judaism teach their followers that the legislation is abrogated for them. But no authority has abrogated it for the people of the covenant.

The Holy Spirit

The form of the Torah is peculiar, to say the least. One starts in Genesis with a powerful vision of the birth of the universe. Mystic tales follow: a serpent speaks, the fruit of a tree can bestow knowledge or immortality, men live nine hundred years. The climax is a world deluge, ridden out by one six-hundred-year-old man and his family in an ark filled with beasts for repopulating the earth. After the deluge and a thousand years of genealogy we start breathing our own air, the men are like us, and we recognize the landscape. Hebrew history starts with a tale of Abraham, the father of the nation. The adventures of the patriarchs take up the rest of Genesis. In Exodus the story of Moses begins, and the Torah tells the escape of Israel from Egypt and the blazing event at Sinai. Then, just when the plot is getting really good, as it were, one runs into a stone wall: civil and criminal legislation, the construction of a tabernacle hook by hook and curtain by curtain, and a handbook of rules for priests. Here and there, all through Leviticus and Numbers, a patch of shining narrative emerges from the dense-packed legal part, but then the laws close in again. Last comes Deuteronomy, the farewell address of Moses; a long oration, half retrospect and half prophecy, with a summary of the main laws of Judaism. The Torah closes with twelve verses that describe the end of the Lawgiver.

Now this is a very odd way to compose a book. Law is law, and narrative is narrative. The mixture of the two, apparently helter-skelter, is jarring. Not long ago a publisher made a lot of money by putting out a "Bible, Designed To Be Read As Living Literature." The editor fixed up the books of Moses by simply cutting out all the laws. Leviticus, as I recall, was reduced to half a page or so, including one verse that seemed worth holding on to: Leviticus 19:18, "Thou shalt love thy neighbor as thyself."

The jurists of the Talmud questioned the form of the books of Moses, but their interest was opposite to that of the living-literature editor. They wondered at narrative diluting a law code. The question occurs in the comment of Rashi, the French exegete, on the first verse of Genesis: why doesn't the Torah start where the laws do, midway in Exodus? The answer is rather gnomic. Israel's claim to the Holy Land rests on the existence of God. If it was not God's will that they possess Canaan, the nations can reproach them as mere conquering brigands. The Torah has to start at the creation to show Israel's founding in a just light.

The ancient Hebrews knew nothing of the Greek muses. The only subject worth mentioning was God and man, in the link which is moral law. If in the course of exploring that subject they happened to strike off dramas and epics and poetry, they made no account of it. The living-literature editor kept the tale of Joseph and cut out the laws of agriculture because the Joseph narrative is brilliant by Greek standards and the laws dull stuff. The Jews have never cut a word of the Torah. The blueprint of the tabernacle and the splitting of the Red Sea have for them the same value.

I am not saying that the writers of the Bible, or the men who compiled the canon, were unaware of the literary power and grace in the holy books. There were many narratives, prophecies, psalms, and wisdom books that failed to survive. We know the names of some. The books that lived radiate a certain inner authority that has compelled lasting notice. The West calls that quality inspiration. The Hebrews called it almost the same thing: the holy spirit. The holy spirit is an event, a process, the hand of God touching a man and enabling him to rise above himself to become a direct instrument of the Providential will, whether as king, prophet, lawgiver, or scribe.

The Rest of Hebrew Scripture

I will make no attempt to describe the Hebrew Bible in detail. The books cover thousands of years. Empires, dynasties, gods, rise and fall. The narrative follows the fortunes of the house of Israel through the stress of great events, and it builds a picture of human nature drawn from all sides. Its chief figure has no match in the writings of the world; it is God.

In the Jewish faith, Scripture after the Torah is commentary, illumination, and sequel. The books of Moses shadow forth the future of Israel. In the rest of Scripture it all comes to pass. Time unfolds triumph and trouble. It brings human spirits that gleam out like stars: Samuel, David, Isaiah, Jeremiah, Ezekiel, and the rest, a constellation of religious genius that still lights the world. The theme sounds in the last words of Malachi, the last of the prophets: "Remember the Torah of Moses my servant that I commanded him at Horeb for all Israel, laws of faith and laws of justice."

The Hebrew Bible read as living literature is a tragic epic with a single long plot: the tale of the fall of a hero through his weaknesses. The hero is Israel, a people given a destiny almost too high for human beings, the charge of God's law. The weaknesses are the ordinary faults of people: shallowness, ignorance, lack of long purpose, lack of strength, lack of imagination, love of pleasure, love of comfort, love of power, love of sloth. The tragic climax is national destruction. Unlike all other epic tragedies, it does not end in death. The hero has eternal life, and the prospect of ages of pain, in which to rise at long last to the destiny which he cannot escape. He begins as a single man, the rich sheikh Jacob at the ford of the Jordan, wrestling in the night with an angel and given his name and his destiny. He ends as the immortal individual that is the Jewish people, the suffering servant of Isaiah. The vision of the whole is the vision of Moses in his farewell address, before he ascends the mountain to die. He tells there the whole long tale that we are still living, with a happy end of redemption that we steadfastly hope to see.

So it is that we have in the Bible a number of very different books, the surviving library of the great days of an old people; and so it is that the whole library, which we call the Bible, seems to be one book. For it has one subject, the discovery of God's law in the tale of Israel, and one author, "the holy spirit." Kings is history; Job is a drama; Lamentations is a dirge; Psalms is an anthology of poems. Yet the unity of the Bible is not disturbed by the inclusion of all, for the spirit is in all. If you want to see the line the Hebrew canonizers drew, read Ecclesiasticus, also called Ben Sirach. A brilliant work of wisdom, Ben Sirach is but one cut below the level of the canon. The Hebrews were content to let this masterpiece go; it survived in the Apocrypha, in Greek translation.

Hebrew Scriptural literature, then, is all moral law, from one angle or another. Every form of literary composition falls within that frame. The law itself is called *halakha,* or the way.

The rest of this literature is light on the law: *hagada,* or the story.

The Theory of Evolution

Two world religions much younger than the Hebrew faith, Christianity and Islam, hold that the Jewish Bible is but a prologue to their own holy books: the New Testament for the Christians, and the Koran for the Moslems. Both faiths in the past have tried hard to convert the Jews to their view, sometimes by persuasion and sometimes by bloodshed. Now there is peace among the three beliefs as they turn their attention to the new faith that threatens to swamp them all, the strong and canny new Marx-Lenin dispensation, the credo of which is the three terrible words of Nietzsche, "God is dead."*

I am wholly unequipped to discuss either Christianity or Islam. The abiding Jewish position can perhaps be stated so. Israel did not find in the Koran of Mohammed light that was not in its own Scriptures. It was unable to worship a man, Jesus of Nazareth, as the Supreme Being. These are the cardinal points at issue with the two faiths. That both contain wisdom and power to give them major positions in the story of mankind cannot be denied unless one chooses to be blind.

But it cannot be maintained, I think, that Judaism on its own basis, with its own Scriptures, is not a whole religion. For others it may seem a halfway house. But we have our covenant, our law, our faith, and our destiny, our Mosaic vision of first and last things — and by these, as God gives us light, we live and die as our fathers did before us.

* The credibility of the Marx-Lenin pseudo-faith has strikingly waned since this was written; and to borrow from Twain, the reports of God's death were greatly exaggerated. — HW (1985)

The idea of Judaism as a halfway house brings almost as a corollary the thought that there is a rise of religious insight in the Hebrew Bible, from a rather low start with Moses to a peak in Isaiah, who still falls short of the real thing, though coming fairly close. I understand the persuasiveness of such a picture to those of other faiths. Without entering the morass of theological dispute, I would note here one or two points that strike me. In our own tradition, and on the basis of the words of Hebrew Scripture, there is not the faintest doubt that Moses is not only the source of Judaism under God, but its high reach as well. The prophets all state that their aim is to call Israel to the Mosaic law, not to supplant, improve, or change the law. Their criticism of empty formal sacrifice echoes the warning of Moses against mechanical religion. God is the God of Moses in the books of prophecy. The law is the law of Moses. Down to the last fading cry of Malachi, all Scripture ever says is, "Remember the Torah of Moses my servant."

If such an evolution had happened in Judaism, the religion would be dissimilar from any other faith that has lasted. Great faiths are born when a master spirit comes to the earth and unveils a new way of looking at the world and at God. He passes, and as long as his vision burns in the souls of men, a new faith lives. Christianity does not evolve upward from the teachings of Jesus; nor does Buddhism rise above the Buddha; nor is Confucius a low beginning for a higher and wiser Confucianism. Change there has been in all faiths, yes — new teachers; new apostles; new history; shifting forms as the years roll. It is a long way from the Mount of Olives to St. Peter's in Rome and St. Paul's in London. But it would be a bold Christian who would say that that way is upward.

Wellhausen's crude fantasy of historic evolution in Israel from the stone-worship of the benighted heathen Moses to the semi-Christian Isaiah is no longer taken seriously.* But one still encounters the general notion of Judaism as an evolved religion. We Jews make no sense teaching it to ourselves. It is against everything we know about our own faith, and there is nothing in world history to support it.

The true analogy to the history of religion is in the arts, as Santayana said: a few peak spirits, and troughs for long centuries between. If the British drama rose from Shakespeare to Noel Coward, or sculpture climbed from Michelangelo to Epstein, or music ascended from Mozart to Stravinsky, then the Hebrew faith may have evolved from Moses to Malachi.

The Text in Hand

The Magna Carta and the Declaration of Independence can still be seen under glass — yellow, wrinkled, faded. But the Declaration and the Carta have their true being not on these parchments but in the nature of Great Britain and the United States. These would not change if the glass broke, the damp got in, and the great documents crumbled overnight.

We do not have under glass the tables of stone, nor the book of the law that Deuteronomy says Moses wrote before he died. Too much time has passed. The bulldozers of conquest have levelled and levelled again the temples, the museums, and the archive halls of the Jewish people. Very little was left after the sack of Jerusalem by the Babylonians twenty-five hundred years ago. Nothing was left after Titus razed the holy city again six centuries later. All we have of the Torah of Moses today are very, very late copies, the earliest fragments being less than two thousand years old. Then we

* The rise and fall of the Wellhausen theory are described in a note to this chapter.

have copies of the Talmud, which quotes the Torah all the time, but these copies too are late.

The Torah comes to the Jewish youngster who starts studying it at six or seven in a printed book, perhaps set in type only last year, more or less ringed with the commentaries of the ages. As he grows in years and wit, he delves into the commentators. His first task is to master the text itself. It is the same text that all present Jewish law rests on. How authentic is it?

Scholars call it the Masoretic text. The Masoretes were Hebrew scribes of the first centuries of the present era. They fixed the wording and spelling of the Bible; since then it has not changed. It has long been a matter of critical controversy as to just how accurate the Masoretes were; for one thing, did they have a true text from ancient sources, or did they invent and corrupt? Opinion has swayed back and forth on this point. The excitement over the Dead Sea Scrolls came in part from their substantial authentication of the Masoretic Isaiah.

If one lives by the Torah we have in hand, one is living by the law of Moses, so far as anybody can. The Torah comes to us authenticated by external evidence to some extent. But its unstained pedigree in Jewish tradition goes back and back, a clear single line, until it vanishes into the smoke of the burning First Temple. Such a pedigree, bearing in mind the devotion of the Jews to this law, is its best authentication.

Chapter 15

The Talmud

Down from the Shelf

UNLIKE the Bible, which is part of the culture of the world, the Talmud is a sealed book, except to those who start studying it early in their lives and grow old over the volumes.

Translations exist. The Soncino edition in English, a great recent feat of scholarship, has become a useful tool to halting American students. But let the uninitiated reader open any one of the thirty-five thick Soncino tomes. With the best will in the world, he will despair after a chapter or two. It is too compressed, too strange, too runic, too abrupt, too zigzag. It is a thousand years younger than most of the Bible. It seems at first glance aeons older.

On the bookshelves opposite my desk as I write is a complete set of the Talmud: an array of twenty-one maroon leather tomes, each about a foot and a half tall. This is a new American reproduction of the great edition of the Widow and Brothers Romm printed in Vilna, Poland, in the late nineteenth century. Farther down the room on another shelf is a real Vilna Talmud, battered and awry, bound in scuffed cracking brown leather. It belonged to my grandfather, who came to America from Soviet Russia in 1928, bringing his Talmud along. He put me to work studying in it, and he promised me that on his death I would inherit the forbidding volumes. He lived to be ninety-four. Two years or so before he died I bought the photo-offset edition. He was living in Israel, in excellent health, and I was tired of studying a much smaller edition with minutely printed commentaries, which he had given me long ago. So now I have two copies of the Vilna Talmud, one a new facsimile on fine white paper, and one the real thing, yellowed and worn in a long lifetime of continued use. I hope to pass on a set to each of my two sons.

I take a volume from the new edition at random. It is heavy and huge. Automatically I use both hands to swing it over from the bookshelf to the desk. I open it, and the pages with their red-marbled edges lie almost flat, in gentle curves. We are looking at two heavy black columns, irregular in shape, of Hebrew lettering, flanked by two narrow columns in smaller print, which again are bordered by still narrower columns of tiny print. There are no vowel points and no punctuation marks.

The heavy column is the Talmud itself. The narrow columns are commentaries, or variant readings, or reference listings. At the back of the tractate more commentaries stand in formidable long blocks of small solid type. On a single sentence in the Talmud, the student can become involved in a debate spanning ten centuries and a dozen lands.

Some living men are supposed to have learned and mastered the entire Talmud with every word of all the commentators — in the Romm edition there are more than one hundred — as well as the rest of Judaism's literature. This seems to me beyond mortal powers. But the resources of the human brain are amazing, and I daresay the thing is so.

If all this seems a little daunting to the reader, he can begin to appreciate my plight when my grandfather came into my life in my thirteenth year.

"Za Rabotu"

I had had a Hebrew schooling which, for my time and place — New York City, early 1920s — was better than average. I could read and translate fairly well the narrative stretches of the Hebrew Bible. My prayers were fluent. My bar-mitzva had been a major spectacle, and I had turned in a star performance. I considered my religious learning done.

My grandfather had not been in America a week — he was staying in our apartment, of course — when he came to me carrying a vast brown book. *"Za rabotu,"* he said. He sat me down at a table before the book and stood over me as he opened it. I stared in stupefaction at the massive columns of meaningless consonants. "Read," said my grandfather.

I have just taken down from my shelves the very volume from the old set and opened it to the very page. Thirty years have passed since I broke my brain over this column. I can read it now without much difficulty; but getting through a page of Talmud is still not easy for me, and never will be. I do not believe it is ever really easy for anybody. The page is quite brown, much browner than the other leaves of this old loose volume. Is it because I pored over the one page for perhaps a month or more in the shafted sunlight of a Bronx flat? There are deep brown spots all over the page. Fruit-juice stains perhaps; I may have been comforting myself with a tangerine as I wrestled with Aramaic that hardly meant more to me than Choctaw. Tears, perhaps, or do tears leave stains on a page?

When my grandfather said, "Za rabotu," he meant it. They are the Russian words for "To work!" He started me — and I have since gathered that it is a favored starting place for budding Talmudists — on one of the most abstruse passages in the whole Talmud, the duel between Rava and Abayi over a question of proprietorship in a found object. The Talmud, with its usual curtness, poses the whole problem in three words. It must have taken my grandfather a week just to explain to me what the three words implied. But he drove me through Abayi's dozen challenges, based on a dozen analogies in Jewish law, and through Rava's ingenious refutations and final surrender; the whole debate being in Aramaic, not Hebrew. I know I reached the end, because the last words of the passage are still embedded in my memory.

To add to my woes, my grandfather spoke no English. The Yiddish I knew was the Americanized jargon, almost a different language from his. How we two managed to communicate remains a mystery to me. But on the whole, in my lifetime nobody has communicated to me more effectively than my grandfather did, starting with that terrible phrase that haunted my entire adolescence, "Za rabotu." His main instrument was the Talmud.

What the Talmud Is

To begin with, the Talmud is not one book, but two books run together. They are the *Mishna* and the *Gemara,* a pair of very old classics of Jewish law, some three hundred years apart in time. Both books have authors, in the sense that we know who wrote them. But neither one is an original work. Both are compendiums of law.

The Mishna is a report of the legal decisions of a line of analysts and judges, the *Tanna'im,* or Teachers, stretching over some four hundred years. Out of mists that shroud Jewish history after the close of the Bible, the Tanna'im appear, successors to an older group of jurists, the Men of the Great Synagogue, who in turn relayed the tradition across the wastes of time from the failing hands of the prophets. The Tanna period falls in two centuries before and two after the start of the Christian era. Rabbi Judah the Prince, a wealthy sage of Palestine, compiled the Mishna (the Review) about the year 200.

Seldom has one work so swiftly and wholly captured a nation. With the Mishna, the Old Testament era in Hebrew ended. Rabbi Judah set the style for all composition in the language after him. Seventeen hundred years later, Hebrew is still Mishna Hebrew. Learned journals to this day use no other. The popular Hebrew in Israel, the language of newspapers, radio programs, and daily conversation, is of course very westernized. But I have been told by a successful Israeli novelist that for him the secret of good modern style is still in the Mishna.

While the Mishna purports to be nothing but jurisprudence, it is much more. With a sentence or a phrase, it can magically bring to life a scene in the Second Temple, a festival night in the streets of Jerusalem, the manners, the morals, the philosophy, the costumes of people dead two thousand years. I suppose there is no literary intent, in the modern sense, in Rabbi Judah's work. To a great extent he was merely writing down a lore rubbed smooth by generations. But in his accuracy and clarity he achieved immortality within his own people, and he set the course of the hoary Scriptural language in a new direction which it still takes.

Through several more centuries a second great line of sages, the *Amora'im,* or Commenters, explored Rabbi Judah's work, debating it line by line within academies, and between national settlements, and from father to son to grandson. That is how the Talmud came to take its present form. We have four or five sentences of Mishna, laying down the law. Then follows perhaps a page, perhaps twenty pages, of close legal analysis, in Hebrew and Aramaic, which can branch off into tales, poems, prayers, history, reminiscence, science, or table talk. This is the Gemara, the Completion.

The discussions of the Amora'im snowballed, adding to

the memory burden each decade. Toward the end, the task must have become about like memorizing the Encyclopaedia Britannica. At this time the Roman world was breaking up. Mediterranean life was a swirl of wars. The continuity of Jewish communications, and therefore the life of the whole nation-in-exile, was in peril. Rav Ashi and Ravina, two of the last Commenters, broke with a firm tradition of keeping the Gemara an unwritten body of learning. They recorded everything they remembered of centuries of Jewish debate on the Hebrew Bible and on the Mishna. So they created the Talmud which fourteen centuries later my grandfather sat me down — an American boy of thirteen — to start learning.

More than anything else, the Talmud reads like transcribed shorthand notes. Debates, conversations, monologues follow each other, racy, pithy, stripped to essentials, worded in strong rhythms that linger naturally in the mind. The form is dramatic; that is, the Gemara is all in dialogue.

The talk always starts with the strip of Mishna in hand. But it does not necessarily stay there. A phrase, a word, an idea in the Mishna will start a new subject, and that subject can engross the Talmud — and all its train of commentators across the centuries — for the next half dozen pages. This is in the nature of oral learning. It would tend to shift from topic to topic as a fresh and interesting notion cropped up, instead of moving along a course diagrammed by one mind.

One can almost see the two compilers packing into their manuscript all the material that occurred to them as they went along, writing down the memorized lore of a lifetime, ransacking their recollections, while they were on a topic, for every scrap of related learning. Perhaps they intended someday to sort it into a form nearer a code. More likely it never occurred to them — as it did to the medieval codifiers — that this was a needed further step. The very writing down of the

Talmud must have seemed to them such a learning aid that thereafter Judaism would endure however low the general level of wit and training would fall. If the laws of mourning were found in a tractate on festivals, and the jurisprudence of the New Year was broken up with a stretch of rabbinic astronomy, what of it?

In time the Talmud was shaken down into codes by many master hands. But no code ever replaced the rambling, encyclopedic, complicated, profound, gossipy Talmud in the affection or the attention of the Jewish intellect. At this point in the very long history of Judaism's legal literature it seems clear that the center of gravity of authority is fixed in the Mishna and the Gemara; just as the final faith of the Jews is fixed in the Torah.

The Talmud is very alive, precisely because it was memorized from life. It has the fascination of court proceedings, or of talk overheard, or of a vehement argument in one's own home. It is charged with the rapid-fire logic of able men thrashing out big issues. It glances off into the colorful reminiscences of travellers, the conversation of scientists and wise men, the strange experiences of judges, the tales, anecdotes, and parables of scholars enjoying lighter moments between grave disputes. And though the course seems zigzag and undisciplined, it is all very tight. Each word has been weighed over many generations.

This, then, in the briefest skimming outline, is the Talmud.

The texts of the Talmud and of its commentaries bear deep marks of the weathering of the centuries. There are hundreds and hundreds of variant readings. Some passages have been eroded by time, the errors of copyists, and the faults of printers, to an indecipherable state; but these are few. On the whole, the abstruse law debates have managed to last out the years and come down to us, still filled with vitality.

The Hagada of the Talmud

There is plenty of hagada in the Talmud too: the distilled parables, fables, sermons, homilies, fantasies, and allegories of perhaps a thousand years. These frequent patches of "easy" Talmud, which the student comes to with delight after racking his skull over complex law questions, are windows into lost worlds. Long ago tradition drew a line between the law of the sages and their opinions on physics, anatomy, commerce, astronomy, and politics. The distinction seems self-evident today. In questions of natural law, we are closer to the best information than they were. In recovering the Jewish law, they were closer to the sources than we are.

The natural world holds still, as it were, while men learn all they can about it. The body of truth keeps growing. But the past recedes every moment, carrying with it Lincoln, Washington, Caesar, Isaiah, Moses. The exact recoverable truth grows ever dimmer. Talmudic law is our lifeline to Sinai. Talmudic science and social criticism illuminate our past, and our forefathers were right to preserve every word. They were equally right, and in their time quite advanced, to distinguish this material from the law. Had the minority won out who wanted to make every word of the rabbis infallible, Judaism would in time have endured the crisis that struck the church when the discoveries of Galileo confronted its fixed Ptolemaic world.

On the whole, Talmudic science — so say the few experts who know both the Talmud and the sciences at first hand — is of a high order in its epoch. The sages freely took from Persia, Syria, Greece, Rome, and Egypt all the scientific information they could get, and evidently did keen original research in matters that touched Jewish law. The calendar they evolved, for instance, ticks on to this day, keeping time with the sun and the seasons. Talmudic political judgment often shows the bitterness of a people trodden by wave after wave of oppressors. We who live in the wake of the Hitler catastrophe hardly know how to quarrel with them. Since the Talmud reports the sayings of hundreds of savants over many centuries, it abounds in contradictory maxims, in conflicting metaphysical guesses, in baffling switches from cynicism to poetry, from misanthropy to charity, from dislike of women to lyric praise of them. It is, even by the standards of today's lending library, appallingly blunt about sex. And yet it has its streaks of reticence and euphemism.

In a word, one can say almost anything about this tape recording of the talk of wise men through seven centuries, and then find a passage to support it. The enemies of Judaism in all ages have snipped out the harshest, strangest patches they could find, run them together, and offered the result to the world as the true face of the Jews' mystery book. The same technique could make a preposterous dummy of the New Testament or of the Old, of the works of Plato, Shakespeare, or Dickens, or the utterances of our American presidents. The Talmud is not only an encyclopedia of law but a work of folk art, a hymn to the Lord rising out of many generations of men who spent their lives in the quest for him. This quest for God, the confident search for the holy in every busy detail of life, is its grand single theme. The Talmud recaptures a long golden age of intelligence and insight, and it is to this day the circulating heart's blood of the Jewish religion. Whatever laws, customs, or ceremonies we observe — whether we are orthodox, Conservative, Reform, or merely spasmodic sentimentalists — we follow the Talmud. It is our common law.

Chapter 16

Jewish Common Law

COMMON law is the usage of the people, the community memory of judges' decisions and ancestors' practice, traversing the years in the charge of a learned guild. Blackstone calls it *lex non scripta,* the unwritten law, and Judaism calls it almost the same thing, the oral law. In time, of course, the "unwritten" law takes form as a written mass of rules, ordinances, and case law. Eventually it sifts down into codes and digests, which grow year by year as new cases bring new decisions.

The core of the common law is precedent. Precedent makes a parade of people born at odd times over hundreds of years into one society.

It sometimes happens — as it did with the Jewish people, and ages later with the United States of America — that a new nation begins with a fairly short founding document. Common law then works out the shape of everyday things in the light of that document.

The Question of Amendment

But analogies between the American and Hebrew law systems cannot go deep at all. At the root there is the difference of north and south. United States law is a man-made system, to be remade or unmade by men. Judaism offers itself as an act of God in human history. In the end nobody follows the Torah who does not find the light of eternity in it.

People who question the force of Jewish law often point out that the American Constitution can be amended, whereas the Hebrew law, claiming divine inspiration, is in its nature unalterable. This difference does not hold, as I think I can show. In developing this point, I would not be understood as ignoring the radical differences that exist.

The Jewish law has markedly changed over the centuries. The Torah, for instance, allowed slavery; Jewish law no longer does. The Torah prohibited buying or selling land in Israel, allowing only leases within fifty-year cycles; today real estate sales in Israel are a matter of course. The Torah permitted polygamy; our present law forbids it. The Torah forced a man to marry the childless wife of a deceased brother; our present law forbids this marriage. (A small Oriental sector of Jewry never ratified, and does not conform to, these two amendments of marriage law.) The Torah required remission of debts every seven years; our law now does not require it. Such changes — there are dozens of them — have revolutionized the family life and the economic structure of Jewry to meet new times and manners.

The enabling clause for amendment is a passage in Deuteronomy which instructs Israel to abide by the Torah as taught to them by their sages. The Torah, therefore — whether you take it as God-given or not — itself sets up the authority for interpretation of its laws in changing times by human jurists. Amendment in Judaism is *takana* or *gezera,* the regulation or decree of the wise. It is limited by the rule that "a gezera is not decreed unless most of the people can support it." Gezera and takana usually work to recognize an existing new need, so that community consent follows. When a gezera has laid on the people a burden it cannot support, the decree in time has been withdrawn.

What we have then is a system of amendment originating with "the wise" and subject to ratification or annulment by the law-abiding community at large, in a quiet referendum that is continuous and effective.

The question straightway arises: who are these "wise," and by what power are they ordained?

As in the learned guilds of Western law and medicine, the process is one of admission of new young men by eminent jurists after a searching test. The conferring of the degree is *semikha,* the laying on of hands. The line of semikha starts from Moses, who ordained Joshua, the priests, and the elders to carry forward the teaching and interpretation of the Torah. We can with confidence trace the line back from the great yeshiva heads of today to the medieval authorities. These authorities inherited and brought forward the legal force of the Talmud jurists.

This scheme I have written abstracts from the real state of things, which is elusive, like so much of our faith. But one fact is unmistakable. The community of those who keep the law is, in the last analysis, the informal supreme court of Judaism. They decide, without casting ballots or taking polls, who the jurists of prime authority are, and what gezeras are within the spirit of the Torah. They do this by funnelling their ultimate religious challenges to a few men in each generation, and by following or not following their rulings. This court of the faithful has been large and it has been small; powerful at times, weak at others; now in command, now despised. But the Torah has lived on only in their lives, so they have passed the enduring judgments on the amendments to it.

The power of passing such judgments comes with keeping the faith. There is no other workable franchise. The worst thing about an irreligious time like the present is not the irreligion. That is between each man and God. The worst is that some of our best minds drop out of the court when they are most needed to give strength for shooting a new rapids of history.

The whole arrangement will seem loose by Western standards. But here it is today, not much different from what it was in 200. Perhaps its very lack of hard outline has helped it last so long. You hear people object that Jewish tradition is a steel shell of unchangeable practices. Actually, Judaism has modulated in form almost like an amoeba through the centuries, responding to different pressures. But, like the amoeba, it has always remained the same single living thing, made of the same fluid immortal stuff.

The Slow Veto

There is no army to keep the main lines of the Torah intact by force. There is not even an organized church to cry down heterodoxies. There is only the formless communion of the faithful.

The one limit to amendment, therefore, is the slow public veto I have described. One might call it the veto of the long run, or of social process. Many gezeras have been passed by the wise which in the end have not carried. Much Talmud study consists of rejected legislation, with the reasons for the rejection. There have been movements in Judaism which have defiantly struck out a new path, with whole new bills of amendments — liberalizing or extra harsh, as the case might be — undertakings like Sadduceeism and Karaism. They have gone their ways and passed their amendments with some name-calling and hot words and nothing more. Their new communions, with a sharply amended Judaism, have flourished for a while. The veto has come imperceptibly. Where the amendments have put the communities outside the living frame of the Torah, there has been a dimming of identity, a loss of vigor; the amended Torah has eventually withered away, and its community with it. This is the only effective veto Judaism has. Denunciations and anathemas mean nothing. My word is as good as yours, say the amenders, and they denounce and anathematize back most heartily.

It is obviously not possible to declare in an amendment that there is no such thing as the Sabbath, or that the Torah allows one to eat anything edible. That would be mockery. The words are there. Radical amendment traditionally takes one of two lines: rejection of the common law, or the contention that all the laws of the Torah were meant only for a limited time.

The Torah with its common law has traversed and survived many societies, which indicates that it is pretty viable. It gives one a pattern of habits and practices that have sufficed to keep Israel alive; but the continuance of even these limited laws through times of sudden and big change always makes for trouble. Life in the new state of Israel bristles with queries. What about trains, post offices, and power plants on the Sabbath? What of the soldier in the field; how far is he freed of rite? Passions boil over swimming pools, the draft for women, the legal definition of a Jew. This ferment will prove, I believe, the greatest boon to Jewish jurisprudence in modern history, though it is a hard time to be a jurist. The demand grows for a Sanhedrin to face the massive challenge. But those wheels have been frozen since the days of Vespasian. They will be slow in turning again.

The major amendments through the years have touched those things in life that evolve: economics, politics, manners, social structure. The defining symbols and rites of our faith have hardly changed in all these great transitions since the end of the Temple service. Symbol goes to the things that lie under change: birth, love, work, rest, light, darkness, the turn of the seasons, the quest for bread and for God. Palm branch and esrog, ram's horn and matzo, Sabbath and food laws, morning prayer and evening prayer, have never lost their old meanings.

In the past century and a half we have had an era of extremely strict construction in Jewish law. The long-stable social forms of Jewish life have been cracking up, faster and faster every decade. The leading rabbis have held not only to the Torah but to all the minutiae of the safety factors, in a desperate resolve to keep the law from being swept away by the flood of change. Critics have argued that this attitude has been fatal intransigence; that it has created the dissenting movements as well as widespread apostasy. Defenders have replied that dissent and apostasy are inevitable in a skeptical age; that but for this strong stand of the rabbis the Jewish religion would have been lost. This debate is at its height today.

To keep the faith livable is of the first importance. Everybody agrees to that. "You shall live by these laws," Moses said; from which the Talmud deduced that construction of the law must never be so strict as to render it beyond the strength of the people to uphold. To be livable, however, it must above all go on living. Deciding where the limits lie in these questions is the crux of the present-day crisis in Jewish law.

The Method of the Talmud

The old Semitic common law going back to the time of Abraham, which the Torah presupposes, was not available in writing to the Talmudists. The tablets and pillars that the diggers are now bringing to light were buried deep. Nor could the sages take down from the shelf the decisions in David's time or the codes of Josiah's law. Not even the case books and briefs of the almost contemporary Hillel school were at hand. In all those years — under Moses in the desert, under the Judges, the Kings, and the Prophets, under the Sanhedrins of the Second Temple era, the common law had expanded into a broad detailed tradition. But there were no written records. The immemorial legal method was oral transmission.

To fix the common law in writing, the Talmudists had three main sources to draw from. There was the Torah itself, and there was the library of Israel's great days preserved in the later Hebrew Scriptures. Beyond these two canonical sources, they had the enormous memorized body of common law.

Certain teachers of this oral law were foremost in intellectual and moral prestige: Rabbi Judah the Prince, Rabbi Jokanan ben Zakkai, the Academy of Hillel, and so forth. In disputes over the oral learning, where one of these authorities took a side, the Talmud usually ruled that the halakha, the law, would follow their opinion.

So it is that much Talmudic combat bears on which authorities made certain decisions. Each disputant tried to prove by close logic that his view derived from one of the prevailing authorities. If he won his point, his tradition entered the halakha. This hammering out of a single line of law was what kept the nation-in-exile from falling apart in a welter of conflicting common-law traditions.

For every point that was in doubt, of course, there were dozens beyond dispute. These were the clear practice of the people, to which the Talmud alludes only in passing — being concerned, as legal minds are, with defining limits and unravelling knots. The Talmud at first seems to dwell on farfetched cases, unlikely emergencies, hairline decisions. But from these limiting cases we see what the broad practice was, and we recover a full picture of Judaism coming down in substance from the days of the prophets.

Difficulties in the Talmud

A learning that is so very old brings peculiar burdens. Its principles are stated in terms of a vanished civilization. The very names of some things have become doubtful. We have simply lost the Aramaic. The most earnest student can falter and reel in the ghost-world of the Temple: the orders of priests and Levites, the different sacrifices, the varying purity rules for wine, bread, fish, water, metal, glass, wood, clay, leather, textiles; the times and immersions of purification — a network of laws fully as involved and as searching as the U.S. Internal Revenue Code — applying to the premises and personnel of a great sanctuary that was destroyed in the year 70.

If it occurs to the reader, "Why not simply skip those parts?" he can forget that offhand solution. Oral learning flows in and out of different subjects like water. Long ago Jewry called their common law "the sea of the Talmud." Principles of law that we need today may show up in the most recondite stretch of Temple practice.

Moreover the Talmud scholar is not simply fishing through the books for decisions that touch the life of the hour; he is re-creating in his own experience the quest for the holy that is the spine of the Talmud. The Temple premises were for many centuries the capitol of the Jewish religion. Serious Hebrew scholarship continues to delve into every detail of Temple life that has been saved from the wear of time.

Then there is the logic of the Talmud. The formal logic is tough and exact — a fortiori, general to particular, and the like. But some of the legal reasoning, especially in tying precedent to written statutes, can prove baffling to the young student. I had some warm disputes with my grandfather over the Talmud's text analysis of the Torah. It was many years before I learned enough about general legal logic to understand the place of exegesis in all law systems.

The Talmud tells us, for instance, that "an eye for an eye" is a statement of principle, a clause of theoretical liability. When I studied this particular page of the Talmud with my grandfather, I grew incensed. I was at that time a contentious crusader against the Jewish law, because it was keeping me from going to the movies on Saturday and generally hemming me in. The barbarity of "an eye for an eye" I treasured as a proof of the obsoleteness of Mosaic law. Accumulate enough instances like this, I thought, and I would break the system. Along came the Talmud, ridiculing the notion of legal mayhem. It showed the impossibility of arriving at equity in loss of earning power, loss of work time, cost of healing, and pain. It pointed out the risk of excessive injury or even infection and death. All this was in the course of an academic dismissal of the mayhem idea; from the start nothing but money damages was even considered, for that was the plain common-law rule, descended from the times of Moses.

I do not suppose sensible people see the hacking off of arms and legs, the gouging out of eyes, as a conceivable result — at any stage — of the law that started with the Ten Commandments and included loving one's neighbor as oneself. "An eye for an eye," like the U.S. Navy regulation that a man who sleeps on watch may be shot, is certainly a harsh ultimate-liability clause. I caught many a sailor sleeping on watch during wartime, but none was ever shot, nor have I ever heard of a sailor losing his life for the offense; yet the words stand in the statute.

The *lex talionis,* as the scholars call eye-for-eye, gave the ancient court a formidable theoretical basis for collecting damages. The money was a commutation of the injury the malefactor in equity deserved for wilfully mutilating his neighbor. The Talmud found texts to fix this point on a basis of Holy Writ. If the Talmud had not so reported the old common law of Israel, if it had in fact described the legal steps for taking a man's eye out, the critics of Judaism — and also irritated fourteen-year-old boys — would have, it seems to me, a case against Talmudic law.

The Torah abounds in possible death penalties. Then we come to the common law, and we find capital punishment in effect abolished by the obstacles to a death verdict. "A Sanhedrin that condemned one man to death in seventy years was called a Bloody Sanhedrin," the Talmud says. The chains of witnesses required in a capital case, the rigid rules for proving knowledge of the law and premeditation, the restricted admissible evidence, the special voting procedures of the court, all combine to make death a theoretical punishment almost never reached. These hedges, again, were common law handed down from remote antiquity.

In the Sinai desert, in a precarious military situation, with a community that was a newly freed mob of slaves, a draconic code of possible death penalties was the first basis for survival. Every nation has such codes for siege, war, or disaster. With the code, Jewish common law handed down the safeguards which kept the land from ever being festooned with the burnt, strangled, and dismembered corpses of criminals — as Greece and Rome were, as the most civilized nations in Europe were until a hundred and fifty years ago. The nailed-up victims on crosses along the highways of Judea, in the era of Pontius Pilate, were the objects of Roman military justice in a conquered province. Crucifixion was impossible under Jewish law. But the Romans had long since broken the power of the Jewish state and replaced it with their own death penalties and executioners.

In short, one can no more understand, or even picture, Jewish jurisprudence as it actually works by reading the Pentateuch than one can envision the present-day United States by reading the Constitution. In each case it is the common law that brings the founding documents in touch with our lives here and now.

After the Talmud, of course, the common law has a very long line of descent.

Chapter 17

✦

From the Talmud to the Present

The Great Change

IN the epoch that followed the crack-up of Rome, the Jew became the Wandering Jew; and the thousand-year analysis and reconstruction of the common law in the schools broke off. Thereafter the Jews had to look to a book to find the laws that were binding, the common culture that meant survival in broken groups, the words that spelled life for a people who by all the rules of history should have died.

Christianity and Islam rose in the ruins of Rome, and their wars scattered the Jews like leaves. There would be now invasions, now peace; now kind rulers, now tyrants; now tolerance for the Jews, now conversion or death; now a spell of safety, now panic, pillage, and a new mass flight or expulsion. Without the Talmud to give them identity, discipline, and force, it seems hard to believe that the Jews would have gotten through the vast long ordeal.

This disorderly era created two new strata of jurists.

The Reasoners — the Hebrew term is *Savora'im* — were the final editors of the Talmud. They put in order what the Commenters had left to them, looking to the text of the Talmud as the source, rather than to the debates of the schools. The reliability of oral tradition was giving way in the anarchy of the times. Luckily the Talmud was in hand. There could not be a more authentic Hebrew jurisprudence, descended from Moses to the sinking academies of Babylon, and there preserved in writing. All the care of the Savora'im was to save this legacy.

The *Gaonim* were university presidents, heads of the two major Babylonian academies. The Jews have never had a papacy, but the nearest thing in moral force in our history was the Gaonate, which lasted from the close of the Talmud to about the year 1000. The decisions of the Gaonim, clarifying and spelling out Talmud law, shaped the life of Jewish settlements all through Europe and Asia. The Gaonate came to an end with the disasters that overwhelmed the community in Babylon. After nearly three thousand years, the religion of Abraham at last left its home in the Middle East, not to return until our own lifetimes. The mastery of our learning, with final legal authority, passed westward to Spain and France.

The word "Gaon" survived as a term of honor among Jewish scholars. I often heard my grandfather called a Gaon by other rabbis, but he never considered himself one. It is almost a mark of courtesy today among the devout to refer to an aged man of learning as a Gaon. The once supreme title has undergone change over the centuries, like the term Doctor of Philosophy. There are many more than there used to be, but the honor is not what it was.

"The First Ones" — Maimonides

We have come — in Jewish time — to the recent past.

It may seem stretching it a bit to include in modern times a period that goes back six hundred years before Shakespeare, five hundred before the discovery of America, two or three hundred before the language in which I am writing this book even existed. But let us see. The United States has now passed its bicentennial. Would it be reasonable to call the years since 1914 the recent past? I think so. Applying the same proportions, Jewish history breaks into the recent past around the year 1000, with the coming on stage of the legal lights known as the First Ones — in Hebrew, the *Rishonim*.

Why call these men who came after the Talmud, after the Reasoners and the Presidents, "First Ones"? I do not know who invented this odd term, but it is part of folk discourse. I suppose it has lasted because it says vividly that with these men our own time starts. They are a hall of fame in rabbinic learning. To tell of them in order and in detail would take another book. One figure looms tallest, the Spanish Jew known as the Rambam.* The world calls him Maimonides.

On the bookshelves opposite my desk stands the great code of Moses ben Maimon of Cordova: five thick volumes bound in dark red, ranged beside the Talmud, as tall if not as broad — his Strong Hand, or *Mishna Torah* (Law Review), written toward the end of the twelfth century.

In this work we have left the Orient. We have left the Holy Land and the lively debates of an old people still on their own soil or in neighboring Babylon, turning over memories of their forebears' ways and laws, living out the last flares of nationhood in the manners, speech, and spirit of Semitic countries. We are in Europe. The rational tone, the inquiry after abstract principle, are Greek. The method, the orderly structure, are Roman. Here the two ancient cultures which seemed Judaism's arch-foes, yet which combined with the Hebrew spirit made the modern world, flow into Jewish law.

Maimonides was not the first of the First Ones — their labors had begun two hundred years before him — but his was the work in which this great change visibly took place. Alfasi of Morocco had prepared a daringly edited Talmud

* *Ra*bbi *M*oses *b*en (son of) *M*aimon. Nearly all the post-Talmud authorities have a short name given to them by the learned, usually a word made of their initials.

hewing to the law, cutting out half the abstract discussion and all the tales and old science. Rashi had already written his master commentaries. Digests and codes of the common law were appearing. The aim in all these First Ones was the same: to set in order the heaped-up Jewish tradition, by the critical standards of Western intelligence. Maimonides did the job definitively. In him Europe does not conquer Judea, but by altering the measuring rods of the mind, it enters our tradition once and for all.

The Mishna Torah is one of the most ambitious literary undertakings I know. In a preface describing the decayed state of learning, the breakdown of communications, and the confusion arising from the difficulty of the Talmud and the tangle of Gaonate comment, the author summed up his job this way:

> Now therefore I, Moses ben Maimon of Spain, have girded up my loins and — relying on the Rock, blessed be He! — have studied all these works. And I have undertaken to write a book making plain what is forbidden and allowed, impure and pure, with the other laws of the Torah; all in clear language and a brief style. So that the oral law can be on everybody's lips, without doubt and without argument; not one authority on one side and one on the other; but clear words, familiar and accurate, the judgment that emerges from all the writings and commentaries from the days of Rabbi Judah the Prince until now.

Maimonides did just that. He took the encyclopedic work of hundreds of sages over a thousand years and recast it in a single book, omitting nothing of consequence. And he did it while practicing medicine and rising to become one of the busiest and best doctors in the Moorish world, eventually court physician to the sultan in Egypt.

The Rambam opens his effort with a Book of Knowledge, a swift broad look at medieval science. His first pages offer a logical sketch of the nature of God; and we see at once that here is a Talmudist who has mastered Aristotle as well as Scripture. His astronomy is from Ptolemy, and his medicine mainly from Galen and Hippocrates, with some of his own empiric wisdom added. The crucial point to note is the way he begins, the frame in which he finds it necessary to set down his code. The Talmud opened by asking when one recited the Sh'ma in the evening.

Through fourteen books the Rambam rears his structure: a new Talmud put together out of the old; symmetrical, orderly, accessible, whole. A meticulous table of contents opens all to the eye. With a flick of pages, the reader can find the answer to any question of law or custom in Judaism. To do this before the Rambam meant a wearying hunt through the forested folios of the Talmud (if one could read the Talmud) and another long search of the Gaonate books to determine the last word in practice. Maimonides did the immense task on every single point of the written and oral law.

He carries out the promise of his preface to the letter. The style is clear and brief. It is Mishna Hebrew refined into little blocks of marble, set in place one at a time to present a smooth gleaming surface. With elementary Hebrew training anybody can read the code. It is in depth, of course, a lifetime study for scholars. But it also sheds instant light from any page, wherever the layman chances to open it.

The Case Against Maimonides

The Mishna Torah swept the Jewish world the way Rabbi Judah's Mishna had a millennium earlier. It also stirred up a storm of protest among scholars. An upstart had laid violent hands on the Talmud. He had presumed to decide hard points of doctrine and practice which had left the greatest Gaonim at odds. He had been brazen enough to lay down the law of Judaism without citing his authorities, asking the house of Israel in his boundless conceit to rely on his judgment for accuracy and finality. He had offered himself as the sole conscience and counsellor of a people. He had introduced the ideas and the methods of the idolaters into the sacred precincts of Jewish law. And so on. Some of the most eminent men of his time raised these cries.

What they said was true enough in a way. All men and all writings have their imperfections. Calumny operates by poisoned exaggeration of real weaknesses and silence on merits. Maimonides later admitted his regret at not having cited his sources, point by point. His aim had been to reduce controversy by cutting out minority opinions and divisive arguments. He must have assumed that the Mishna Torah would justify itself by its completeness and clarity. Calm reliance on his own strength of mind, absolute confidence in powers equal to the huge task, pervade the pages of the Rambam.

The enemies of Maimonides succeeded in denying him the place he sought in Judaism. Perhaps it would be more accurate to say that his own peculiar distinctions and limits — turned against him with inflamed energy by his foes — brought him down. His stated purpose was to give the Jews a codified Talmud, a ready reference book of Hebrew law. His code never quite achieved that place. By a recurring irony of Jewish history, a disciple, not the master, entered the promised land.

Moses Maimonides remains on Mount Nebo. That he led the Jews safely to the ford into the modern world none can deny. The codifiers who came after him could not help following his forms, structures, and decisions in large part, even when they violently opposed his modernism. After Maimonides there could be no retreat to the less orderly Gaonate times. His code remains the main ground for our existing law, and a major tool for teaching the Talmud; and Maimonides stands without question as the mightiest single legal authority in Jewry from the Talmud to the present hour.

My grandfather's attitude toward the Rambam was a mixture of awed admiration and cautious disapproval. He knew the Mishna Torah well, referred to it constantly, but warned me that some of its passages were questionable. He told me that study of the *Guide for the Perplexed,* the Rambam's major work of metaphysics, was unsafe except for a man of exceptional piety and mental powers. This approximates, I think, the standing of Maimonides among devout Jews of the old school.

Was it fair? It was a fact. Had the Rambam won the place he sought, Judaism might have become a more open body of thought from the Middle Ages onward; or again, it might have been locked into a rigid version of science and philosophy, destined to become obsolete in a few centuries. The main body of Jewish thinkers never had to backtrack and abandon the science of Maimonides, never having committed themselves to it.

He was seven centuries ahead of his time; that is my belief. His credo was plain: no part of human knowledge belonged outside Judaism or could be left outside it. If the Torah was God's word, it was linked in every sentence to the natural world; and as knowledge of the world broadened, Torah study had to expand. His opponents feared the shocks of scientific disclosure to comfortably held views. They knew the tendency of young scholars to declare for total overthrow as soon as errors in old learning became clear. From 1300 to 1800 they more or less succeeded in sealing off the modernism of Maimonides within his "radical" books. The price for this was, in the end, an intellectual revolution which shook Jewry. Today the credo of Maimonides rules all serious Hebrew study.

The Shulkhan Arukh

Nobody could have guessed in advance, I think, that this code, of all codes, would be the one to carry the lightnings of Sinai into the twentieth century. To this day, five hundred years after Joseph Caro wrote it, there is no rival in sight. It is the Blackstone of Jewish law. There it stands, opposite my desk, beside the Rambam, four sections in eight tall volumes — the *Shulkhan Arukh,* The Ready Table.

Caro, born some two and a half centuries after the Rambam, was one of his humble armor-bearers; his commentary generally defends Maimonides from the barbs of his enemies. He bore armor, too, for another great code-maker, the Tur, whose popular law digest was the answer of strict tradition to the modernism of the Mishna Torah. Caro's commentary on the Tur's code, the work of a lifetime, was a gigantic display of Jewish legal learning; it is considered by many the most impressive in our literature. Called *The House of Joseph,* it is much larger than the Tur code itself.

In his old age Caro decided that a brief extract from *The House of Joseph* might be useful as a reference manual for laymen. He compiled a book which, he said, was so short, simple, and clear that the average layman could run through it once a month and so keep the main heads of Jewish practice fresh in his mind. This was the Shulkhan Arukh — the work which today occupies every serious Jewish scholar from perhaps his fifteenth year to the grave; which is the backbone of all rabbinic training; which, with its commentaries and the later court decisions, constitutes present-day Jewish law; which the reader is usually appealing to when he consults a rabbi for a ruling.

Of course the huge volume that comes down from the rabbi's shelf is no longer the handbook of Caro. On any page of The Ready Table, the author's words may come to two or three lines of type. The rest consists of bank upon bank of commentaries, extending (in new editions) to the present day. I have more than once brought tolerant smiles to the lips of scholars by citing the text of Caro in an argument. I have thereby betrayed my lack of familiarity with the fine print where authority generally resides. Nevertheless the glory rests with Caro. His code is the locus, the norm, of working Jewish jurisprudence.

Why did Caro's handbook leap to this greatest eminence that any writing has held in Judaism since the Mishna of Judah the Prince? Nobody compares him to Maimonides as a personality or as a thinker. There is indeed a curious half-anonymity about him. I have seen editions of The Ready Table in which Caro's name does not appear on the front page. The Shulkhan Arukh has won an independent life, like the Talmud. In a sense, the height of success for an author is to vanish in this way.

The unpretentiousness of the Shulkhan Arukh is striking. Where Maimonides opens his code with answers to the most terrible questions of theology, Caro reverts to the old tone of the Talmud and starts by telling what the pious Jew does when he gets up in the morning. So he goes on, point by point, largely following his two masters, Rambam and Tur, but leaving out any philosophizing that does not touch action. Often he uses the language of his masters, word for word, and he takes his structure from the Tur. The Ready Table is no triumph of style like the Mishna Torah. It is curt, choppy, cut to the bone, dry; but plain and understandable as any writing can be, and charged with the authority of total grasp.

Caro was born in Spain just before the expulsion in 1492. After some wanderings in Europe, he settled in the city of

Safed in northern Palestine, and there lived out his eighty-seven years, writing, teaching, and studying to the last. A mystic might say that the triumphant code had to be written in Palestine, to fulfill the Scripture, "For from Zion shall go forth the Law"; and that there you have the secret of the success of The Ready Table. The Talmud observes that the air of the Holy Land makes one wise. There is, for a fact, something in the Shulkhan Arukh of the stark and stony hills, the rugged clear landscape, and the crystal air of Safed. As Caro returned to the Holy Land, so his handbook returned to the plain law of the Torah and the Mishna. In his *House of Joseph*, conceived and mainly composed in Europe, Caro traversed the whole huge growth of analytic exile learning. In Safed he reduced it all to The Ready Table and entered on his strange, nearly nameless immortality.

The Law Today

My grandfather's personal law library, when he died, ran to some four hundred volumes. I am told by experts that it is a jewel collection of classics. His prized rarities were the decisions and opinions of the most recent stratum of Hebrew jurists, the Later Ones, or *Akharonim*.

These authorities of the seventeenth to the twentieth century — men like the Vilna Gaon, Haym Volozin, Akiba Eger, Hazon Ish, Hafetz Haym, and a score of other luminaries — wrote many of the commentaries which are banked in the great folios of the Shulkhan Arukh. They also published a quantity of important law in separate volumes. These works of the Later Ones usually came out in small editions and soon vanished from the market into central law libraries in the yeshivas, or into collections like my grandfather's. It is in these books that a rabbi confronted with a decision today is likely to find the law. These works of the

Later Ones presuppose of course, and stand on, the major codes and the Talmud. But their instances come down to the present time and are diverse enough to touch most of the things that happen in Jewish life.

My grandfather took his books with him from Soviet Russia to the United States, and from the United States to Israel, where he is buried. To say they were his pride is to understate the case. They were his life. He was well known for his legal mastery. He served on rabbinic courts often, and he was consulted regularly on difficult questions by younger rabbis.

When my grandfather reached a decision, he spoke as the voice of all the volumes on his shelves, stretching from several published in the 1950s back to the Torah itself, written about three thousand years ago. He came to a decision with exacting care, poring over the books, taking down first one and then another until they piled high on his table. His research ranged from the opinions of living authorities through the decisions and codes of the later legal masters in Poland, Germany, and Palestine; then back sometimes through the First Ones of Italy, France, Morocco, Egypt, dead — it might be — five hundred or twelve hundred years, to the Talmud and its contemporary learning. When he was at all in doubt, he called on other sages, gray scholars like himself.

My grandfather was known as a *maikil,* a liberal jurist. Wherever it was possible, he took the way of permission, of acquittal. He reconciled many couples who came to him for a divorce; he brought about some divorces in embittered and stalemated cases. With his reputation for liberality in decision, and humanity in judgment, went an extreme personal strictness. His way was to allow others the easy side of a doubt and to construe the law on the hard side for himself. There was no evasion or self-aggrandizement in this. A rabbi assumes before God full responsibility for the acts of people who do as he says. But he judged with kindness and with an accurate sense of the limits of human nature. It is not pride of family, I think, but a reasonable judgment that makes me say he was a Jewish jurist in the best tradition, the kind of man who has sustained the Mosaic law through many eras.

Retrospect

My survey of Jewish law — which will seem skeletal to those who know the field — must end here. Because I had no space to do more, I have tried to make but one fact clear: that Judaism is no mere skein of charming folkways, but a working jurisprudence.

The important living doctors of this law are for the most part deans of rabbinic schools in the United States and Israel. With the colleagues on their faculties, they ordain each year a number of young men. The candidates undergo a bar examination in Hebrew law — the semikha test — of appalling length and strictness, covering the Talmud and the major codes and decisions, early and late.

Intensive training for semikha begins during the first year of high school. It runs parallel to the candidate's college education as well as to the graduate studies needed for the ministry today: sociology, speech, community service, and the like. I have taught some of these lads advanced English composition. They are, I believe, the most hard-driven students in the world. Some of them, I have to say, are unequal to the double task. Some are very brilliant.

These young men who pass the Hebrew bar are not only ministers, but doctors of religious law. They inherit a continuous line of statutes, common law, codes, and case law, stretching across a hundred generations, the oldest living law there is.

Such long life does not in itself show that the law fits the present hour. It does argue rare vitality and a congruence with human nature in many proving grounds. Roman law was perhaps the high reach of civil lawmaking for order, scope, and equity. It arose when the Mosaic law was old. It disappeared more than a thousand years before United States law began. The Mosaic law has been a contemporary of both.

We set out to answer three questions about the Jewish law: what it is, whence it comes, and what force it claims.

It is the body of jurisprudence which men like my grandfather, and doctors of the learned guild of older times, carried forward down a long chain of generations; and, dying, handed on to new jurists. It comes from a legislator of world stature, Moses, who set together elements of ancient Semitic law, and an inspired vision of a moral order under God, in a new constitution of a unique religious family-nation. This constitution is the Torah. With its common law evolved over a thousand years and set forth in the Talmud, and then broadened and amended by fifteen more centuries of codes and judicial process, it has come down to the present day. It is the religious guide for those people who hold to the identity it created and who accept Moses in their own lives as the Hebrew lawgiver.

With the fall of the Jewish State in the year 70, the Mosaic civil and criminal law, by the edict of its own jurists, gave place to the civil and criminal laws of lands where the Jews lived. The law in these lands has for Jews, under Talmud enactment, the full force of religious law, except when it challenges their right to worship God in their own way. The laws of Moses on the service of God remain binding. There are no sanctions to force compliance. The power of the law of Moses is today, and for many centuries has been, wholly moral; and in this too the legislation is unique.

That power, such as it is, has kept in life and identity the people known as the Jews, who now number some eleven million, having recently lost one third of their ranks in the twentieth-century massacre by Hitler.

Part 4

THE PRESENT

Chapter 18

✦

The Present

THE present day in Judaism means from 1800 onward. That was when the Enlightenment struck the ghetto; the Enlightenment, that bolt which shattered old Jewry into the boil of parties it is today. Writing the tale of Judaism after 1800, one must write an Iliad, or one must be brief as a telegram.

Chapter 19

✦

What the Enlightenment Was

THE ghetto Jew in Europe created a stockade culture, centered on his religion and taught in his holy tongue. Through the dark ages the ghetto was bright with literacy; and Jewish knowledge was as good as anything the outside offered, or better. There was no enlightenment, because there was little enlightenment to be had.

All this changed with the coming of Copernicus and Bacon, of Galileo and Descartes, of Newton and Voltaire. There were blazing suns outside the ghetto. Light shafted through the heavy timbers of the stockade. The first reaction of the leaders inside was to seal every chink and try to shut out the light. Whether this was an inevitable reaction or the mistake of weak vision can be argued. But it happened.

It is not hard to imagine the state of mind of the leaders. The impact of the new learning on the painfully won, smooth-running ghetto culture would, they feared, be destructive. The preservation of that culture was a life-or-death matter. Modernism had been suspect ever since Maimonides had thrown Jewry into a two-century turmoil. The rabbis heard the rumors that the new learning was laying waste to Christian piety. They took up a delaying action. It was instinct.

They could not have foreseen the catastrophe of their

policy. Nothing in their experience allowed for the freeing of the Jews. But the new ideas of the Renaissance, the liberalism of the eighteenth century, and the loosening society of the industrial age meant the end of the ghetto. At the time the emancipation probably seemed to come at a crawl. Looking back on it, we see it as happening almost at once; Jews one moment shut into the twilit pales, in the next moment blinking around at the open light of the Western world.

In Germany and France, when Jews found it was actually possible for them to get the new learning, there was a swift and terrible rebellion against the curtainers. As fast as the bars went down young men poured out of the yeshivas into Western schools. In the yeshivas there was Talmud and Shulkhan Arukh, commentary and supercommentary, a vast body of learning growing heavy with rings upon rings of more and more minute distinctions. What hope was there of holding within this range the attention of young minds, sharpened on this very whetstone of hard legal logic, when the new learning was at hand?

Germany, the stronghold of the old school, the place of one of the stablest Jewish communities, became a center of apostasy. A Hellenizing epidemic raged. Educated Jews dropped their religion, their learning, their very names. They became agnostics or Christians in droves; or they adopted semblances of the old faith resembling synagogue Judaism as little as possible, and polite Western churchgoing as much as possible.

The process was delayed for a while in Poland and Russia because tyrannic regimes held the Jews in their pales. But yeshiva boys immured in the ghetto somehow heard tales of the new knowledge. They got hold of the forbidden books, smuggled them into the study hall, and read them inside the great folios of the Shulkhan Arukh, under cover of a pious Hebrew chant. A thirst for wisdom possessed them. Did not

Proverbs say, "With all your strength get knowledge"? Their teachers told them this knowledge meant the supercommentaries. They did not believe it. What did they care if the rabbis who found them with the books of *haskala,* of enlightenment, called them epicureans, atheists, breakers of the wall? These old epithets they began to take as names of honor. Out of their ranks came the minds and spirits that created modern Zionism. The fact that Zionism was cradled in rebellion against the separatist learning of the old yeshivas colors the state of Israel to this hour.

We are very close to this hurricane in Jewish life. One can almost say we live in its aftermath, digging out from under the debris, with the wind still whipping wreckage about. There are surviving teachers of the old school who inveigh yet against modern learning as the destroyer of the Jewish religion. There are white-haired rebels who see red when they see a rabbi. But though such quarrellers live, they play at armchair war of a day gone by. History has swept past them, and the issue of survival is posed today in far different — and deeper — terms.

Chapter 20

✦

Orthodoxy

"I Should Have Learned English"

THERE is in Jerusalem today a tiny band of diehards called the *Neturai Karta,* dedicated to total rejection of change. Their name means Guardians of the City. They number perhaps five or six hundred souls. Their few streets and alleys are a living stage-set of the ghetto that was: wooden market booths in an open cobbled square, little boys with earlocks and long black caftans chasing the chickens, shawled and wigged women passing with downcast eyes, and from open windows the chant of children translating the Torah into Yiddish by rote. The dwellers here (and their little knot of supporters in the United States) are certain that they are the only authentic Jews left on earth. It is they who have sallied forth on the Sabbath to stone cars, rioted over playgrounds where boys and girls disport together, run advertisements in American newspapers denouncing the land of Israel as fascist, and so forth.

Some people believe that this group holds the "orthodox" viewpoint. But the orthodox are as appalled by them as anybody.

The Neturai Karta are doing their very best to live as though the past two centuries had never happened. Yet a ghetto Jew of the eighteenth century transported to those streets would be stunned by the changes that have crept in, along with the cables of the telephone and lighting systems.

One cannot live in a time capsule after all. Existence is change. Not to recognize the government of Israel is to recognize it in a way; to forbid listening to radios is to adapt to the radio. Once adaptation starts, it has its own laws. Time does the rest. Moses in his wisdom marked off only a few things in life that would endure. The rest he left to change. He did not freeze Jewish manners for all time in the cast of Egypt or of the desert.

But several times in Jewish history our people have lived long enough in one way to make it seem natural, inevitable, and at last sacrosanct. In the ghettos of Europe a man who wore his coat shorter than the average was suspect, so stylized had manners become. The laws of Moses had blended with a colorful speech borrowed from Germany, and a dress adapted from the medieval gentility, into a living whole, an inviolable way of life, *Yiddishkeit*. The difference between the enduring laws of our faith and the manners of a temporary environment had dropped from sight. Discovering that difference again has been an agony.

My grandfather maintained pretty well unaltered in his own life the life of the East European pale. His black coat reached to his black shoe tops. His black round hat never was violated with a Western crease. His beard did not know the touch of the barber. He was, in short, to the best of his ability, a walking replica of the East European Jew of the past two hundred years. Most certainly he did not dress or talk or act like Joseph Caro, or Maimonides, or Judah the Prince, or Ezra. He took the norm that he found and gave his life to it.

He had no clear program for the future. Integrity for him was all. For him it lay in the law, and he held to the manners, dress, and language in which he had first studied. The price he paid at last was an evaporation of his congregation in the Bronx, as the younger members looked around for a rabbi who spoke English. He did not mind that. But he could not hold the attention of the young people in his own family after a while. That cut deep.

When we rode together in a taxi to the ship that was to take him to Israel, almost the last thing he said to me was — the old man, looking back over twenty-three years in America, the last decades of his vigor — "I should have learned English. But the sound of it was so harsh to me!"

Who Is Orthodox?

To ascertain how many Jews "really" hold to the religious law is not possible. There is no way to pry into the inner chambers of personal life. And there is some disagreement today on what the law commands, and what counts as obedience. The word "orthodox" lacks precision. It falls into too many sections.

The Neturai Karta would perhaps report a census of eleven or twelve hundred orthodox Jews in all the world. The zealous followers of the Rabbi of Satmar might expand the number to fifteen or twenty thousand. Neither group approves of the very religious Agudists of Israel, a small political party, because they sit in the Israeli parliament. Journalists sometimes call all these groups ultra-orthodox. Of course they would reject the label.

The main body of orthodoxy, several million strong, also has shades of belief and lines of division. At the moment one hears of the Mizrachi, the modern orthodox, the Sefards, the Hasidic, the neo-Hasidic, the neo-orthodox, the traditional, and so on. I doubt that the patience of the reader will permit me to describe the differences that separate these bodies. But the divisive points are not always minor to the people in question.

Irremediable splintering does not occur in this main Mosaic

communion, because the old magnet holds the factions together: the law. There is bad waste of energy in internal discord. Funds melt away in duplicate efforts, when hardly enough money is at hand to get the main jobs done. The emancipation, the Enlightenment, the shift to America, Zionism, Hitler, the birth of Israel — these tremendous events have whirled the orthodox body dizzily. There has been heavy attrition. There is as yet not much pulling together. But an impressive remnant holds to the law: in Israel possibly half the people, in shadings of observance that are endless; elsewhere, perhaps a third. These figures are crude guesses. There are no figures. Observance of the chief laws of the faith, with serious training of the young, more or less defines the people we are talking about.

The Decline of the Old Learning

But the training of the young that our grandfathers knew — Torah, Talmud, and code law in infinite depth, and little more — is all but gone. The revolution in pedagogy is so great that advocates of old and new alike are as yet rather stunned.

The big wave of ghetto immigrants in the early 1900s brought the old learning to America with them. There was nothing else to bring. The battle was then locked between old and new: it was yeshiva *or* haskala, Jewish *or* Western knowledge. The laws of the new land quickly ended the argument. The children had to go to public school, and they went. Religious studies were pushed to the afternoon and the night. This was the death blow to the old learning, though it lingered for a generation.

And in what a sad form it lingered! It meant for small children the *heder* and the *melamed,* the schoolroom and the tutor. For anybody who knew the realities, the words are full of dark bitter tones. The melamed was usually a poor misfit, unable to find a well-paying job even in golden America. More often than not he was ill-informed, heavy-handed, and short-tempered. The schoolroom was his own squalid flat or the back room of an impoverished synagogue. The contrast with the bright classrooms and crisp teachers of the American public school was devastating. Worse yet, what the children learned at school fitted the life they saw around them. The melamed's dronings were queer echoes from an unknown world. His doom was swift. He gave way to the Talmud Torah, an afternoon school manned by younger Americanized teachers, with blackboards, chalk, bells, well-printed books, and the beginnings of system.

It was the yeshivas, the higher schools of the old learning, that took the worst beating at first. They offered the ancient curriculum. By contrast there was the glittering array of Western arts and sciences beckoning from public high schools and colleges. Yeshivas drooped and closed. The air was like that of the years of the German collapse of Judaism. To many a Jewish thinker the end of a road of three thousand years seemed at last in sight.

The Jews have a way, when all is lost, of finding a path through the Red Sea. It occurred to a few old rabbis that American law prescribed Western education for all children, but not where they were to get it. Private schools existed. What if the yeshivas took the new knowledge within their walls? Then they might mark out the hours so that both learnings could go forward. They asked the public authorities and found them willing.

And so, in the persons of young teachers of English, geography, American history, science, and higher mathematics — teachers not necessarily religious, nor even Jewish — the learning of the Western world, after two thousand years, officially crossed the threshold of the yeshiva. This unheralded, matter-of-fact, diffuse event, which happened on the Lower East Side of New York in the early years of the twentieth century, marked an irreversible change in the history of the Jewish people. It was the triumph of the credo of Maimonides, seven centuries delayed. It led to swift and startling results.

The New Learning

A pyramid of the new learning has appeared almost out of nowhere in recent years, all over America: nursery schools, elementary schools, high schools, colleges, and a major university. These have no national structure and very little interconnection. Each raises its own funds.

The base of primary teaching is in the all-day or day schools. Here the children encounter American education and Jewish learning as one thing. Arithmetic, Bible, geography, composition in English and in Hebrew, geometry and Mishna, mean alike homework, tests, and report cards. The great question, when the movement began to roll, was this: would not the day schools cripple the children for life in the open American society? The first schools were crudely organized, badly run, and short of funds. Some parents took the chance and enrolled their children anyway. Year by year the schools improved, and by now some decisive results are coming in.

The graduates of the day-school system have nearly all passed into general education at some point, most often in the advance to high school. These students on the whole do as well as their peers in the public schools and colleges, sometimes better. They have the advantage of coming from a severe discipline. They have taken academic honors, and have had success in life, proportioned to their gifts. They possess Jewish knowledge that the last generation lacked. That is the difference.

Capping the pyramid is Yeshiva University, a Torah

school taking all human knowledge as its domain. The plant, with a value running into the tens of millions, is a network of buildings branching all through New York City: preparatory schools, a college of arts and sciences, a theological seminary, laboratories, graduate schools, and the newest medical center in America, the Albert Einstein College of Medicine.*

The new education has sparked the rise of a so-called modern American orthodoxy, a movement which was as hard to imagine when I was young as world peace is at the moment. The energy and momentum come from young people, thirty-five and under, mostly college graduates. They form clubs, and start synagogues, and build mikvas, and organize lectures and seminars, and found day schools, and altogether comport themselves like discoverers of a new world. Their manners are wholly American. Possibly because they are aware of the paradox of their way, they go in very hard for fashionable clothes, current reading, and suburban amenities. The synagogues they build are more in the spirit of Frank Lloyd Wright than of the great European shuls. The sexes sit separately, with women placed as advantageously as men. As yet the movement has no consistent form. Old Jewry was a mature body with defined ways and customs. The new American orthodoxy is a spreading experiment. The main Mosaic community, with a loose but immense

* This university is by no means the only major center of Jewish learning in America. The Hebrew Union College, which ordains Reform rabbis, and the Jewish Theological Seminary, the center of the Conservative movement, both stand very high in the estimation of general scholarship. Brandeis University, a non-sectarian institution under Jewish sponsorship, is also well regarded. Torah Vodaas is an orthodox yeshiva of international prominence. Yeshiva University is the largest of these undertakings, and the broadest in scope. But its real distinction lies in being — so far as I know — the first center of the higher Hebrew learning in history which is committed to the Mosaic discipline, and equally to the disciplines of Western arts and sciences.

structure of synagogues and Talmud Torahs all over the world, uncounted thousands of buildings old and new, grandiose and small, holds to the familiar forms; but manners are generally westernized, and preaching in English, or French, or Spanish — whatever the local language may be — is the common thing. The liturgy remains Hebrew.

In Israel the orthodox range across all the population. There are isolated knots of the old Jewry, keeping up the European manners and the Yiddish tongue. There are orthodox communes, trade schools, and experimental farms; there is a network of religious schools, and there is a university, Bar Ilan, on the pattern of Yeshiva. There are orthodox sailors, generals, engineers, scientists, bricklayers, nightclub entertainers, newspapermen, cabinet ministers, and taxi drivers. Synagogues dot the cities as churches do in the United States. Whatever religion exists in Israel is orthodox, in many variations. There is of course the large body of Sefard Jewry from Africa and the Middle East, who bring an infusion of the exotic to the inherited forms of the European exile.

But Israel is not a religious land as Spain is. The dominant parties are socialist. The culture is a free and extremely skeptical one. In a later chapter I shall return to this remarkable land of the Jews. Here the point to note is that orthodoxy, with the usual maelstrom of conflicting opinions and emotions, is painfully taking hold in Israel as a modern way of life. It disconcerts both the old people with its changing manners and the agnostics with its firm stand on Mosaic law.

The Hasidim

An exception to this general picture of orthodoxy is the party known as the Hasidim. The Hasidim today defend the place in Jewry once occupied by their angriest opponents, the diehard leaders of the old learning. Of all the diverse branches of Jewish opinion, only certain Hasidic groups hold out in a mass against Western education.

Hasidism rises in the *Cabala,** that strange efflorescence of magic, mystery, and poetry in Jewish lore. The movement sprang up around the figure of a mystic wonder-worker, the Baal Shem Tov, who was born in Poland in 1700. Himself a man of great learning, the Baal Shem sparked a romantic revival within Judaism. Learned and unlearned alike, he taught, could please God with an offering of love, with the service of the heart. Joy, song, fervid worship in company, under a beloved and holy leader possessed of special magnetism and cabalistic powers — this was the way of Hasidism which the Baal Shem created, and it spread swiftly in the ghettos. It opened a path of Judaism for a great number of people who could no longer cope with the complex and almost infinitely detailed learning of the yeshivas.

The Cabala's whispers of worlds beyond this world, of close-hovering angels, of miracles worked through old secret incantations, had a strong lure for the prisoners of the muddy ghettos, doomed to poverty and ostracism. To attach oneself to a Rebbe, a wonder man to whom the Cabala truths were open, to whom the angels spoke — a man whose every word had the timbre of magic, whose small gestures bore instruction and beauty, whose table scraps brought a touch of his inner light to those lucky enough to eat them — to live close to such a man, in the circle of his disciples, was to escape from a brown world into a golden one.

The real force of Hasidism lay in the fact that men arose with the gifts to fill the role of Rebbe, all through the pales of eastern Europe. Their sayings grew into a folklore, charming, fresh, and wise, with a novel color half of this world and half

* For a description of the Cabala, see Notes, p. 317.

of the moon. The acts of the Rebbes became, even in their lifetimes, a body of legend, a sort of Jewish Lives of the Saints. Their names melted into place names, as though they were earls; they were the Lubavitcher, the Lubliner, the Berditchever. They founded dynasties; often as not their sons or sons-in-law succeeded them in their religious office.

Hasidism in its early years took forms that shocked the majority. The ecstatic manner of worship, the oddness of dress and manners, the changes in prayers, were disturbing enough. But the whole séance air of wonder-working, of amulets and ineffable names, of superhuman powers — feats like invisibility, levitation, clairvoyance, and second sight were common in Hasidic legend — seemed to open wide in Judaism a door slammed shut by Moses the Lawgiver, the bar against the superstition and the magic practices of old Egypt. Above all, the doctrine that study of the law pleased God less than simple fervor — a distortion of the Baal Shem's thought, but a popular one — was a call to war. It meant the end of Judaism. Hasidism never convinced the main body of Jewry, but it won a life and a place of its own.

To this day, wherever they go, some of the more zealous Hasidim cling at every point to the dress and manners of the Polish ghetto: long earlocks, fur hats, and the rest. But more and more the adherents, as they move in the business world, take on a Western look, though their loyalty to their Rebbes does not dim. Some Rebbes still ban television and movies, and they all have reservations in varying degrees about Western education. The best-known and strongest group today is built around the Lubavitcher Rebbe, who lives in Brooklyn. They have a liberal tradition; the incumbent Rebbe studied at the Sorbonne. Their network of schools uses modern teaching aids, and they have developed vocational training highly. My grandfather was a Hasid of this group. His studied withdrawal from Western dress, his reluctance to learn English, may have stemmed from his Hasidic leanings. But he was committed to learning as the most important thing in life, and he never objected to our acquiring the best general education we could.

The Hasidim came to the United States and Israel in force during the Hitler terror. They have felt the impact of modern life for more than a generation. The movement remains alive and vibrant. A school of Jewish existentialists claims its folklore as new philosophic ground. The sad-sweet, lively music of the Hasidim has passed into all Jewish life; it has given many a Tin Pan Alley drudge a hit; it has even been clothed in the dinner jacket of sonata form and brought into the symphony hall. But in general, Hasidism has yet to meet the shock of the Enlightenment, which the rest of Jewry has absorbed and moved beyond.

The question is, What will the light do: shrivel it, or stimulate it to its best growth? At present the dynastic leaders seem to answer the question by rejecting it. They see a large measure of withdrawal as the price of continued integrity, and they are willing to pay it. Whether time will accept such a high fee for the continuance of Hasidism in its old form remains to be seen.

Chapter 21

✦

Dissent

REFORM Judaism began in Germany early in the nineteenth century. A movement which broke off from it in its first decades gained little ground in Germany, but took hold in America as Conservative Judaism. These denominations are today the two religious structures in Jewry outside orthodoxy.

Reform drew its energy, which was at first very high, from two sources: the new freedom of the Enlightenment, and the strong stand of the rabbis against change. As thousands of Jews went streaming through the break in the ghetto wall to apostasy, some scientific scholars and leading preachers started casting about for means to harness the flood. An obvious solution was to make the religion easier and more attractive in German terms. In the teeth of all the traditionalist objections, they went boldly to work.

At the start the changes were mere touches of ritual: prayer in German, the use of an organ, uncovered heads, attractive vestments for the rabbi. But the appetite of the Enlightenment was not to be appeased by such crumbs. There ensued a rapid jettisoning of laws and customs. A new credo emerged with these changes. The essence of Judaism was the worship of the one universal God. The rest of the work of Moses was temporary machinery, no longer in force in the present day. It followed that the common law too was out of date, since it rested on the Torah. On this premise, German Jewry within a single generation worked out an undemanding religion, freed of any ritual inconvenience, housed with elegance, and invitingly Western in tone and language. Traditional rabbis fought Reform hard, mainly with anguished emotional onslaughts. Shaken and depleted, German orthodoxy closed its ranks, but Reform won and kept a large following.

It is hard for us to imagine now the élan, the brilliant excitement, of the first years of German Reform. The brotherhood of Jew and Christian must have seemed for a while to be in sight. The Reform Jews were discarding all the distinctive ways of their old faith and merging into the manners and esthetics of the West. Surely the German citizenry would meet them halfway, and together they would usher in religious peace! The German Jews who immigrated to the United States in mid-century brought Reform with them. Here it chiefly survives, a stable way of life for a sizable community. German Reform was obliterated by Hitler.

Conservatism Overtakes Reform

Within Reform itself, early in its growth, there was a serious reaction at the immensity of the change, at the wide sweep of the knife. Major Reform scholars set themselves against the trend. They argued — anticipating ideas that are common in today's sociology — that a working faith had to be more than an abstract idea, that life went deeper than logic. They made little headway against the jubilant tide of change at first. But today Conservative Judaism has drawn abreast of Reform.

When I briefly attended a yeshiva high school around 1930, the senior students were full of dark talk about an alluring place called "Schechter's Seminary." To go there, the rumor went, was to flirt with apostasy; on the other hand, one might acquire the suave charm that would lead to a pulpit in a wealthy Conservative temple. Among the lads who intended to become rabbis, this temptation caused great soul-searchings.

Solomon Schechter, the father of American Conservatism, was a scholar of great ability. He was a disciple of the moderates in the German Reform movement: hence, the name Conservative. To this day the seminary he founded is a most conservative graduate school of divinity; not at all the glittering mixture of Monte Carlo and the Left Bank which the yeshiva lads fondly imagined it to be. The young men keep up traditional observances and forms of worship, and get a grounding in Jewish law. They are trained too in the historical criticism of religion, which was Schechter's forte.

Schechter's ideas really took hold in the early twentieth century, when the nature of American Jewry radically changed. The fugitives from the pogroms and the revolutions of East Europe, perhaps two million strong, arrived fresh from the ghetto. In the bewildering new land, many of them were not at all inclined to drop the old faith pell-mell. They rather clung to it; it was a familiar anchor in a sea of strangeness.

All the same, as they became used to America and won a place in the land, the tug between the old way of life and the new grew strong. They wanted to hold to their faith, but they also wanted — somehow or other — quick relief from the strain. Reform was cold and queer to them. They could not comfortably pray in English with uncovered heads. A rabbi who ate pork, and smoked a cigar after the Sabbath service, was a shocking figure, however fine his discourse might be. They had to look elsewhere.

The disciples of Solomon Schechter offered, in their new Conservative temples, certain of the attractions of Reform.

Husbands sat with wives; an organ played; English enlivened the cut-down liturgy, but there were some old familiar Hebrew prayers too. The young rabbis, smooth-shaven and well-spoken, were clearly of the new world. Immigrants who were being pushed by circumstances to break the Sabbath laws and to eat banned foods could hardly bear to face the Holy Ark and the rabbi of the synagogue. They were less uncomfortable in the temple. There they felt good about the Judaism they were managing to retain, rather than guilty about the laws they were violating. While Reform gained but a few adherents in these years, the newcomers made of Conservatism, in a decade or so, a movement equal to Reform in strength.

If the first generation could find the Conservative pattern attractive, their children naturally found it more so. The Jewish education of the young being so scanty, their ties to the old faith were largely sentimental, twined with love for their parents. Some of them were ready for the step to Reform, but so long as one parent remained alive, the Conservative compromise was the clear choice. When they did join Reform temples — as many did, and are still doing — they were accustomed to more ceremony, rite, and Hebrew than they found. The Reform leaders, pledged to the doctrines of the German Enlightenment, could not acknowledge the force of the Mosaic law. But there has been a trend for some time in Reform to renewal of rites and symbols, and to a greater use of Hebrew, for cultural reasons.

The Blurring of the Lines

So it happens that the lines between the two movements sometimes blur. In what might be called the liberal Conservative congregations, the distinction from Reform may be a matter of caps and prayer shawls for the men, and more

Hebrew. We have it on the authority of *Conservative Judaism,* an able and wholly sympathetic study by the sociologist Dr. Marshall Sklare, that the observance of Sabbath, diet, and other disciplines in these congregations falls off steadily and steeply. This tends to merge the worshippers with Reform Jewry in practice.

Conservative use of Reform innovations and its own departures, like permission to drive cars to the temple on the Sabbath, are defended as minor changes adopted to save the faith. The Conservative rabbi does not smoke on the Sabbath. He observes the laws of diet, and enforces them in temple catering. In his personal life he keeps up traditional duties and customs. He is thus vulnerable to the Reform challenge that there is a double religious standard in his movement: one for rabbis, which is practically orthodox, and one for the laity, which is practically Reform. But the theoretical standard of Conservatism is the same for rabbi and layman. The difficulty lies in the facts of human behavior. The mingling of the sexes, the playing of the organ, the permission to drive cars, and the abridged prayers somehow suggest to the layman a general release from the ritual law. The wide differences in practice from temple to temple, and the lack of any Conservative law, make the task of correcting this impression very hard.

Orthodoxy and Dissent

Between the dissenting movements on the one hand and the large and various bodies of orthodoxy on the other, there is at present a sort of polite peace. The anathemas of the nineteenth century have died away. Naturally the contest for minds, or at least for memberships, is keen under the amicable surface.

That there will be a major change in this picture in the near future seems unlikely. Reform cannot admit authority in the

Mosaic law without vanishing. The Conservatives cannot drop their innovations without merging into orthodoxy. Both dissenting movements have nationwide plants: temples, divinity schools, Sunday schools, afternoon schools, and large bodies of members. It is not usual for an establishment to vote itself out of existence.

Will the orthodox discard their fealty to the law and acknowledge the wisdom of Reform or Conservative improvisations? The time for that would seem to have been in the nineteenth century. Orthodoxy has survived and recovered from the impact of modern dissent. Individuals, indeed, continue to drift away. There has been a well-known cascading from orthodox to Conservative, and from Conservative to Reform groups. But Reform does not swell as it might, because of attrition into lack of interest and loss of identity. Nor, curiously, does orthodoxy seem to diminish. It received massive new strength from the refugees of the Hitler terror; and since then it is, if anything, on the rise. The prospect so far as the eye can see, at least in the United States, is that the three denominations will continue for a long time.

The dissenting movements can scarcely wish for the disappearance of orthodoxy. Their existence more or less depends on a main body of Mosaic followers who write the Holy Scrolls, study the classics, keep the faith at its picturesque maximum, and provide a pool of strength and renewal for the less demanding denominations. The great weakness of both Conservative and Reform Judaism — at least this is my impression — is their tendency to run down without constant infusion of orthodox-trained new blood.

It is widely argued today that both movements were shock absorbers of the Enlightenment, and kept great numbers of Jews from being utterly lost to the ancient House. If, as the orthodox believe, the Mosaic law has a decisive inner force, they ought to await with tolerance and with confidence the coming return of dissenters, beginning with the most intelligent. But that is asking a lot of human nature. When a temple opens in a neighborhood where a synagogue has reigned for a generation, and attracts away some husbands and wives who like to sit side by side, the reaction is usually less than philosophic.

The dissenters have had a very good thing in mixed seating. Against orthodoxy it has been until lately their trump card, because it is so much nearer to the manners of the American majority. For the orthodox, this detail of synagogue custom has become a rallying ground. Since the invasion has struck at them here, it is here that they dig in. It is the hallmark of the new orthodox edifices that the men and women worship separately. The issue may seem a small one on which to divide a community as ancient, and as rich in ideas, as Jewry. But one never knows in advance, marching into battle, which of the many hills on the field is going to become Bloody Nose Ridge.

A Personal Note

I have here done my best to portray the Reform and Conservative movements candidly and accurately. My portrait should perhaps be corrected in the reader's mind by a fact that will be obvious to him; my general sympathy is with the main tradition, and so I view these movements more or less as an outsider. Individuals in these movements have contributed magnificently to scholarship, to Jewish rescue and survival, and to the physical plant of Jewry in America and in Israel. How can men who score such achievements be in error, if they are? The answer would have to lie not in any lack of wisdom or talent in them — and most certainly not in any superior insight ascribable to me — but in the large social forces that have created the movements of dissent. In the history of every people, men of the best energy and wit, and of the highest value to their fellows, have been on the wrong side in long-range issues. Perhaps the orthodox are out of step with history, not they. History will decide. My object here has not been to criticize any party in Jewry, but to tell the truth as I understand it.

The American Jewish community works together in rescue and philanthropy, whatever its religious differences. Whether the task is helping Israel, or building hospitals, or supporting community projects, the orthodox, the Conservative, and the Reform Jews fall in side by side and get at the job. Vigorous leaders often come from the dissenters, or from the large group that does not worship at all. Major service organizations like B'nai Brith and Hadassah, renowned for energy and achievement, are not committed to any one religious party. A minor point, but one that illuminates the underlying good will in the community, is this: even when unobservant Jews happen to outnumber religious ones in a project, they usually make their catered affairs kosher, sometimes at high added cost. The instinct that suggests such conduct is worth high praise, but nobody thinks much about it.

If charity, healing, rescue, and welfare work were all of Judaism, the bulk of the community would be orthodox. These things are not the whole Torah, but they are much of it. Pietists sometimes despair of American Jewry. I for one am proud to be part of the community, and I think its great days lie ahead.

Assimilation

"The best thing we can do is intermarry and disappear," a fraternity brother said to me when I was about seventeen. It was the first time I had heard the slogan of assimilation spoken loud and clear. It froze me. I peered at him, wondering whether he could be serious. He was. The assimilators are always quite serious, though some Jews find their state of mind almost unimaginable.

Assimilation is, and for the longest time has been, a main party of dissent in Jewry. It does not seem a party, because in its nature it has no organization, no temples, no schools, and no books of doctrine. But in periods of freedom like the present — and there have been several such interludes in our history — it sometimes wins half of the Jews, and occasionally more than half.

To call the assimilators turncoats, weaklings, traitors, breakers of the faith, is to substitute abuse for the effort to think. Assimilation is not only a popular way, it has weighty logic on its side. The real surprise is that the Jews have not wholly evaporated in one of these times of tolerance. What, to be given the chance to lay down the burden of ostracism and disappear among the billions of mankind, and not take advantage of it with a rush and a cheer? Where is the sense — in view of the sombre history of the Jews — in behaving any other way?

With all that, the assimilator seldom states his position in the cold blood of my fraternity brother. Nor does he, as a rule, plot a course of vanishing. He allows it to happen. This is achieved simply by doing nothing about being Jewish. Three or four generations, and the family ceases to count as Jews, unless bloodthirsty lunatics like the Nazis start up a grandfather hunt. Remaining Jewish in a free society takes work. If the work goes undone, Jewishness dims and dies. It is the exceptional assimilator who tries to speed the death by such devices as changing his name and obscuring or denying his background.

Assimilation, like frostbite, begins at the extremities of Jewry. Settlements far from centers of the community almost always fade away fast. In the social body it is the wealthiest and the poorest, the best educated and the least educated, the brightest and the dullest, who tend to go first. Ignorance and low intelligence cause loss of grip on the faith. Carried along in the ghetto by the current around them, the ill-informed and the incapable drift into non-observance when cut loose, and into oblivion. Poverty drives people to suspend observance, and grinds away their identity. At the other extreme the rich and the gifted make their way swiftly into the non-Jewish world. Judaism being an encumbrance on the way, they tend to drop it. It is in the middle that Jewish identity persists longest, whether as Zionism, orthodoxy, or religious dissent.

Yet here too assimilation at last takes hold. When professors and governors, movie stars and millionaires, writers and judges openly give up their Jewish ties and ways — these in America, and their equivalents in Germany, Spain, Morocco, Rome, and Babylon in other days — the wonder is that anybody at all remains behind to carry on the faith. Yet a remnant always does, and Judaism in time renews itself with the greatest struggles — if only to produce, in the next age of tolerance, another wave of gifted assimilators. It is even argued that this is the true mission of the Jews, the secret of the Messiah symbol — that they must go on relinquishing to the world St. Pauls, Spinozas, Freuds, Disraelis. It is a fetching idea. One weakness of it is that if assimilation ever won a round of history, the milieu and the human strain that produce such luminaries would disappear, and the world would see no more of them.

The loss of these intelligences in the van of a new assimilation surge is each time foredoomed. Quickest to see the conflicts of the old way and the new, they are the first to decide that Judaism is dated. They find in their mastery of the new life, in the welcome granted to their talents, a whole answer to existence. They create a climate in which assimilation becomes first a smart, then an ordinary course. Masses of plain people follow them without the compensations of high achievement, simply because it is always easier not to be Jewish, once the communion weakens.

The odd thing is that this momentous rejection by the able few is almost never a well-considered act. Often they are born of parents already adrift, so that they never get a chance to know Judaism. Or if they find a received form of it in their homes, it loses out swiftly to the interests generated by their special talents. By the age of fifteen they have swept into a life, and a state of mind, which exclude forever an adult estimate of their Jewish identity. It is a freakish occurrence when — as with Heine — a man of genius has second thoughts about assimilation, reopens the case with all his energy, and reverses the verdict. And such a rare event comes too late, both for the man and for the people who have followed him.

The Assimilator Speaks

"What you say here is quite true, and on the whole well put. I respect your knowledge of Judaism and your ability to respond to it. In an abstract way I envy you — not your life exactly, but the knowledge of a lore and the experience of a belief, which are quite strange to me. But it is out of the question for me to reopen the matter. As you know, I have never denied being a Jew, and I am proud of an ancestry which, as you say, is ancient and distinguished. I'm sorry to say the Jewish mission means nothing to me. It is a curiosity of intellectual history, no more.

"I'm well aware that my children will probably slough off their Jewish identity, and that my grandchildren most certainly will. At the risk of offending you, I have to say I think this will be a good thing for them. My talents, such as they are, have not protected me from certain stings and stabs that come a Jew's way. Life is hard enough. To forgo a disability seems sensible to me. Again, all of you who prefer to make it the core of your life have my respect and puzzled admiration. You may even have a point, in the eyes of the God you believe in and I don't. But to me you are all Quixotes, carrying on an obsolete code of honor in rusty armor on a collapsing nag, with a mad and sadly comic energy. I wish you well. If you turn out right and there is a beyond in which we will compare notes, you may have the laugh on me, assuming there is laughter there. But I do not think I will ever hear that laugh, and for the life of me I cannot change my views, which are as clear and inescapable to me as the sky above.

"You want me to re-examine 'my heritage.' Would you have me also examine in depth Mohammedanism. Buddhism, Catholicism, and Zoroastrianism? When, then, will I get my day's work done? Judaism means exactly as much to me as one of those. It is a collector's item in the gallery of comparative religion. I know its general picture: Abraham, Moses, one God, the Exodus, the Torah, no ham, all that. No, I have not studied the Talmud. But I claim to have a contemporary intelligence. If the West has put those special Jewish studies aside and taken only the Bible, that verdict must be mine. Does the Rambam have anything to say to me on the far side of Kant, Nietzsche, and Whitehead? If so, where are his discoverers? I gather he is a sort of Jewish Aquinas. Aquinas is an old story to me. My integrity requires that I know the best in current thought, and by and large I do. I will not go back to the yeshiva and sit among the boys. I am a man, doing a man's work, and I am aware of no gap in me that needs such a drastic and melodramatic repair."

I have, of course, deliberately invented a thoughtful assimilator to speak for his party. It would be stacking the cards to select the poor chap living in an echoing Tudor-style mansion in a New York suburb, who said to the visitor from the United Jewish Appeal, in a slight accent, "Who told you I was Jewish? Get out of here, please, and don't bother me again." Or the girl who sued to break her grandfather's will, which barred from his legacies any grandchild marrying outside the faith. The girl's parents had given her no Jewish training. She wanted her Gentile sweetheart, and also her ancestor's stocks and bonds, but not his awkward religion. I believe she won.

These people — the imaginary one who speaks so well, and these others whose acts speak just as eloquently — are lost from Judaism, that is all; lost down a road which has swallowed many more Jews than the Hitler terror ever did. Of course they survive as persons. But from the viewpoint of an army, it makes little difference whether a division is exterminated or disperses into the hills and shucks off its uniforms.

Our faith teaches that God can revive Judaism in a Jew to his last hour. But in the ordinary course of things, we must say of the assimilators that the nerve of Judaism is killed in them. It has happened all through our history to many people. Lack of training, lack of will, sharp changes of environment, persecution, absorbing interests, intellectual alienation — all these things can kill the nerve.

The given reason is almost always the last — intellectual alienation. But most of the time these are words that follow the events. The Spinoza figure is so rare as to be almost single — the man who plumbs Judaism and passes through a crisis of rejection. Most people lose their Jewishness because they have never had a chance to get a grip on it. The Talmud called this large group "children raised in captivity," holding them innocent of religious violations. Among these "children" in the Talmud's day were some of the most prosperous people in the Roman Empire.

The Uncertain

There is a class of Jews just as large as the assimilators today, but wholly different. In them the nerve is damaged, but alive. They may speak and act as the assimilators do. Usually they belong to no temples, and they follow no rites. They may be eloquent in the parlor against the conformity of religion, and the supernatural God of Moses. For all that, they cannot regard with calm their own fading Jewishness. The thought that their children may be lost from the Jewish tale darkens their peace, though they cannot say why. They are almost ashamed of their own survival instinct. These are not assimilators. They are vital Jews, thrown out of orbit by the cataclysms of the past two centuries. Their retention of identity and feeling is a marvel. They testify as much as the observant to the strange endurance of the spirit of Abraham's House.

Chapter 22

✦

*Israel**

I HAVE said that Israel is not a religious country, in the accepted sense. Yet the founding of Israel must be the present climax of an account of the Jewish religion. If one could venture the impertinence of guessing at God's ways, one might say that the Enlightenment happened, with all its excitements and disasters, so that Israel might happen.

For it was the Enlightenment that created Israel, the new triumph of the Hebrew spirit, growing year by year in strength and world esteem, the fulfilled dream of sixty exiled generations, the land of the Jews. A hundred years ago it was still a mocking old ghetto vision, with no more presence on earth than the footprints of the Messiah. Today, embattled and racked by too-swift growth, it exists. It sits in the councils of the nations. Its young armies have already wiped out of human thought the picture of the Jew as a cringing wanderer, doomed forever to endure abuse and murder without fighting back. The record Israel has written in its first ten years is imperishable.

After Titus razed Jerusalem, the Jews — father, son, great-grandson — persisted in looking toward Zion as a

* Written in 1958, this account is based on my first visit in 1955. For a contemporary picture see my postscript essay, "Israel at Forty: The Land and the Faith," pp. 271 ff. This chapter contains some historical essentials of Zionism, and a snapshot of the Jewish State in its infancy. — HW (1987)

traveller looks toward home. The rolling centuries never crushed this quixotic dream of a scattered fragment of a nation that it might someday return to the soil God had appointed for it. "Next year in Jerusalem" was the motto that kept the dispersed people in hope. I can remember hearing that refrain at the Passover table in my childhood, and wondering at the empty dreaminess of it. I have lived to see the state come to pass, all the same.

Now that the miracle has occurred, it seems an everyday thing, unless one takes pause. One can reconstruct the visible strands of history that led to the birth of Israel. But it remains for me, and I think for most thoughtful people, one of the stunning occurrences of recent centuries. The United Nations vote that created Israel was, I believe, a just one; perhaps the first great act of international law, a faint pink streak of the dawn of world order.

The agonizing tensions between Israel and its Arab neighbors are outside the scope of this book. The Arabian crescent needs a modern industrial unit like Israel, and Israel needs Arabic trade and raw materials. Time should bring a natural interchange between them. But that outcome now seems to lie beyond a generation of frowning armies balanced on borders.

How Israel Happened

Israel is an incomprehensible place unless one knows at least the bare facts of its creation.

The world changes of the nineteenth century made it possible. The freeing and educating of the Jews, the rise of the middle class and then of the working class gave the Jewish mass new force. Printing presses, trains, telegraphs, better roads, began to link the scattered and sealed-in fragments of Jewry all over Europe. Anti-Semitism, the black plague of that century (which in the twentieth fulminated to kill Jew and Christian on the scale of the old black plague), whipped up a crisis that called for action. Finally, with the new machines, transporting a whole nation no longer needed heavenly magic. In the dark ages eagles' wings and Messianic white steeds had been the dream symbols of Zionism. They stood for the railroad, the steamship, the automobile, and the airplane, which came at last.

The setting for a great event is not enough. It needs the hero. The true founder of Israel was one of the strangest heroes of modern times, a leader as impossible to anticipate as Moses or Napoleon. A free-thinking Viennese newspaperman — a gray-gloved, top-hatted boulevardier, at home in Paris and Berlin, a writer of ephemeral plays, novels, book reviews, and pamphlets — this man, of all men, was struck as by lightning with an uncanny vision of the coming Jewish State in Israel. He wrote off in a few weeks *Der Judenstaat,* the state's true declaration of independence; a little book which even today brings tears to the eyes with its white heat that does not die, its minor cosmopolite follies, its grandiosities, its passion, and its startling bursts of true Hebrew prophecy. Israel today has all the strengths and weaknesses of that book. It is the book come true.

Theodor Herzl died a few years after writing the book, physically wrecked, the discredited leader of a small squabbling visionary movement, massively opposed within Jewry and without, which appeared as far from realizing the dream of the Jewish State as Jews had been since the days of Vespasian. Only forty-five years later — the span of Herzl's own truncated life — the leaders of the new Jewish state brought his remains from Vienna to the Holy Land and laid him to rest on Mount Herzl, looking eastward to Jerusalem.

Today's Leaders

When Herzl wrote *Der Judenstaat* he was so naïve about Jewish affairs that he did not know a Zionist drive was already rolling in the Eastern pales, where the Jewish predicament, under the anti-Semitic Czarist autocracy, was becoming catastrophic. He did not dream that his book had been anticipated by the famous pamphlet *Self-Emancipation,* the work of an Odessa doctor, Leo Pinsker. Later Herzl said he would never have written his book had he first read Pinsker's.

The Lovers of Zion, the party sparked by Pinsker, had as its aim the immediate removal of Jews from the Eastern tyrannies, already bloodied with pogroms. First get the people to Palestine, then statehood would somehow or other follow; that was their idea. They called it "practical Zionism." From the day Herzl rose they opposed it to his "political Zionism," which turned on winning a great power, or several of them, to sponsor the new nation.

Does this split over theory seem minor and foggy today? It nearly killed Zionism at the outset, and it did kill Herzl. Now we see that both sides were right. Israel needed people on the land, and it needed the United Nations resolution, which with the instant recognition by the United States and the Soviet Union gave Herzl his triumph in the grave. The split between Herzl and the Eastern Zionists was one of the tragic false issues of history. People fall in love with different aspects of a single truth and are willing to kill or be killed for their own standpoint. Time passes, sometimes only a few years, and it turns out that the mortal opponents really wanted the same thing and were soldiers on the same side, clubbing each other to death in the dark.

Herzl pursued his aim with spectacular daring and force in the few years of life left to him. He dashed around the European capitals, haunting the back stairs of princes and bankers, trying to enlist support for his vision. He talked to the Rothschilds, the German Kaiser, the Sultan of Turkey, the British Foreign Minister, the King of Italy, and the Pope. He wore himself out in these dazzling interviews, which all ended in what we Americans call the runaround. But if he failed with the men of money and power, his drive set fire to the Jewish masses. He was openly called the Messiah by the oppressed peoples of the pale. He was all the more exciting because he was so remote from them.

The Eastern Zionist leaders recognized his genius and yielded him the prime place in the movement. But they never stopped sending streams of pioneers to Palestine, a policy Herzl fought as a fatal obstacle to peaceful recognition of the new state by the Powers. When the great visionary came to the Sixth World Zionist Congress with a stopgap plan for settling Jews in British Uganda, they battled him to a standstill and broke his power and his heart. A year later he was dead.

The labor Zionists of the East thereupon took the field. To this day they hold it.

Their leaders were the emancipated yeshiva boys who gained their knowledge of the West in the socialist undergrounds that fought the Czar; the idealistic nineteenth-century socialists soon to be crushed by the iron cadres of Lenin. This origin largely accounts, I imagine, for a strangely old-fashioned note in Israeli politics, quite different from the glittering modernism in agriculture, science, and defense. It is the present day at the borders, in the research institutes, and on the communal farms. In the polemic journalism and in the parliamentary debates of nine parties, it often seems to be 1905. David Ben-Gurion, the Prime Minister, is a world genius of action like Churchill; and like Churchill, on domestic issues he tends to sound the rhetoric of his youth in another day.

The Paradox of Israel

So it happens that the land of Israel, the new fulfillment of the most ancient religious dream on earth, was conceived by an irreligious founder and brought into being by men for the most part not observers of the faith.

There have always been, it is true, religious men in the front ranks of Zionism. A large part of the Jewish masses has remained observant in Israel and in exile, while giving their support to the new state. There is a strong Torah party in the Israeli parliament. And Zionism itself comes out of the religion, ultimately rests on it, and is a rootless expense of blood, money, and work except in the light of the ancient tradition which has been its life force.

All this is true, yet it is less than realistic to think of Israel at the moment as anything but a virile little secular nation, one of the many erupting nationalisms in a century full of overthrows and new nations. If it is anything more, it is so despite itself, one might say. It does not aim to give the world a Messiah. It wants peace, independence, and a good life for its citizens.

Zionism in its present flowering in Israel falls readily, all the same, within the long view of the Jewish religion. A wholly religious state in ancient Israel did not exist. There were religious kings and irreligious kings; generals hostile to the faithful and generals kind to them; a part of the populace that held to the Mosaic law and a part that did not. David, after Moses, was the supreme mixture of man of action and man of God. He stands alone in the history books of Scripture. In the time of the Second Temple the very priesthood went into the hands of Hellenists. Visitors to Israel who profess deep shock because they see people smoking on the Sabbath have not been reading their Bible or their Jewish history. Israel is the place where, as we believe, the light of the Lord will someday blaze forth to fill not only the little land but the whole earth. It does not offer itself, at least in Jewish thought, as the place where the event has already occurred.

In the categories of Hebrew law, modern Zionism is a single long action of lifesaving, of snatching great masses of people out of the path of sure extinction. Since the time when the Greeks hit on the bright notion of always attacking the Jewish armies on the Sabbath — for they found at first that they could slaughter the unresisting soldiers at will — our law has held that ceremony always gives way in an emergency to lifesaving action. This is not in the least the declared basis for the acts of irreligious Zionists; but I think it is the underlying truth of their way.

Naturally when men grow gray in a way of living, even such a strained way as dedicated and continuous rescue, it comes to seem a normal existence. The men of action who spearheaded Israel's birth found themselves opposed at many turns by pietists whom they were saving, but whose whole care was the law, and who objected to the Zionists' free-hand attack on events, their lack of scholarship, their carelessness of rite and scruple. The rescuers hardened in their secular rationale and in their contempt for the faith as it confronted them.

Ben-Gurion cannot, like Eisenhower, answer to all parties in Jewry with benign tolerance. In his many daily decisions for running the country — wherever these things touch religion — he either has to do as the rabbis say, or he has to oppose them, or he has to compromise with them. No other path is open to a ruler in Israel. He and his party oppose the rabbis much of the time, and give in all or part way some of the time. That these deep-dyed old socialists oppose the rabbis on occasion out of habit, out of attitudes stamped on them as boyish rebels, is undoubtedly so. But just as often, I believe, their opposition comes from their judgment of what must be done here and now to keep besieged Israel alive. If another younger David rises out of the religious party to the helm of Israel, the same dilemmas will confront him. The stabilizing of this utterly new case of Jewry will take long years, and clashes must be part of the process.*

The socialism of Israel today seems to me a far from crusading ideology. So far as I can gather from the young people, their faces are turned to the West. It is the free experimenting life of the United States that is their heart's desire, not the ant-heaps of China or the ration-card gloom of the iron curtain countries. The spirit in Israel is completely free, uncensored, unregimented. But what choice have they? We in America during the war years went into the gray world of rationing and federal controls. There is no other way in a national emergency. Israel's life is a continuing military crisis, and probably will be in our lifetimes. If the nation's guard goes down for six months, Nasser's armies will be burning Tel Aviv and Haifa. So the socialist trammels and bureaus stay on, and the buoyancy of the people despite them is something of a wonder.

These considerations help explain, I suggest, why the many observant Jews in Israel and outside it support the new nation, though some of its leaders are not formally religious, and some are outspoken agnostics. Men of good heart understand that a new destiny is being hammered out, and that all hands in Israel — saving a few extremists — are working for the survival of Jewry. No matter how bitter the differences are over day-to-day method — and the bitterness now and then rises near the red line of civil commotion — the aim is one, and the people in extremity become one.

What Israel Is Like

The first time I saw the lights of Lydda airport in the dusk from a descending plane, I experienced a sense of awe that I

* These dilemmas have sharpened with the years, and the younger David has yet to arise. See my postscript essay, pp. 271 ff. — HW (1987)

do not expect to know again in this life. Then the plane came to earth, and I was in just another air terminal, all confusion and hurry and official rigmarole and multilingual signs — except that one of the languages on the signs was the tongue in which I had learned the Torah as a boy. Standing at the exit gate waiting for me, erect despite his more than ninety years, dressed in his unchanging black round hat and long black coat, was my grandfather. He threw his arms around me, and that was my welcome to the soil of the Holy Land.

The soil itself, of course, was well overlaid by smooth concrete; but I thought I could feel its electricity flowing up into my bones anyway. This romantic notion quickly faded in the fuss over baggage, the passport business, the rapid exchange of family news, the dizzying official introductions; for I was part of an American delegation to the seventh anniversary of Israel's independence headed by Governor Mennen Williams of Michigan, bringing a replica of the Liberty Bell as a gift to the government. A Foreign Ministry man was waiting for us in the anteroom, to which we were forthwith led. I expected to meet a graying dignitary in formal clothes. He was a boy in his early twenties, in a light suit, with his tieless shirt collar spread outside his jacket.

We had to go up to Jerusalem at once for an overseas broadcast. So I parted from my grandfather, who went back to his flat in Tel Aviv, and I joined the delegation for a hair-raising automobile ride. I have driven cars in Paris, in Mexico, in Rome, on the Riviera, and on the roller-coaster freeways of Los Angeles, and I think I know something about wild driving. But the Israeli driver on the open road is not a driver at all, but an airplane pilot who cannot quite get off the ground owing to the lack of wings. Yet he never stops trying. He sometimes manages a hop or two along the way, about as long as Orville Wright's first flight at Kitty Hawk. There were very few cars on the road back in 1955. The Israeli drivers have been gradually slowing down since then, but their hearts are still in the wild blue yonder. This talented Foreign Ministry driver, by the way, was a boy of nineteen or so.

When we came to Jerusalem, most of the main thoroughfares had been closed down for the dancing in the streets. I supposed during the first few decades of American independence people danced in the streets of Washington and New York too. Now we are mature and have decided that even firecrackers are hazardous, and on July Fourth we have sedate picnics and go to the beach. The Israelis are a hundred years behind us, so they dance in the streets.

The policemen who guarded the closed-off intersections were really police-boys; I never saw one thirty years old. Of the dancing crowd under the huge electric 7 in the main square of the city, about one third seemed to be in army uniform, men and women — that is, again, boys and girls. The most poignant impression I had of Israel that night, after the first embrace by my old grandfather, was the amazing youth of the Israelis. That impression was never quite effaced. Israel sometimes seems to be a land of children and young adults.

Of course this is an illusion; the old are there, as everywhere. But in a pioneering land surrounded by hostile armies, the chief things are energy, quickness, and modern training; and so young people fill the responsible posts, and you encounter them everywhere. When I went to sea with the small Israeli Navy, the commodore who headed the fleet was a man who in the United States Navy might be — from the look of him — a lieutenant senior grade. But his navy's maneuvers were taut and professional, and in the 1958 trouble it fought excellently.

Israel is a lovely land. That is something that is hardly mentioned in the accounts you read, because the novelty and the controversy take all the play. In the north there are lone plunging mountain stretches that recall Switzerland; the middle coast plain is a half brother to southern California; and the dry red empty Negev, with its fantastic Dead Sea, must be a lot like Mars. I find a new place of charm each time I go back. Best of all I like the city of Haifa, white and busy on green slopes around a saucer of purple Mediterranean; then Jerusalem, the solemn magic of which I cannot write down, but its old hills in the dawn will draw me back year after year; and then the mysterious peaks of Galilee, with vistas down to the far blue sea of Kinneret which give you the illusion that Israel must be the world's largest land instead of one of the smallest. If Israel were not already a tourist attraction for its palimpsest of religious memories, it would soon become popular, I think, because it is so beautiful.

It is impossible for me to imagine how visitors of other faiths feel in the land of the Jews. I did much of my travelling during my first visit with a Methodist bishop from San Francisco, and he was enthralled and tireless, always ready for more action in the evening. Surely to a serious Christian the land must be full of vibrancy. But the special feeling that comes to one who has been a member of a minority all his life, and now finds himself in a place where everybody is like him — this extraordinary shift which changes the very nerve signals, as it were — must be a sensation that only a diaspora Jew who comes to Israel can know. Born Israelis cannot imagine it. It is a little like falling in love for the first time, or suddenly understanding Shakespeare, or having a child. The novelty passes, and one is the same person as before; yet never quite the same.

They can nearly kill you with kindness, hospitality, and demonstrative pride. You must see the potash works, and the cement factories, and the auto assembly lines, and the hospitals, and the farm communes, and the sulphur mines, and the yeshivas, and the technical schools, and the children's villages; of course you must, and what is more, you must see every one of them, unless you can beg off with energy and show that your plane is leaving in a few hours. There will be parties every night and you will be up at dawn to go rocketing off to Eilat or Sodom or the northern border. My wife dug in at one point and told the Foreign Ministry lad with desperate defiance that on the morrow she would go nowhere and do nothing, just wash her hair and then sit in the sun all day. It shattered him.

They are a very warm people. Our old tradition is true: the nation is a family. All its disagreements have the sharp note of family quarrels. All its rejoicings are like a wedding or a birthday. The people cannot be induced to take the government quite as seriously as people do everywhere else; after all, it is only Uncle David or Cousin Moshe making the speech. This must drive Israeli officialdom rather wild at times. But it has its points. When the family is threatened it fights like a band of blood brothers.

If I seem to be describing an idealistic wonderland, then I am completely off the mark. I doubt that more profound skeptics and cynics can be found anywhere. The weary wisdom of the Levant has not left the Holy Land. Moreover, the acrid lessons of the ghetto centuries, the horror of the Nazi massacres, the twists and turns that the nations displayed, even in the drifting smoke of the Hitler Holocaust, before granting the Jews the few square miles that they now call a homeland, the unrelenting and pointless hatred of the Arab leaders, the wavering of the great powers between the call of justice and the call of oil — all these things have deeply marked the Israeli spirit. And there is an edge of defensive bitterness that comes from the knowledge that the land needs resettlement and construction money from the diaspora Jews, and will for some time.

Israel is the place where daily news, yellow-journal gossip, spicy magazines, movie subtitles, billboard ads, radio jingles, business argot, and all the commercial underside of a modern society must find tongue in the language of Holy Scripture. The tension is too great. When it snaps, the reaction is to cynicism without bottom. Israel also has some of the cynicism that is the special vintage of the iron curtain countries, and that comes of seeing bright socialist slogans dissolve into heavy bureaus, privileged cliques, and the unyielding power-mass of the Organization.

These less than utopian facts are all part of the land of the Jews, under the rosy first picture that the visitor encounters. Yet in the end, the first picture is true. The eye does see what it sees: a land of sunlight and rapid growth, of old stony deserts turning green, of children as abundant as apples in October, of vigorous young people in charge of brave experiments and tough armed forces and hard undertakings, of new universities and factories springing up on ancient hills, of blossoming expanses in the country and cheery throngs in the city. In Tel Aviv there seems to be a bookstore on every other block. Such reading, such drinking of coffee and tea, and such talk one finds only in Paris, if anywhere. A taxi driver courteously and ably explained to me where I had gone wrong in writing *The Caine Mutiny,* in terms not much different from the first American reviews. I was his cousin, you see; he could speak freely.

The little land, by the far stretch of planning, can some day support four million Jews. American Jewry, like the Jewry of Babylon during the time of the Second Temple, will evidently remain more numerous. Whether it will also be the stronger in works and in learning, as Babylon Jewry was, nobody can say. The Jews of Israel have immense vitality. Problems in religious law find their deepest analysis and most searching tests today in Israel — naturally, since the very life of the nation is being tested. Both communities seem vital to Jewish survival, this side of the coming of the Messiah.

Epilogue

"How Will You Survive?"

BEN-GURION said to me in his office — the wise, tough old builder of Israel, with the floating white hair of a dreamer and the hard jaw of an army general — "You Jews in the United States are different from any Jewish community that has ever existed. You are not strangers, or no more strangers than anyone else in your land. America consists of immigrants. You belong like the rest, and you will prosper. But how will you survive as Jews?"

Without thinking I answered, "Through the religion."

The old socialist looked at me aslant with an unfathomable little smile, and laid his hand on a brown leather-bound book. "I keep the Bible on my desk and at my bedside. Israel will be a land built on the Bible. That I can promise you. As for the religion . . . that is a great mystery." He shrugged, and his eyes had a far-off and, I thought, troubled look. We talked of other things.

In that interview I caught a ray of light that helped explain my own odd life to me.

Though I have lived as an observant Jew, I have never been able to pretend to religious certainties. I have found it impossible to join in cheerleading condemnations of Reform, Conservatism, and irreligious Zionism; and for all my too-frequent public speaking, I have never denounced the assimilators. The words of Tennyson:

There lives more faith in honest doubt
Believe me, than in half the creeds . . .

have had the ring of truth to me. Possibly to my Jewish friends whose cooked meats I would not eat I have seemed a remote fanatic, but I have felt quite at home with them. I have understood their doubt, if they have not understood my abstinence.

It was my lot to reach quite young what many people consider the dream life of America: success by my own efforts, a stream of dollars to spend, a penthouse in New York, forays to Hollywood, the companionship of pretty women, all before I was twenty-four. It was nothing impressive I did: I was only a staff writer for the great radio humorist Fred Allen: but there I was in the realms of gold. I dreamed of higher success as a playwright or novelist — like my Noel Airman in *Marjorie Morningstar,* all I wanted was a succession of hits — but even as I lived this conventional smart existence of inner show business, and dreamed the conventional dreams, it all seemed thin. I was not sated or revolted. But I found myself unable to believe, deep down, that hits plus random pleasure would ever add up to a life. It left out my identity. People who chase pleasure, money, and hits and have no other dimension are interchangeable ciphers, more or less. It left out my grandfather, the most impressive man I knew. It left out most of the sensible books I had read. I began to read again, following an interlude after college which had been all chase and no thought. Without reaching any conclusions, I moved into a freely chosen observant life.

I was gambling my whole existence on one hunch: that being a Jew was not a trivial and somewhat inconvenient accident, but the best thing in my life; and that to be a Jew the soundest way was the classic way. This was a leap far ahead of my reading and my thinking at the time. I was all Nietzsche, Veblen, Shaw, Marx, Dewey, Dostoevsky, and so forth. Nevertheless I took the chance, saying to myself, "I may be wrong." Living this way, on a gamble, I learned things about Judaism that no other procedure could have taught me. The faith would have remained a closed book to me — except as childhood nostalgia — had I not made the experiment. There are many things that you can come to know only by trying to do them.

Here are some of the things I learned. One can observe the laws of Moses and lead a life in the everyday world. Judaism presents steep difficulties, intellectual and practical, and its present state is disorganized; for all that it is on balance a delight, a path of integrity and of pleasure. For children born Jews, the faith taught authentically is without question a master resource of mental health and personal force. I also became convinced that the secret of Jewish survival under long stress lies in the laws of Moses, whether this survival matters to one or not.

On the point of the children I want to pause. I have heard people justify not training children in Judaism because, as they say, "We don't want to warp them. When they grow up they can make their own choice." But this view dictates the most total warping they can condemn a child to. They warp him to a lifetime of rationalizing his ignorance. What adult sits down among the school children to learn the Hebrew alphabet, the Torah, and the ways of Jewry? It is the easiest thing in the world to drop one's early religious training, as many of my readers know. It is sheer mountain-climbing to regain ground lost in childhood. It ought to occur to such parents that they may be wrong about the faith; that it makes no sense to cement their children into their own attitude of denial. Judaism was in my possession when I reached the point of wanting it — like arithmetic, like geography, like all the things I learned long before I had the slightest desire or need for them.

Let me suggest that the words "I may be wrong" are words that our present day needs, outside Judaism as within it. We are overloaded with shallow certainties. But where are the deep doubters? To echo the agnostic questions of the past two centuries is not to doubt, but to recite classroom lessons. I claim the capacity to doubt. It is the one mental asset I am sure of, beyond the skill with words that gives me my living. I doubted at twenty-four the commitments of the show world to which bright people all around me uncritically gave their lives: more money, bigger projects, new pleasures, more involved plans, and so on to death. I doubted the popular naturalistic creed of my college days, about fifteen years before the existentialists made a public noise by doing so (though a hundred years after serious philosophy had undermined it), and I left it for something that seemed more likely to be true.

The New Permission to Believe

"Judaism as wisdom, as a source of identity, as noblesse oblige, as survival machinery, yes," said one of my good skeptical friends. "If only you leave out the supernatural God, we might have a meeting of the minds."

He speaks by the book; he is an unreconstructed naturalist.

Naturalism offers two dogmas: first, nature is the only book of revelation, a book of perfect harmony and order once one learns to read it; second, it came about by chance, and nobody wrote it. If someone produced a copy of *Tom Jones* and claimed that nobody had written it, that it was a chance growth of wood curiously shaped and marked, I suppose he would encounter some incredulity. The universe being somewhat more intricate, beautiful, and impressive than *Tom Jones,* the same incredulity has caused rejection of the chance-nature dogmas, century in and century out. This is the old argument from design. It is as ancient as human thought. So is the chance-nature creed. The dialogue between them never ends, though now and then there is a thoughtful silence on one side.

Without question naturalism, triumphant in the past two centuries, has brought forth science, with its glories and its terrors. The tough mind, the exact analysis, the confidence of finding stable law under random appearance, the replacement of easy formulas of faith with hard thinking and stubborn experiment, the resolve to leave nothing in life unexamined, to take nothing for granted — these intellectual disciplines have created modern times. Humanity cannot backtrack from them; it would be madness to do so. Science is the prime tool we have found for ending poverty and illness, and for controlling natural disaster. The discovery of new forces, it is true, creates new hazards, some of them frightening. But we are not likely to improve our lot or increase our safety by diminishing the skilled use of our minds.

Whether the discoveries of science serve in the end to deny or to affirm God remains a great open question for scientists as well as for philosophers. Science does not, in so many words, look for God's truth as theology did. It does, however, seek with unshakable faith a truth and a harmony assumed to lie under the world's random color and buzz. In this quest, despite all the persisting paradoxes and mysteries, it has had stunning success. To some deep and sober minds, God is "an unnecessary hypothesis"; to other minds of equal force, the existence of such pervasive truth and harmony, and above all of the very *possibility* of truth, implies a final truth-teller, the God who imposed form on chaos and old night, and who sustains form.

But the argument from design as a formal proof of God's existence has been pretty much out of court ever since Hume and Kant riddled it with logical holes. All this happened within the rules of the philosopher's game. It was shown that evidence of design, in exact formal logic, did not prove a single good designer, or even a number of good ones; design in the universe, especially with the apparent mistakes and imperfections, could as logically prove what pagan religion more or less taught — that the world was made and ruled by a number of powerful but whimsical and slovenly demons. Kant contributed the famous analysis of how reason prints an appearance of design on a universe we can never really see or know. The intelligence works in categories, and all sense experience streams in through these categories. The designs men see are to an unknown extent the workings of their own minds. The thing-in-itself they will never grasp.

This was hard and persuasive arguing — at least the world found it so in the books of Kant; I cannot tell how it appears reduced to a cursory paragraph. Technically, the religious thinker remains with the presentiment of godly design, and the neatest analysis cannot talk him out of that. This presentiment pours forth in the Psalms, Job, and Isaiah; it seldom fails to sound in the great poets of the world; and most men feel it at one point or another in their lives. Their reaction to it is likely to decide whether or not they are religious. But they cannot use it to buttonhole an agnostic and make him change his mind, on logical grounds.

The purely mechanical universe, certainly, is as outmoded as the notion that the earth is flat. The godly universe, it seems, cannot be logically demonstrated. In the novel currents of existentialism, one finds deeply religious and wholly atheistic thinkers. It is a new, interesting, and extremely unsettled situation. "Nothing is strictly true, and everything is permitted," is a recurrent cry of the baffled intelligence; and unless I am mistaken, it is the present cry from the academic groves, if one cry rises above the conflicting voices.

And by everything they mean everything. You would appear to have the highest intellectual sanction of the hour even to believe in the God of Moses, provided your belief is "an existential choice" and not merely an echo of your grandfather's naïve views. So a dress that looks like one's grandmother's 1925 aberration can either be an unwearable rag from the attic or the newest thing. It all depends on details of style.

The God of Moses

Now the God Moses taught us about is much like the modern God of Nature — a single originating and unifying force — with one big difference. Moses said that the force behind the appearances was not a blind grinding computer, but a purposeful Creator who was interested in men, loved them, and in moments of revelation expressed his will in human affairs. This is not a formal argument; it is a teaching. Those who follow Moses — the Jews, the Mohammedans, the Christians — are convinced that the Creator gave him a necessary view of the truth for the good of men.

The objections to the God of Moses are clear to anybody who has lived in the world twenty years. The Book of Job sums them up for ever, and it does not answer them. The earth rolls in law and beauty; Orion is a gorgeous spectacle, and the horse is a marvel of constructed cunning. Nevertheless, innocent children die, the world is full of seeming random disaster, and righteous Job suffers. A Jew has to absorb Job as well as Moses, to stand solidly on his religion. Voltaire and all the great rationalists took the line of Job to batter down a theology that had become a prison for the inquiring intelligence. But the teaching of Moses stands with medieval theology knocked away. You may not follow the ontological argument; the Rambam's proof that there is no evil in the world may leave you cold; the Torah preceded these things and transcends them.

The Outer Limits

Consider for a moment Voltaire's point that mankind is so small, so lost in the vast black of time and space, such a brief wriggling jelly on the surface of a tiny ball, that the notion of

God interesting himself in men is merely funny. This vivid argument rests on the notion of comparative size. But if you think size has meaning only for us and not for God — because if size interested God he would only be a very sizable fellow, and not a total force — then the argument falls. Of course we are minute; but Betelgeuse is no larger to God, if he exists.

It makes clear sense that he would provide a stage for human destiny broader than our reach. "He has made everything beautiful in its time," Ecclesiastes said, "and has put eternity into men's hearts, except that a man will not find out the work that God has done from the beginning to the end." The men at the microscopes and the telescopes now confirm the report.

After three centuries of the dizzying freedom of Copernicus, science has locked us back into a slightly larger Ptolemaic prison. This time it has thrown away the key. We will never get out. There is no guesswork in the new picture of our round prison. It is a fact that any college man can show in a couple of pages if he takes the right subjects. We live inside a small crystalline sphere. The radius is the speed of light — a mere crawl in view of the big distances it has to go, yet the highest speed there can be — multiplied by the time of a human life. The Columbian voyages of the rockets, at their long stretch, can conceivably get out to the nearest stars. That is the very end of the line, the transparent boundary of heaven. Beyond that, spheres beyond spheres, stretch the Happy Hunting Grounds, for hundreds of millions of light-years.

What lies beyond? Infinity, chance, "nature," the God of Moses? Take your choice. The game will never be over, and admission is free.

But the hopeless limits lie not only beyond our closed round crystal heaven. They are everywhere around us. There are enough of them in a glass of water to make the machine universe a joke. Measure down to a certain very small size, the scientists tell us, and beyond it precise measurement ceases to exist as a possible scientific fact. Yet inside that limit big things go on, great forces swirl, decisions occur that we can only guess at. In the multitude they come to an average that we can call laws. But the inexorable ticking of observable cause and effect gets lost on the way; a memory of the nineteenth century, like the Grant administration.

The stark mystery of form hangs over all. Darwin taught us how forms change and adapt. But why form occurs, in matter and in life, we cannot tell; and the overwhelming, the paralyzing puzzle, is why form persists. *"And the earth was without form, and void . . ."* That is exactly what one would expect, given random chance as the world's law. What happened?

The paradox of existence stands. Take one side of it, and go on your way with the chance-nature dogmas. Take the other side of it and — if you are a Jew — you will probably find the Lawgiver in the end waiting for you. He will greet you with the smile and the embrace of my grandfather. "What kept you so long?" he will say. And you will sit down to study the Torah together.

"This Is My God"

You may well say:

"Please leave me alone. Your pleasure is fooling with words and reading books, and it has led you to follow the law of Moses. Good luck to you. I am a very busy man. I am moving into a new house, a very handsome one, but it costs a little more than I can afford and I must attend to my business. My sons and my daughters are growing up, and they are darlings, although a little silly. I could wish they knew more of Judaism, but I wish a lot of things for them that are out of the question. I am a reasonably happy man, glad to be alive, and living a full life. You go your way and I'll go mine. Fair enough?"

Fair enough. One word more, and my book ends.

In the death camps of the Nazis, Jewish doctors, publishers, businessmen, composers, writers, lawyers — the cream of German Jewry — sometimes took to reading the Bible, and even to painful mastering of the Hebrew alphabet, in an effort to learn, before the darkness closed in, who they really were and why they were about to die.

There will be no death camps in the United States that we live in. History is a phantasmagoria, and anything can happen. But the civilization we know will have to be obliterated before a Hitler can sit in Washington. The threat of Jewish oblivion in America is different. It is the threat of pleasantly vanishing down a broad highway at the wheel of a high-powered station wagon, with the golf clubs piled in the back . . . *"Mr. Abramson left his home in the morning after a hearty breakfast, apparently in the best of health, and was not seen again. His last words were that he would get in a round before going to the office . . ."* Of course Mr. Abramson will not die. When his amnesia clears, he will be Mr. Adamson, and his wife and children will join him, and all will be well. But the Jewish question will be over in the United States.

If this should happen — and I do not for a moment think it will — would it be a solution that either the Jews or the United States would welcome? Does America want the disappearance of its people of Abraham?

Hitler was unique. There was nothing accidental or merely maniacal in Hitler's great effort to kill the Jews. It was the crown of his career. Hitler saw himself as the apostle in action of the prophet Nietzsche, whose creed was "God is dead." Nietzsche in mid-nineteenth century saw where the ideas of his time had to lead. He predicted, and in his mind's eye lived through, all the horrors of our century. It may be that because he was the first to see them the experience drove him mad. We have learned to take these things numbly and go about our business. His solution of the problems he foresaw was as spectacular and as wild as his visions. He embraced the "death" of the Jewish God (and therefore of Christianity) as a necessary step of the human race toward a higher existence, the day of the godless superman. He wanted to lay the axe to the root of what he thought was a doomed society and morality; and he did a brilliant, terrifying job of it.

He did it with his pen. Hitler did it in earnest. An insane genius of politics, a whirling void of a man, senseless and terrible as a typhoon, Hitler moved along the path Nietzsche drew, parodying and prostituting his ideas, drenching them in blood, but following their contours as a typhoon follows the pressure lines of a barometric map. Six million Jews died. This was the tribute of nihilism to its own picture of the Jewish God. Through all history the strange persistence of the Jews had been taken as a witness to the presence of God in the universe. If God was dead, there was only one way to prove it, one event that would stamp the fact for ever on the hearts of men — the death of all the Jews. It was the logic of lunacy; but it could not have been, in its own terms, more rational.

Hitler is gone like a typhoon, leaving behind wreckage, mass graves, crumbling crematoria, and haunted minds. Like the spinning wind he was, he simply vanished, dissipated into his own emptiness, leaving no human grave. He did not kill the Jews. If we are God's witnesses, God still lives.

What else are we? What does our long history mean? Does it all point to five million Adamsons in the United States, driving cars, watching television, leading honest lives, and exhibiting no trace of a terrible and magnificent origin; and four million Hebrew-speaking Adamsons in Israel, with their own cars and television, and with no memory of Isaiah and of Sinai? Was it for this that our fathers endured for two millennia the worst shocks that flesh can take, and yet lived on?

As for me, I declare my faith that our history is not

meaningless, and that nihilism is a hallucination of sick men. God lives, and we are his people, chosen to live by his name and his law until the day when the Lord will be one and his name one. We are nothing at all, or we are a people apart, marked by history for a fate embracing the heights and the depths of the human experience. We live; and we live in a time when we can draw breath in freedom and renew our starved-out strength.

"Chosen for what?" the captain of an Israeli luxury liner said to me with a bitter smile that showed he came from Nazi Germany. "Chosen for sorrow?"

For that too; that is a truth we know. This choosing was not a choosing that — to this hour — any other nation would ask for. The Jews had descended from Abraham. The knowledge of God was in their blood. They said yes at Sinai because they could do no other, and they entered on a history more dark than bright, more bloodstained than green. But that history is their name, their meaning, and their glory.

Ben-Gurion had all the wisdom of greatness, and his memory will live because he led the Jews in raising the flag again on their own soil. Between his socialism and the law of Moses there is no choice to be made. Social justice is a law of the Torah, and it is the great cry of the prophets. Its working out in a machine age is a challenge to the applied common law. Above these questions, near and vexing as they are, towers the religion that created Zionism, that cradled Ben-Gurion, and that is at once the life and chief ornament of our nation. What are we but the pettiest of the peoples, except for our Law?

I am not pleading here for one way of Judaism. All ways are in turmoil, but the Torah stands. In the hearts of most Jews, there is the instinct to survive as Jews. It is to this instinct that I speak, and that I want to honor. A few decades ago that instinct seemed to many people something to be ashamed of. It was not rational. God was dead. But since then, godlessness having gone insane and done its best to murder us all, we have a right to think again. This ancestral voice in our hearts — I put it to my Jewish brothers — is not imaginary or misleading. It is the call of our deepest, truest, best selves. There are fools who call it our shame. It is our immortality.

Our old House is going through immense changes. The day of the black-coated rabbi with the silver-topped cane, the ghetto aristocrat of learning, is dying fast. Before the century turns, the law of Moses will be in the hands of young men who are now chaplains in the Israeli Army and Navy, or candidates for doctorates in American universities. They will be as religious as the leaders who are departing, but they will make new decisions. The shifting amalgam of ghetto custom and Western manners that marks the observance today is a step toward the firm reestablishment of the law in a strong frame. This process will be long and hard.

It will be effective in direct proportion to the number of first-class minds that are among the faithful in the next two or three generations. That is why, in this book, I have risked tedium to appeal over and over for the training of the young, whatever the views of the parents. As a nation in battle needs arms, our faith today needs inquiring intelligences. If they are mostly excluded through lack of knowledge, a major renaissance of Judaism can be lost.

For the great modern Mosaic referendum has already begun. The followers of the law, the people in whose lives it continues, will be the shapers of the result. All Jews — orthodox, dissenting, agnostic — will have a gravitational effect on the event. But the men and women in the Mosaic communion will most directly give their brains and force to the outcome.

If I stand up to be counted in that communion, it is not

because I hold it perfect, or because I miss the stresses that have sent many into dissent and assimilation. It is because I sense in my bones that Jewish survival rests with the law. It is for this reason that I did not join the dissenters. The formulas of dissent make a pleasant compromise for people who want an easier life than the law asks, or who have little training and yet want a taste of Judaism. But the formulas die away in the training of the young. They are of the hour. The law is of eternity; in any case, this is how I see it. Nor do I understand Zionism without Moses as anything that can long endure. Once a life is saved, the question remains: what is to become of the life? The destiny the Bible gives us is the only answer I can find, and it seems to me a gleaming answer.

I may be wrong, wholly wrong. What is at issue is the central truth: where does Jewish strength really lie? A hundred years will give the verdict. We who will not live a hundred years must choose, and act. Our children stand waiting to be shown what to do, and where to go. Tomorrow we will be gone, and they will be Abraham's House.

Now my hand slows. The task needed an Ezra, and it found only this poor pen. I have done the best I could to tell my brothers that our law of Moses is great and honorable, now as when it first came to us.

"This is my God, and I will praise him; the God of my father, and I will exalt him."

Afterword, 1969, on the Six-Day War:

✦

THE ASHES AND THE GOLD

The Ashes and the Gold

AFTER ten years, I take up the "poor pen," to write a word about the decade that has passed.

We Jews are living our most momentous century since the fall of Jerusalem in the year 70. In the past ten years a remarkable — some would say miraculous — deliverance occurred: the Six-Day War. We live in the precarious aftermath of that famous victory. No man knows yet what the outcome will be. But the effect on world Jewry has already been radical.

Down the centuries we survived exile from our homeland, and the scattering of our people, through the unique folk treasure which is the theme of *This Is My God:* our faith. From the fall of Jerusalem to the French Revolution, a stretch of 1700 years, we were united by loyalty to the God of our fathers, and to a strong cultural structure centered on the Mosaic Law. That structure, detailed in the Talmud, was a world consensus of scattered Israel. It kept us alive and together, though separated by seas and continents.

Since the French Revolution, a progressive weakening and breakdown of old institutions has corroded men's faiths. Judaism has not escaped. In the nineteenth century, the consensus that welded and preserved our dispersed nation collapsed. I describe this modern crisis in my chapter "The Present." For almost two hundred years our people has been seeking the way to go on living, while bereft of its old basis for existence.

I think we have found it. After a quarter century of quaking instability, caused by the German murders, the center of gravity of the Jewish people has come to rest in Israel. As I see it, Jewry has by instinct reached a new consensus that Israel has become our heart and that Israel must live. In this national resolve, after two centuries of divided counsel and disarray which in part led to our catastrophe, Jewry is one again.

By destroying the Jews of Europe, the Germans struck our unique dispersed nation to the heart. The diaspora might have withered and died in two or three generations; but now it will not. Providence has given us a new heart, transplanted back where history first placed it. The thunder of the Six-Day War was the heartbeat of old Jewry, starting up again after the paralytic shock of the Holocaust.

Not all Jews feel that heartbeat. The indifferent ones and the determined assimilators keep dropping out of ranks, now as in former days. On our right, anti-Zionists so fear the charge of double loyalty that they still repudiate Israel and proclaim themselves pure Frenchmen, pure Americans, or pure Australians of the Hebrew persuasion. On our left a loud few condemn Israel as a militarist "aggressor"; they remain pathologically deaf to the public Arab vows, repeated for twenty years and still blaring, to reduce the Jewish homeland to ashes. These two minorities flee the living center of our folk in opposite directions. Their sound much exceeds their weight.

The implications of the new consensus, for the rest of us, go to the root of our lives. When I wrote *This Is My God,* the Jewish people still groped in the modern blackout of religious belief, still staggered from the German bloodletting. Now we are not in the dark, and we do not stagger. We know how matters stand, and we are braced. We look to our brothers in

Israel for heart and hope, and most of us look to God — in our different ways — for his continued grace to Israel, the Third Jewish Commonwealth on holy soil.

Zionism of the Spiritual Center

In this sense Zionism, once a party cry in Jewry, has in the past ten years taken the central ground. Not the Zionism of Herzl, which called for a transplanting of all the world's Jews to Palestine; that is still doctrinaire Zionism, but the emerging folk consensus is something else. Seventy years ago, Herzl's great opponent, Ahad Ha'am, foresaw the new Jewish state as the spiritual center of a regenerated diaspora. For this moderate aim he was attacked and scorned by the all-out Zionists. Now he appears to have been a prophet. The return of all Jewry to the Holy Land remains a messianic vision, but Israel already exists as our new spiritual center. Since the Six-Day War migration there has increased; from America, the number has risen from one thousand to four thousand a year. The young, the adventurous, the inspired, find Jerusalem the Golden a magnet. But so far, this is an elitist, not a mass, phenomenon.

Whatever the divergences in Zionism, the movement did grasp the modern Jewish problem. It foresaw catastrophe in Europe, and urged return to Palestine as the way out. International politics hobbled the desperate Zionist drive. As the sky blackened and the typhoon came on, inertia and complacency held all too many Jews on the European continent. A few went up to the Holy Land against all odds, and saved themselves; in effect, Israel is the Warsaw Ghetto that rose in time, and survived. Zionism created this new Remnant, and therein lies its somber historic triumph.

But the dangers to our people remain so great, that we are almost compelled — even the most secular among us — to hope for more miracles. Beleaguered Israel has won three armed clashes against huge odds, but her enemies still rearm, still make war on the borders, still vow her swift bloody end; and the Soviet Union openly aids them in the field, as though the odds against the tiny Jewish state were not stupendous enough already.

Soviet Jewry suffers under a cultural throttling, an attempt at a cool holocaust, in which bodies will survive but identity will gutter out. A strange, malign obsession compels the present leaders of the great Russian people to allow no monument over Babi Yar, no Hebrew schools or press to three million Jews; and yet to forbid emigration to those who wish to preserve their Jewishness. The imposing of this cruel dilemma, on a Jewry that suffered so much under the Germans, is a disgrace in the world's eyes, a stain on Russian honor. All men of good will look for this horrible aberration to pass. Meantime, the very existence of Israel is a steady beacon of hope to this mute, darkened Jewry.

In the haven of the greatest democratic power on earth, the American Jews are safe. But the tidal pressures of conformity slowly, constantly erode our heritage. For us, too, Israel is a providential new wellspring of culture, spirit, and — to the faithful — faith.

What of the Faith?

Well, what of the faith? "Tell me," said the man on the Fire Island beach, meeting me after ten years in which these dangers have all sharpened, the ten years that have passed since I wrote this book, "are you still religious?"

I speak for myself, as I have throughout this book, to say that I hold to our Law with love through all these giant changes in Jewish history, all these marvels and perils. I can see that our ways of life and worship are mutating; as they did when we passed from Egypt to the desert, from the desert to the judges' days, from the judges to the kings, from the First Temple to the Second Temple, from the Second Commonwealth to the long centuries of dispersion. Judaism is very stable, and very adaptable. What new forms and teachings will arise in the Third Commonwealth, what word of God will come forth from Jerusalem, I cannot foretell. I believe the Torah will be a pillar of our nation in this new era, as it has been in all other eras, some as irreligious as our own, some even more savage and dissolute.

Of one trend, I am sure: the new consensus is causing a cultural revival. The decline struck bottom some time ago. To learn Hebrew and even Yiddish is not, for the new generation, a burden and a bore, but a thing to do, if one has the wit. That is not a return to the religion, by any means. But once Hebrew comes back to life, in the diaspora as it already has in Israel, our classics await, charged with Godliness. I do not foresee a near messianic era, though I can hope for it. But I see with my own eyes a shattered nation pulling itself together, taking stock of its resources. The final resource of the Jews is, and has always been, their heritage.

But the blocks to Godliness, interposed by modern thought and some gruesome modern realities, are at least as formidable as those set forth in the Book of Job. I know that well. To some challenges, as in that immortal book, there will perhaps be no answer, ever, but broken Job's, *"I know that my Redeemer liveth."* The great philosopher of history, Vico, saw the Jewish people as an exception to the law of the decay of nations. Their secret, in his view, was their possession of the true word of God; which gave them no relief from the accidents and horrors of history, but only a way to live through them. This is my God.

Israel was his dwelling place in ancient days. The faithful trust that the Redemption has started, and that however long the fulfillment will take, the mission of Jewry is no longer just to survive — as it was for almost two thousand years — but to work as one at restoring Zion, the fit future dwelling place for the prince of peace.

The Jews are a curious sort of pilot-people. The whole world seems to approach a time of judgment, when mankind will emerge, perhaps in the lives of babies already born, into an age of gold or an age of ash. We Jews have had our age of ash, and we have survived; barely, but we have survived. With struggles and dangers that still mount, we have found our way to Jerusalem the Golden, and we are rebuilding it. From this wonder of history, all men can take hope.

Washington
14 November 1969
4 Kislev 5730

Postscript, 1987, on Israel at Forty:

THE LAND AND THE FAITH

The Land and the Faith

IN its fortieth year, Israel remains in a state of war with several Arab neighbors. That is bedrock. It must never be forgotten in discussing the Land and the Faith. No guns are going off as I write, in March 1987, but formal hostilities exist with no end in sight. The Jewish populace has grown in forty years from half a million to more than three million. The Israel Defense Force has become a military power without peer for its size; considered comparable, in some aspects of tactics and technology, to superpower forces. That is probably why the guns are not firing at the moment.

Since I wrote "The Ashes and the Gold" in 1969, the remarkable chronicle of the Jewish State has been punctuated by further military exploits. The brilliant but scary and very costly turnaround victory in the Yom Kippur War of 1973, the airborne rescue of hostages from Arab terrorists at Entebbe in 1976, the controversial expulsion of the PLO terrorists from Lebanon, the surgical bombing of the nuclear reactor in Iraq, the air strike on the terrorist headquarters in Tunis; such high combat drama has repeatedly made world headlines.

The Israelis would gladly trade all that adventure and glory for peace. They have proved it. I was present at the lowering of the flag at the Sharm El Sheikh naval base in April 1982, a final step in their peaceful evacuation of the Sinai peninsula, under the Camp David agreement. A son of mine was serving in a *Wasp* patrol boat based there. After the ceremony I sailed with him up the Red Sea to Eilat, the new base for his vessel, having witnessed the most impressive sacrifice for peace made by a nation in modern times. I will never forget the sight of his *Wasp* squadron, circling round and round full speed offshore with sirens eerily wailing, in the farewell ceremony for a lost ship; nor the ranks of girl soldiers in white dress uniform on the wharf, standing at attention and weeping as the Star of David flag came down. Egypt lost the war to regain Sinai by force of arms. The Israelis gave back this strategic buffer of their own accord, to fulfill their part of a breakthrough peace on one front.

I once asked an Israeli general how it was that his tiny new nation had so swiftly acquired remarkable military prowess. He replied, "We had to." That is the long and the short of it. The oil-rich Arabs can buy all the weaponry they require from other countries, mainly the Soviet Union. The Israelis have to build their own tanks, and much of their defense matériel. So they have learned to make armaments, and to excel in advanced technology, scientific and agricultural as well as military, for one and the same reason: they have had to.

Israelis can sometimes strike one as rushed and prickly people. But the cliché about the *sabra* — same word for native cactus fruit and native Israeli — is true: thorny outside, pleasant and piquant inside. Is it any wonder that they are prickly? American aid notwithstanding, they pay sky-high taxes to carry their military budget. Struggling to make ends meet, they moil away at their jobs, sometimes two or three jobs each, never forgetting that at short notice they may have to hustle on their uniforms and fight again. They give weeks and months to reserve military duty. They waste days bucking *pakkidim*, sluggish tea-drinking bureaucrats, the locust plague of their convoluted politics. Their democracy is strong and stable, and unique in a region of absolutism and dictatorships; but an obsolete electoral system, frozen between two big minority parties, gives splinter factions the swing votes that invite patronage, sleazy bargains, and an ever-greater load of pakkidim. The Israelis will surely rise up and throw out this system in due course, with whole warrens of pakkidim, but meantime there it is.

So being an Israeli is mighty wearing, one would think. Yet despite the ongoing burdens and tension, they take most things with a smile and a shrug. When I am there, I feel at home in a sort of huge small town, where the living is exciting and good, if not exactly easy. This hometown feeling may come from the fact that nearly everybody seems to know nearly everybody else. In certain ways Israel can be a rough tough place, but the family warmth after forty years is still strong and striking.

If Israel has changed a lot since my first visit in 1955, so have I. I have lived in Israel, I have lectured there in Hebrew, and once I even appeared on Hebrew television. I have acquired a base in Jerusalem where I come and go. In short, I am no longer the dazzled tourist who wrote Chapter 22 of *This Is My God.* But I live there, when I do, as a foreigner; free of taxes and military obligations, free to leave any time, free to roam the world with an American passport. I still write as an outsider; one who loves the land and the Israelis, and has come to know them better.

A Deep Rift

In the matter that concerns this book, our old-time religion, pious and secular Israelis remain gravely at odds. Close quarters exacerbate the rift. The gap between old traditions and modern times is a worldwide crisis, but to the Jews, who have survived nineteen centuries of exile by clinging to their faith, it is a life-or-death matter. Grievous open clashes still occur, head-on collisions of politics and tradition. President Chaim Herzog has called this Israel's worst problem, worse even than the conflict with the Arabs.

For the Arab problem has a paradoxical positive side. World Jewish solidarity with Israel is recent, and in large part the work of Arab enmity. Zionism was founded about a hundred years ago by a small group of fervid ideologues. Most Jews at the time regarded them as troublemakers. The Holocaust and the birth of Israel gave Zionism some credibility, but not until a second Holocaust at Arab hands threatened in 1967, and Israel won the astounding Six-Day War, was there a radical change. At that historic moment, and not before, the diaspora Jews turned in a body to Zionism.

The root of Zionism was and remains the religion. Of that there is no doubt whatever. What Jewry responded to in Zionism — however hesitantly at first — was the call for a Return to the Land. It struck a note that had been reverberating in our Bible and liturgy through all the long centuries of exile. The Land of Zion is the setting for the grand Scriptural drama of God and Israel. The central message of the prophets is that in the latter days, in a Messianic time of world peace, our people will return to the Land, to dwell in Zion for ever.

But the political agenda of modern Zionism, its rhetoric, and its ideology, were derived from the great nineteenth-century revolutionary movements in Europe, nationalism and socialism. These were mainly secular, even anti-religious, in thought and action. In that sense, Zionism has sometimes been called the Jewish Revolution, or Risorgimento. Most of the early Zionists, in their uphill struggle to found a Jewish State, abandoned the religion. That is the heart of the schism. And so in the Land today, the Faith is being field-tested by the breaking stresses of modernity.

The stresses are harsh. To believers, the Torah is a constant in our destiny, like the natural constants in physics. The world changes around the Torah, and perceptions of it change, but it is a *given* of God. To non-believers, including leading present-day Zionist thinkers and writers — humanists, they tend to call themselves — the universe is a product of chance, and the Torah a product of human genius, part of our national literature. The two camps have been at loggerheads since the Enlightenment, as I have described in my book. Hotheads occasionally embarrass and disgrace both sides. At one extreme they stone cars on the Sabbath, at the other they vandalize yeshivas. Violent fools we have always with us.

No simple solution is in sight. No shrill slogans help. The hope in the long run must lie in the day-by-day responses of all the Israelis to the unprecedented religious challenges of a democratic Jewish State; in the folk instincts of the people, drawing long breaths of the air of the Holy Land — which, the Talmud tells us, makes a person wise.

On the evidence of the centuries, we believers have reason to hang on, with tolerance and affection for those who disagree. The Zionist secularists once wanted to have a Zion without holiness. I know some of the best of them, and I hear second thoughts being quietly spoken.

The Present Picture

For many American Jews, Israel's well-being is almost their Judaism today. Their attendance at synagogues, temples, and community centers is up, but nothing brings them out, engages their spirits, and unifies them, like the annual drives for Israel. Ben-Gurion used to declare that nobody was a Zionist who didn't come to Israel to live. If the Old Man were alive today, I wonder whether he would not put that slogan on ice. American Jewry is a large dependable support crew, as it were, for the three million Israelis in their endurance march through history.

And for all its troubles, all its tempestuous passages, what a march it is! Today people under fifty cannot remember when Israel did not exist. To youngsters in school, Israel is a real geographic presence, like Norway or Greece. It is *there;* and more *there,* actually, if media attention counts, than most countries on earth. This world awareness of Israel is the triumph of Zionism; and in a sense, perhaps, the culmination of it, as the seed ends in the flower. The Messiah will bring all the Jews to Zion, the prophets tell us. Zionism will not do it, that appears plain.

What about *aliya*, then? Are the world's Jews not coming to reinforce the embattled Israelis, who have so long been the vanguard of the Return? Not, it would appear, in the Messianic mass that Herzl prophesied and Ben-Gurion querulously demanded. Not now, not yet. The Messiah tarries. But they will come. In numbers that vary with the years and events, they have been coming.

Israel arose, above all, as the place of refuge for the Wandering Jew. The half-million Jews of turbulent Latin America, even if they are born and die there, live out of their suitcases; and there is the great imprisoned pool of more than two million Soviet Jews. If in any numbers they are freed or forced to wander, some will go to North America, Australia, or Western Europe; and nobody can blame them for that, but they will head for Zion, too. Ben-Gurion said to me in 1955 that Israel needed four million Jews to be secure. They will be there before the century ends, with more coming. Such at least is my instinct.

Young American and European Jews, caught by the majestic magic of Israel, are also joining the great adventure of the Return, year by year. My son who served in their navy came back smarting over business misadventures, yet with an unquenched love of the Land, a yearning to try again, and a glorious Israeli bride. He once said tartly, "Israel is all Jewish history, focused into a laser beam." Not bad! Well, such intensity is not for everybody. Israelis are born into it. Intense living is their meat and drink. If it becomes too wearing for the few who emigrate, I don't call those few fainthearted, I call them only human. And I honor the many who follow the beam undaunted, who love the Land, who raise families and work, and rejoice in good times and fight when they must; and I honor the Jews from all over the world who come to join the brave ranks of the Return.

To this awed observer of Israel, the miracle still gleams. Doomsayers abound to point to the problems: the social clash of Ashkenaz and Sefard Jews, the chronic political cleavage of Labor and the nationalists, the recurring religious confrontations, the tangled West Bank question, the periodic economic difficulties, and the hostility of implacable Islam. All true.

Yet with all that taken into account, Zion is stronger than ever. Life in the Land is stimulating and colorful. Its enemies are in disorder. Some are at each other's throats. The greatest country on earth, in an extraordinary relationship with sharp ups and downs, calls Israel ally and friend. Other nations more and more accept the fact that the great Return has happened; that the Jewish State is *there,* and worth dealing with. The Arabs resist this trend with dwindling success. By the time this sketch appears in print, events may have bypassed what I have written here, but this is an honest word about the beautiful, flourishing Land of the Jews as of March 1987.

As for the Faith, for all the turbulent clashes produced by swift change, it lives in the Land. I see Faith and Land as two sides of one coin: the half-shekel collected to count the newly freed children of Israel, in their first census at Mount Sinai. There is a wry Israeli byword in which I believe heart and soul; and with that I close an eyeblink glance at troubled radiant Zion, in the fortieth year of the Return: "*Yih'yeh b'seder*" — "It'll be okay."

Herman Wouk

Palm Springs
15 March 1987
Purim 5747

NOTES

Notes

MY book is over. The notes that follow are amplifying statements, and suggestions for further reading. The curious reader who has time to look through these random comments may find a sidelight here and there that will interest him.

The notes do nothing to change the bare sketch of a world religion into an adequate account. Each chapter of my book treats a subject that commands many millions of words in Hebrew literature, and in some cases in world literature. It may be that a short book on Judaism is impossible, or it may be that I have fallen short of the task. But whoever undertakes to tell the general reader about the Hebrew religion in candor and brevity will find himself omitting volumes, as I have done.

Though I have performed extensive research for this book, I have not relied on myself. An outstanding American Talmudist reviewed the manuscript chapter by chapter, through all its stages, for technical accuracy. Then, knowing that scholars tend to differ on interpretation, I submitted the completed book to three other critical and well-informed rabbis. The passages on archaeology and scientific Bible criticism were checked by an expert who has published in the field. The references to classic and current philosophy received a fairly violent going-over by the head of the philosophy department of a major university. On technical points and matters of fact, I yielded to expert correction. In expressing viewpoint I often stood on my own ideas.

While the book is offered as a general guide to the Jewish faith, it has no force, I need hardly say, on doubtful points of law. Ordained masters of Hebrew learning must be consulted in any such question.

The transliteration of Hebrew words in the book is popular rather than exact. My aim has been to find a word that would read smoothly and yet be close in sound to the Hebrew, which defies perfect transliteration anyway.

In editing the book I have dropped literally hundreds of points of information into the notes; and then I have cut them from the notes. To include all such qualifying comments and interpretations would have been, in the end, to write a voluminous concordance, not a brief guide. I have cut and cut again to present the reader with a clear basic outline of this gigantic subject.

After some thought, I omitted reference numbers to these notes in the book itself. I myself welcome such numbers in a technical work, but not in a book intended to be read straight through in a few sittings.

PROLOGUE

p. 5. Kierkegaard . . . stands now in the van of new thought.

I cite his vogue as a symptom. I am not quite as ready as the new thinkers to jettison traditional philosophy, the long line of analytic insight from Plato and Aristotle to James, Santayana, and Whitehead, for the inspired lava flow of Nietzsche and Kierkegaard.

The fact that existentialism, along the line of Kierkegaard and Dostoevsky, reopens a "respectable" path to religious belief does not excite me. Pascal did so long ago; and anyway the paths were never really closed, just somewhat clogged with piles of thick books. I do not believe the way to religion for a modern man necessarily lies through sick despair, though I am a stunned admirer of the literary brilliance of some of the existential writers.

One should at least read *Fear and Trembling* to know what all the talk is about; and Kafka's *The Trial,* which is not only a sort of gospel of the new thought but one of the few wholly original novels of the past hundred years. *The Myth of Sisyphus* and *The Rebel* by Camus will bring the reader up to date in the spirit, if not in the letter, of this field.

CHAPTER 1. WHO ARE WE?

p. 8. The Jewish people is over three thousand years old.

For a long general history of the Jews, I know of nothing that equals Heinrich Graetz's colossal eleven-volume book, available in America in six volumes. This is not to say that I recommend it as reliable or even as professional history. Graetz was a vivid and impassioned writer, off in a world of his own, freely expressing his opinions and prejudices, and taking haymaking liberties when he chose. All the same he makes his subject live; and when you want a clear survey of any stretch of our three-thousand-year narrative, you do well to start by reading Graetz. Then, depending on how far you want to enter the subject, you must go to the libraries and see what work has been done by scientific historians in the period you want.

Hinduism as a continuing tradition is reported to reach back as far as Judaism does, or further; and there are Chinese sacred texts which are said to antedate the Pentateuch. Neither India nor China offers, to my knowledge, a case of a people originating in the unique way of the Israelites, or surviving, as they have done, through a fantastic series of historical predicaments which would have dictated extinction in the ordinary course of things. It is this very long survival in the teeth of historical logic which is most remarkable and needs accounting for, though the longevity is in itself striking enough.

p. 10. Then the science of archaeology arose.

THE VERDICT OF ARCHAEOLOGY

Here is the late Nelson Glueck, an American archaeologist with major discoveries to his credit, writing in his work, *Rivers in the Desert:*

> It may be stated categorically that no archaeological discovery has ever controverted a Biblical reference. Scores

> of archaeological findings have been made which confirm in clear outline or in exact detail historical statements in the Bible. And, by the same token, proper evaluation of Biblical descriptions has often led to amazing discoveries. They form tesserae in the vast mosaic of the Bible's almost incredibly correct historical memory.

Dr. Glueck was criticized for this statement by some educated men who fear it gives people carte blanche to go back to fundamentalist reading of the Bible, and perhaps to try Dr. Scopes over again. It is quite true that the fundamentalists, who once regarded archaeological investigation of the Bible's historicity as blasphemous, now look a bit silly hailing its results. But their position has never made sense, and Judaism has never held to it. (On this point see *Guardians of Our Heritage,* edited by Leo Jung; the introductory essay by the editor, "The Rabbis and Freedom of Interpretation.")

Dr. Glueck is a Reform rabbi, but Reform was not committed to the verbal infallibility of Hebrew Scripture. His statement agrees with the sum of what I have gathered from my reading in archaeology. There are serious gaps still in the archaeological record. The situation on the dating of the fall of Jericho is, in the word of my consulting expert, "parlous" at the moment, but revisions of these situations keep occurring. In general, a retreat to the old position that the Bible is a congeries of unhistorical myths and legends is scientifically unthinkable.

The Bible is first of all, and will always be, a grand religious document. It reveals its religious message in part in a historical narrative. The verdict of twentieth-century science is that the narrative, so far as it can be substantially reconstructed at the site from ancient ruins and records, is true.

CHAPTER 2. THE PREVALENCE OF SYMBOLS

p. 24. We are going to spend a lot of time on symbols and ceremonies.

Anybody who has read Thorstein Veblen will recognize the source of much of this chapter. I can hardly imagine what it is like not to have read at least *The Theory of the Leisure Class,* but I recommend it to the reader most forcibly if he has happened to miss it. The magician's patter and false whiskers of Veblen's style will put one off for a while, but that is all a fine crabbed joke, and one becomes used to it. I used to compel the students in my graduate English seminar to read it, and I took pleasure in seeing it dawn on them that they were encountering satire.

Tocqueville's *Democracy in America* really made the same points much earlier, and some deeper ones, in a straightforward way. This work seems to me required reading for anyone who wants to think seriously about American life. It is beautifully written, but dense and hard and long.

p. 30. conformity . . . has at last ousted insecurity as the final hurled curse of parlor talk.

On conformity, if the reader hasn't read *The Lonely Crowd* he isn't in it, and he had better have a look at the book soon.

The authors think that other-directedness is the most prevalent mode in American conduct today. It is the aimless, shapeless pursuit of "the right thing," the thing that the crowd at the moment seems to be doing. It occurs in people whose tradition-direction or inner-direction breaks down, and who lack the mental or moral force to shape their own destinies.

They oppose to this undesirable mode of conduct *autonomy*, the conscious and self-directed choice of values in the light of mature critical intelligence. This is a lot to ask of people, maybe, but they ask it; and moralists down the years have always made the same hard demand.

Certainly they would call a Jew who practises Judaism without questioning or thinking about it "tradition-directed." Whether they would grant autonomy to a Jew who has examined the matter seriously and finds Judaism the most intelligent way of life for himself, I cannot tell.

CHAPTER 4. THE SABBATH

p. 44. The blue laws surviving in Anglo-American society . . .

An ironic sidelight on the so-called blue laws: Where Christian communities strictly keep up this ordinance founded in Judaism, observant Jews are likely to suffer the worst constraint. They observe the Hebrew Sabbath, and are also required not to work on Sunday. The Jewish merchant has five days to earn his living, the Christian merchant six; a competitive margin which nowadays is destructive. In New York State, which has more Jews than Israel has, there was no legal relief on this point for many years; now the law has been liberalized. The conventional reply to petitions for relief is that Christians are greatly in the majority — which is certainly so; and that therefore Jews must accept the Christian work week — which does not follow at all, as one ordinarily understands the American system. The problem is a knotty one, and will magnify as serious Jewish observance increases.

p. 50. Its essence is a ceremonious abstaining from all acts . . . of workmanship.

Meticulous observance of the Sabbath by those trained in piety extends as far as not touching workaday objects, and using roundabout means, arranged before Sabbath begins, to obtain heat and light. The customs and manners of the Sabbath are complex. One has to remember that the heart of it all is first rest, and then the mystic idea of the day. The laws and the customs are long-established means to these ends. A man resuming his Judaism makes a start somehow, and as time passes reconstructs his Sabbath. Then one day he finds it is second nature. I have known pious men all my life, and I did not know one whose marginal pieties on the Sabbath did not differ in a detail or two from those of others. My grandfather had a special manner of putting away his prayer shawl.

p. 51. Such themes throng the writings on Sabbath . . .

Rabbi Dr. Moshe David Tendler, an American scientist and also an orthodox Talmudist of some note, kindly reviewed the manuscript of this work, and observed about the Sabbath chapter that I seemed to have missed all the main points. I will do better paraphrasing his comment here, I think, than attempting to introduce into my text ideas that did not occur to me.

"The Sabbath expresses four basic ideas," he said. "In the first place, observing the day is an expression of faith in the act of creation, and so it is an affirmation of our creed. Equally important is the denial it offers to human pride — 'My power and the strength of my hand have wrought all this.' The fact is that men can do nothing but use the existing forces and substances of nature. To stop such use one day out of seven restores mankind's perspective on itself as nothing else can; and if modern society desperately needs one thing, it is this recovery of humility and perspective.

"In the third place, abstaining from work and from the mechanical toys of leisure forces a man back on the things in life that are purely human — the use of one's reason, for one thing, and the family affections eclipsed by busy-work and busy-play.

"But the most dramatic thing about Sabbath seems to me the way it presents the paradoxical texture of Judaism in a single cyclical event — the balance of asceticism and luxury, of solemnity and pleasure. People are always trying to ticket our faith as merely restrictive, or merely worldly. Judaism's at-homeness in the here and now and also in the disciplined service of God offers a balanced way of life that is unique. We escape pigeonholing, and so does our Sabbath. It is both a rejoicing in the best things of this world and a formal restraint in the use of them. This pattern runs all through Judaism."

The reader may think this is better than anything in my chapter, but I cannot help it. If this man had already done a book on Judaism I would never have taken on the task. But he is too busy, between Talmud and microscope.

CHAPTER 5. THE NATURE FESTIVALS

p. 53. Their legislation is . . . somewhat more lenient . . .

The underlying leniency of the holiday legislation lies in the force of the ban on labor. Violation of the Sabbath carried more serious punishment. Certain labors which pertain directly to festive preparations were specifically permitted by the Torah, including the use of fire and the carrying of burdens.

p. 54. a leap month . . . proclaimed by the Sanhedrin.

One would think leap years would have been proclaimed by the king rather than a Sanhedrin. But the common law stopped the king from taking any part in the decision on leap year. The king was held to be an interested party, and therefore excluded from this judicial process. His soldiers received their wages in an annual lump sum. On leap years he got thirteen months' service out of them for the price of twelve.

p. 59. In the interval, called the week of the festival, most work proceeds as usual.

On working during the week days of the festival, the regulations are complex. The nub of the matter is that where financial loss could occur, work proceeds; and so in everyday life most people go about their business. Strictly pious people avoid as much work as possible. My grandfather, a great letter writer, wrote none during festivals.

p. 61. An old tradition is the serving of dairy foods . . .

The custom of eating dairy foods on Pentecost is hoary. The explanations I have heard seem to come after the fact; as the suggestion that new humane slaughtering methods enacted with the giving of the Torah could not be employed that same day.

It seems to conflict with the general practice of eating meat on feast days, the conventional token of luxury; but it is universal among the observant. One man of exceptional learning whom I know has a brief serving of dairy foods, pronounces a benediction, and after a short interval commences a regular meat repast as on other holy days, thus carrying out both customs. Perhaps I would follow his way in this matter if I were as abstemious as he the rest of the time.

The Vilna Gaon, a great latter-day authority of Polish Jewry, interdicted the use of floral decoration on Shavuos because it resembled church practice in Poland; but the custom has revived and is growing in the United States and in Israel.

p. 62. You can construct the hut in your own yard.

The technical requirements for building a suko fill many pages of the law codes and much of the Talmud tractate *Suko*. These rules mainly list errors to be avoided. One can easily learn the right way to build the hut from one's rabbi, or from manuals such as Meyer Waxman's clear and indispensable *Judaism: Religion and Ethics*.

An ancient tradition links the suko to the "clouds of glory," the sheltering presence of God, that protected the Jews in the desert.

p. 66. vivid acts like clearing the home of leaven and marching with the palm branch.

Regarding the symbols of the nature festivals, a few readers may miss here an exploration of the inviting Freudian possibilities: leaven as semen, the phallic imagery of palm branch and esrog, the suko as the womb, and so forth. For all I know, there are learned essays somewhere on these pregnant ideas, but I have never run across them. While I am a great admirer of Freud, as any sensible person is today, I do not quite share the orthodox Freudian faith in his doctrine as a universal solvent, so I do not labor these points.

Others may regret that I have not elaborated on similarities in savage or archaic fertility celebrations to Jewish rites. This I would have done if space had permitted. There is no better way of demonstrating why Judaism has survived where other ancient religions have long ago disappeared. The forms of celebration of a harvest are limited and predictable; if the ancient Jewish symbols bore no resemblance to the recurring ones in human experience, Judaism would be a religion of another planet than the earth. But the differences are spectacular and decisive. There is no magic in the Jewish religion, no obscenity, no conjuring of the deities, no hope of manipulating nature through poetic tricks and incantations. The Torah offers you nothing for waving the palm branch but a sense of identity with all Israel, and of worshipping the Lord with pleasure. The fact that our rites come down from the dawn of time seems to me an argument for their lasting power as symbols. I do not understand the contention that their antiquity dims their stature.

Sir James Frazer's *The Golden Bough: A Study in Magic and Religion* is by far the most colorful and interesting book I know of in this field, though savants consider his views somewhat old-fashioned. It comes in twelve vast volumes. Few readers are going to plow through them, but a one-volume abridgment prepared by Frazer is available.

CHAPTER 6. THE HIGH HOLY DAYS

p. 69. white vestments for the worshippers . . .

The white vestments of Yom Kippur in tradition stand for the white burial garments of the pious Jew, the *takhrikhim.* These symbolize purity; they are modelled on the white linen garments worn by Aaron and his sons in the sanctuary.

p. 73. The first shrieking blast of the ram's horn . . .

The symbolism of the ram's horn has in itself generated a literature. Legend links it strongly with the binding of Isaac, and the last-moment substitution of a ram for him in the sacrifice on Mount Moriah. The binding of Isaac (the *Akeda*) haunts our prayer books as a supreme event in our history, and the Rosh Hashana liturgy is full of it. It is a little startling to find the Danish existentialist Kierkegaard sharing the old Jewish view of the Akeda. *Fear and Trembling* is very like an old maggid's harangue on the theme.

p. 75. Immortal Israel, however, is something more.

My section on "the immortal individual" owes much to Sir Henry Maine's *Ancient Law,* though that superb book dwells on Roman jurisprudence and has little to say about Hebrew tradition.

p. 77. "The Moving Finger writes . . ."

It is worth comparing the famous quatrain of Omar about the

moving finger with a curiously similar figure in the Talmud, ascribed to Rabbi Akiba:

> He used to say, Everything is given on loan, and a net is spread for all the living. The shop is open, and the merchant gives ready credit, and the ledger is open, and the hand writes. And whoever wants to borrow, comes and borrows. And the collectors make their regular rounds each day and collect from a man, with his consent or without it, and they have ample security to force collection. And the judgment is a true judgment; and all is a preparation for a feast.

The startling turn of the last sentence is the difference between Judaism and pessimism.

CHAPTER 7. THE MINOR HOLY DAYS

p. 81. The occasion is . . . the famous deliverance of the Persian Jews from . . . Haman.

Some Bible critics question the reliability of the Book of Esther, as others once questioned the real existence of Moses and the events of the Exodus. Such critical theories come and go with the years as archaeology turns up new facts. The reader will find a comment on the general theory of Bible criticism in the notes to Chapter 14.

Purim, like the Exodus, marks a quasi-military operation; and like Passover, it occurs on a full-moon night. The date was selected by lot by Haman, probably out of several full-moon nights, for a sort of St. Bartholomew's massacre of the Jews. By the king's decree the Jews were at the last minute permitted to arm and defend themselves, and in the rioting they won a major victory over their foes. In the Second World War, battle plans by land and sea were often drawn to take advantage of the full moon; and if we ever have another war, moonlight will come into the planning again. Our other full-moon celebration is Sukos, the harvest feast.

CHAPTER 8. THE PRAYERS, THE SYNAGOGUE, AND THE WORSHIPPERS

p. 92. . . . Moses prayed and Miriam was cured of her leprosy.

The "leprosy" of the Bible can hardly have been the disease we know by that English term. The symptoms and course of *zora'as,* the Hebrew word for the illness that struck Miriam, are minutely described in Leviticus. They differ markedly from leprosy, though there are some resemblances. For one thing, zora'as could clear up in a few weeks; for another, it could visibly infect clothing and walls, which had to be destroyed if cleansing failed. The description indicates a virulently infectious mold or fungus which plagued the Near East in Bible times and which to my best knowledge is dormant or extinct today. That it existed and was an extreme menace in ancient days is self-evident from the Levitical isolation rules. We are well rid of zora'as, if we are. Modern Hebrew uses the word to describe leprosy.

p. 94. there is no reviving Yiddish as a community tongue . . .

THE FUTURE OF YIDDISH

A general revival of Yiddish among Jews in the United States I believe to be most unlikely. The renaissance of Jewish culture which is under way centers on modern Hebrew. The gradual dwindling of the once-great Yiddish press and theatre in North America is tragic, but it is an event that grows from causes everybody understands. I count it a privilege that I grew up when this culture was still strong, so that I gained possession of Yiddish without any effort.

Yiddish is a brilliantly expressive and racy vernacular constructed on a base of High German, full of loan words from other tongues, and impregnated with the maxims, idioms, and commonplaces of Hebrew learning. These many layers of reference give the tongue a remarkably ready vividness. Everybody who speaks it sounds a little like a poet or philosopher. It is written and printed in Hebrew characters. In Israel more than half the older people know Yiddish. For the small group of the ultra-orthodox all over the world it remains the everyday tongue.

It is a mistake to predict the extinction of Yiddish in the near future. At least one world genius of letters, Sholem Aleichem, wrote a large body of work in the language, and there were many excellent authors in the nineteenth century not far below his standard. Such a literature in itself fights to keep a language in being. More important — for people who like to reason from economic causes — is the fact that Yiddish is the lingua franca of the sizable and growing Jewish communities in South and Central America. There Yiddish study and the Yiddish press retain current vitality. I was charmed in Mexico to hear babes of four in well-to-do and cultivated families speak at will in Spanish or Yiddish. Buenos Aires has scholarly Yiddish publishing of high quality. The language will survive, I think, for a very long time, though it may be that its literary zenith was in the nineteenth century. In our own time we have had at least two authors of world repute, the Nobel laureate Isaac Bashevis Singer and the late Sholem Asch, writing in Yiddish; even Asch's Christian tales were composed in this vernacular.

The misfortune is that the great Sholem Aleichem, put into English, dims out like Molière, and for much the same reason; humor and poetry are the least translatable qualities in literature. Asch, on the other hand, a straightforward novelist, survived admirably in translation. It is said that Sholem Aleichem retains all his value when put into modern Hebrew. I have not read the translations but I hope it is so.

p. 99. The Creed and the Service

FULL TEXTS OF THE SH'MA AND THE SHMONE ESRAI

This is the complete Sh'ma:

> *Hear O Israel, the Lord our God, the Lord is One.*
> *(Blessed be his name, whose glorious kingdom is for ever and ever.)*
>
> And you shall love the Lord your God with all your heart, and with all your soul, and with all your might. And these

words which I command you today shall be upon your heart. And you shall teach them to your children, and you shall talk of them when you sit in your house, and when you go on the way, and when you lie down, and when you rise up. And you shall bind them for a sign upon your hand, and they shall be emblems between your eyes. And you shall write them upon the door posts of your house, and upon your gates.

And it shall be, if you truly hear my commands that I command you today, to love the Lord your God, and to serve him with all your heart and with all your soul; that I will give the rain of your land in its season, the early and the late rain, that you may gather in your corn, and your wine, and your oil. And I will give grass in your field for your cattle, and you shall eat and be satisfied. Beware lest your heart be deceived and you turn aside, and worship other gods, and bow down to them. For the anger of the Lord will kindle against you, and he will shut up the heaven and there will be no rain, and the land will not give its fruit. And you will perish quickly from the good land that God is giving you. So you shall lay these words to your heart and to your soul, and you shall bind them for a sign upon your hand, and they shall be emblems between your eyes. And you shall teach them to your children, speaking of them when you sit in your house, and when you go on the way, and when you lie down and when you rise up. And you shall write them upon the door posts of your house, and upon your gates. That your days may increase, and the days of your children, upon the land which the Lord pledged to your fathers to give them, as the days of the heavens above the earth.

And the Lord spoke to Moses, saying, Speak to the children of Israel, and tell them to make a fringe upon the corners of their garments down the generations; and they will put a thread of blue on the fringe of each corner. And it will be a fringe for you, that you may see it, and remember all the commands of God and do them, and not turn after your hearts and after your eyes, which you stray after. That you may remember and do all my commands and be holy to your God. I am the Lord your God, who took you out of Egypt to be your God. I am the Lord your God.

This prayer is a compilation. The first verse is Deuteronomy 6:4. The second is the traditional response uttered in the Temple after a blessing. The first long paragraph is Deuteronomy 6:5–9. The second is Deuteronomy 11:13–21. The third is Numbers 15:37–41.

These are the Eighteen Benedictions of the daily service:

(1) Blessed are you, O Lord our God and God of our fathers, God of Abraham, God of Isaac, and God of Jacob, the God who is great, strong, and awesome, the most high God; who bestows goodness, and owns all things, and remembers the goodness of the fathers, and will bring a redeemer to their children's children, for his name's sake, in love. King, helper, savior, shield!

Blessed are you, O Lord, shield of Abraham.

(2) You are powerful for ever, O Lord, quickener of the dead, mighty to save. You support life with kindness, quicken the dead with great mercy. You raise the fallen, heal the sick, free the prisoned, and keep faith with those that sleep in the dust. Who is like you, master of mighty acts, and who compares to you? O King who kills and who brings to life, and who makes salvation flower, faithful are you to give life to the dead.

Blessed are you, O Lord, who give life to the dead.

(3) You are holy, and your name is holy; and holy ones praise you each day, Selah!

Blessed are you, O Lord, the holy God.

(4) You grant man knowledge, and teach humans understanding; grant us then knowledge, understanding, and sense.

Blessed are you, O Lord, the giver of knowledge.

(5) Return us, father, to your law; draw us near, king, to your service; and bring us back in whole repentance before you.

Blessed are you, O Lord, who delight in repentance.

(6) Forgive us, father, for we have sinned; pardon us, king, for we have done wrong; for you are he who pardons and forgives.

Blessed are you, O Lord, gracious, and amply forgiving.

(7) See our distress; plead our cause; redeem us soon for your name's sake, for you are a mighty redeemer.

Blessed are you, O Lord, redeemer of Israel.

(8) Heal us, O Lord, and we will be healed; save us and we will be saved; for you are our praise; and raise a whole healing for all our ills, for you are God and king, the true and merciful healer.

Blessed are you, O Lord, who heal the sick of your people Israel.

(9) Bless this year to us, Lord our God, and all things growing for food, and send a blessing on the face of the earth, and satisfy us with your goodness, and bless this year as in the good years.

Blessed are you, O Lord, who bless the years.

(10) Sound the great horn for our freedom; raise the banner to gather our exiles, and gather us together from the four corners of the earth.

Blessed are you, O Lord, who gather the banished of your people Israel.

(11) Restore our judges as of old, and our advisers as at first, and remove from us grief and suffering, and reign over us, you alone, O Lord, in kindness and in mercy, and justify us in judgment.

Blessed are you, O Lord, the king who loves right and judgment.

(11a) But for slanderers may there be no hope; may all wickedness perish as in an instant; may all the enemies of your people speedily be cut off; may the rule of violence soon be rooted out, smashed, thrown down, and humbled, soon in our time.

Blessed are you, O Lord, who break foes and humble men of violence.

(12) For the righteous and for the good, and for the elders of your people the House of Israel, and for the remnant of their teachers, and for the true converts, and for us, may your mercies awaken, O Lord our God; and grant a good reward to all who trust in your name in truth, and let our lot be with them for ever; that we may not be shamed, for we have trusted in you.

Blessed are you, O Lord, stay and trust of the righteous.

(13) And to Jerusalem your city, return in mercy, and dwell there as you have spoken; and build it soon in our time, an everlasting upbuilding; and in its midst set soon the throne of David.

Blessed are you, O Lord, builder of Jerusalem.

(14) May the blossom of David your servant speedily flower, and may his glory be exalted through your salvation; for to your salvation we look each day.

Blessed are you, O Lord, who make the glory of salvation flower.

(15) Hear our voice, O Lord our God; spare us and have mercy on us, and receive our prayers in charity and favor, for you are a God who hears prayers and beseechings; and from before you, O our King, turn us not empty away; for you are he who listens in mercy to the prayer of your people Israel.

Blessed are you, O Lord, who hear prayer.

(16) Accept, O Lord our God, your people Israel and their prayer; and restore the service to the Holy of Holies of your Temple; and receive with favor the offerings and the prayers of Israel, and may the service of Israel always be pleasing to you; and may our eyes see your return to Zion in mercy.

Blessed are you, O Lord, who return your Presence to Zion.

(17) We thank you, for you are the Lord our God, the rock of our lives, the shield of our salvation, from generation to generation. We will thank you and we will tell your praise, for our lives which are committed to your hands, and for our souls which are in your charge, and for your miracles which are with us each day, and for your wonders and your benefits which come at all times, evening, morning, and noon; O you who are good, may your mercy not fail; you who are merciful, may your kindness not cease; to you have we hoped for ever.

And for all these things may your name be blessed and exalted constantly, and for ever and ever.

And all life will give thanks to you, Selah! and will praise your name in truth; the God, our salvation and our help, Selah!

Blessed are you, O Lord, whose name is good, and unto whom it is fitting to give thanks.

(18) Grant peace, good, blessing, grace, kindness, and mercy to us and to all Israel your people; bless us all, father, as one in the light of your face; for in the light of your face you gave us, Lord our God, the law of life and the love of good, and righteousness, and blessing, and mercy, and life, and peace. And it is good in your eyes to bless your people Israel at all times and at every hour with your peace.

Blessed are you, O Lord, who bless your people Israel with peace.

The evening litany of Eighteen Benedictions is by tradition optional, because there was no regular evening offering at the Temple to correspond to it. It parallels the nighttime burning of meat from the day's offerings. In our time the evening litany is part of established prayer.

The translation of all Hebrew in this book is my own, and must not be taken as in any way authoritative. For the sake of clear communication I have completely dropped antique English, and I have perhaps too often used plain words instead of splendid ones. But Hebrew is so direct, so colloquial, so immediate that I know no other way even to suggest the true effect.

Within the two main branches of liturgy, the Ashkenaz and the Sefard, there are further minor variations in the prayer books of different countries. The Hasidim, who fall within the Ashkenaz group, use a prayer book all their own, which mixes elements from both liturgies, and draws much from the Cabala. (See note p. 317.)

CHAPTER 9. SYMBOLS OF FOOD, CLOTHING, AND SHELTER

p. 111. Of the creatures in the sea, Jews eat those with fins and scales.

Ichthyology reports four types of scales in fish: cycloid, ctenoid, placoid and ganoid. The first two types mark the edible fishes. Many fish have scales of one of the latter two kinds — sharks and eels, for instance — and these are not eaten. I am informed by a competent scientist that sturgeon too are in the latter class, though I have heard laymen argue for years about sturgeon.

p. 111. Insects are wholly out.

On the eating of insects, the Bible law specifically permits grasshoppers of a certain variety. The grasshopper was widely eaten in the ancient Near East, and it still is. The locusts devour the crops; all the protein and carbohydrate are in them; the people recover their food supply by roasting or pickling the creatures and eating them. A brilliant short novel by David Garnett, *The Grasshoppers Come,* is built on the edibility of the locust. In Jewish common law the exact definition of the edible varieties of grasshopper became obscure, and so these insects passed under the general ban. But in some settlements of the Near East the knowledge of the distinguishing marks of the edible locust survives. I recently heard of a Yemenite medical student in a United States university, devoutly orthodox, who attended a laboratory class where locusts were being dissected. He told the instructor, a Jewish biologist, that the creatures were of an edible variety; and he pointed to a distinguishing mark, the Hebrew letter *hes* clearly marked on the insect's abdomen. He proceeded to prove that they were edible and kosher (at least so far as he was concerned) by eating a few. I asked a rabbinic authority whether this conduct was acceptable. Perfectly, the answer was; based on the Talmud rule, "He has a continuous tradition from his fathers." I gather that if I caught a grasshopper with a *hes* on its abdomen it would not be an available morsel for me, since I have no such tradition. I submit to this deprivation with fortitude.

p. 111. "Kosher means pure" . . .

HYGIENIC EXPLANATION OF DIET LAWS

Maimonides in *Guide for the Perplexed* explains the diet laws almost wholly on two bases: health and the abolition of heathen superstitions. His discussion of the prohibition of drinking blood remarkably anticipates *The Golden Bough* on the concept of sympathetic magic in savage religion. I believe he was the first to point out correctly the importance in Torah law of striking at shamanism.

He cites two Talmudic opinions on this general class of disciplines. One says a rational basis for them can be found. The other rests on their formal symbolism as acts of faith, dedication, and identity.

In adopting the second line through most of my discussion of the diet laws I am not (the notion is preposterous) challenging Maimonides. I readily concede the sanitary and hygienic points. Modern medicine has come much further than Maimonides himself could in substantiating his view. We know that milk and meat mixtures, though esteemed as delicacies in some cooking, are almost a laboratory culture for bacteria, and must be prepared and preserved with great care. We also know that dishes rich in blood are similarly risky. Crabmeat and lobster are serious rivals to creamed chicken as ptomaine generators; and we are just learning the dangers of saturated fat, of which suet is the prototype. The relative indigestibility of pork, and its normally infested state, are scientific observations which Maimonides hit on only empirically.

But though all these things are so, I cannot help maintaining that to the modern mind they seem secondary. Maimonides was a doctor, living in a time when filth and plague were universal. Comparing the careful handling and strict selectivity of the Hebrew diet with the kitchen squalor and indifference which he saw everywhere, he found the health aspect of the Torah laws a main key. Today civilized countries have more or less caught up with the sanitary rules of the Hebrew food code; though large numbers of non-Jews today eat kosher fowl and delicatessen meats because of the extra margin of freshness and guaranteed inspection.

The survival of the Jewish community, in an industrial society with a tidal trend to conformism, is now a major problem; and so one naturally sees how the laws work as instruments of identity and discipline. A different time sheds a different light. Both Talmudic views of the law now appear just. From either viewpoint, giving them up means cutting out a main engine of Judaism for no useful reason. Of course they are inconvenient at times, but not nearly as inconvenient as paying the federal income tax. One does what one must to keep alive the things that matter.

The deprivation of the observance lies almost wholly in the impact of a changeover. A luxurious table can be spread under the Hebrew laws, as anyone knows who observes them.

As to variations in the small details of diet observance, there is again almost no end. Permission and restriction on minutiae vary from rabbi to rabbi, though everyone in the Mosaic communion observes the main laws. An extremely strict teacher of mine once pointed out that, beyond the main laws, meticulousness in observance is an expression of religious temper. My grandfather found it normal and desirable to give up beef for thirty years rather than eat meat which he did not himself see slaughtered, yet he quite approved of my eating such meat. Our tempers were different. Whether his was "superior" or "extravagant," "noble" or "fanatic," the reader will judge depending on the temper he brings to the question.

A Jew born outside these laws, with no training in them or in the rest of Judaism, can begin most effectively to restore his identity — if that is his desire — with the food laws, the same day he makes the decision to do so. Dropping the obvious excluded foods, without worrying about punctilio, will give him a sense of contact with Judaism. He can go on from there in study and in reconstruction of his life as occasion allows.

p. 121. During morning prayers, men wear a four-cornered fringed shawl . . .

A four-cornered garment was conventional in ancient Israel. Now that dress has changed we put on a rectangular shawl to preserve the commandment in its given form.

There is a Biblical prohibition against the mixing of linen and wool in the making of a garment. Maimonides refers this symbolism again to the aim of uprooting practices of sympathetic magic; the priests of idolatry wore clothes mixed of these two materials as a sign of power over the vegetable and animal kingdoms, while carrying a mace made of a mineral. Devout people inspect new clothes to be sure that they do not contain *shatnaze,* the mixture of linen and wool, even in the use of threads or stiffening material.

Certain devout married women keep their heads covered at all times in public, usually by wearing a hat. The *sheitels* or wigs of their grandmothers, which some use instead, have evolved into modish transformations.

p. 122. Shelter

A Torah law requires the builder of a new house to make a parapet around the edge of his roof (Deuteronomy 22:8), "so that you will not bring blood upon your house when the faller will fall." The Talmud derived laws of liability from this verse, and moral comment too. The faller will fall as God wills, the rabbis said; but let not your house be an available instrument for his doom.

CHAPTER 10. BIRTH AND BEGINNINGS: MEN AND WOMEN

p. 132. The ban on musical instruments like the organ . . .

The ban in law against use of the organ falls within a general interdict against use of devices on holy days which may break down and require immediate repair. The abstention in memory of the fall of the Temple is part of a comprehensive tradition. The remembrance of the destruction of the Temple pervades Jewish life; the breaking of a glass at weddings is supposed to recall it; pious Jews in building a home leave some part unfinished in token of the fallen house of God which is yet to be rebuilt.

CHAPTER 11. LOVE AND MARRIAGE: AND CERTAIN ELEGANT VARIATIONS

p. 146. If my reader endorses discreet adultery and sodomy . . .

On elegant variations in sex, I know no more illuminating stretch of writing than Burton's amazing terminal essay to his (unexpurgated) translation of *The Arabian Nights*. It cures the reader of any idea that modern vice is in any way new or even ingenious. The sexual disorder of Egypt and Canaan, at which the Bible code struck, never died out of the Mediterranean littoral. Our novelists and playwrights report today that it remains just the place for such diversions.

CHAPTER 12. DEATH

p. 151. Even in the Talmud the idea of the hereafter is shadowed forth only in metaphors . . .

Though it is a mistake to try to spell out the Jewish hereafter, because nobody knows precisely what the parables and figures imply, a couple of points are clear and worth reiterating. Our tradition asserts that the righteous of all faiths have a share in the world to come; there is no thought of salvation only through our communion. Nor is there the idea of everlasting damnation. The sinner, one view holds, serves his punishment, whatever it is, for a year and no more; and no Jewish teaching suggests punishment without end.

CHAPTER 14. THE TORAH

p. 170. Wellhausen's crude fantasy of historic evolution in Israel . . . is no longer taken seriously.

WELLHAUSEN THEORY: HIGHER CRITICISM

Most college-educated readers probably have a dim view of the Graf-Wellhausen hypothesis of Bible study. Its general effect, when it was believed, was to discredit most of the Old Testament, and especially the books of Moses, as chopped-up conglomerations of very late forgeries, rather than authentic documents of antiquity. I can briefly summarize its background, and its rise and fall, for the occasional reader who may be curious about it.

Looking on the Bible as a collection of very old books, any man can see that it bears the marks of its age, and of its place in time. It contains difficult and obscure passages. Verses contradict each other. Repetitious sections occur. Discrepancies exist in chronology, law, and episode. All this has been plain to Hebrew scholars ever since the canon was fixed. The Talmud abounds with discussion of the difficulties. Running commentaries on Scripture in students' editions point them out. The explanations are sometimes convincing, sometimes forced. Commentators disagree with each other. They freely challenge the exegesis of the Talmud sages. The student in the end is left to decide about these things as well as he can.

In the seventeenth century, when the Bible was used by theologians to block the advance of reason and of knowledge, the emerging scientific intelligence in self-defense went at the Bible and trained its attack on these spots. So far as I know, the general theory of modern Bible criticism was first set down by Spinoza, in his *Tractate on Theology and Politics,* though he owed much to

Hobbes. A Talmud student in revolt, Spinoza knew his spots, and he had one of the sharpest minds — and pens — in centuries.

Spinoza's idea in a nutshell was that the Bible after all was literature, a book like any other book, though perhaps greater than most. It had not been written in black fire on white fire, untouchable and everlasting, by God. That was mere metaphor. It had been set down by human hands at different times with ink on parchment. It was therefore subject to literary analysis. Traditions about its composition were not the final word. They might not be true. Rational scrutiny of the text would show the truth about its authors, and the facts of its origin. He outlined all the paraphernalia of what we now call the Higher Criticism: variations of style, repeated passages, chronological discrepancies, oddities of grammar and vocabulary, and so forth. He leaned much on an orthodox Hebrew commentator of great stature, Ibn Ezra, often taking the difficulties pointed out by Ibn Ezra and putting new corrosive interpretations on them.

This gate that Spinoza opened in 1670 was at first a passage to nothing but trouble. Writing in this vein invited abuse, prosecution, ostracism, and possible imprisonment or even death. But within a century Voltaire went crashing through the opening and bulldozed a broad path. After Voltaire, rational analysis of the Bible was any man's game, and the run was on.

The distinction of first proposing forgery as an important motive in the composition of Scripture belongs, I believe, to a German theologian named de Wette, who in 1806 published a scathing attack on the reliability of the Book of Chronicles. But the forgery theory of Scripture documents will always be linked with the name of another German, a history professor named Julius Wellhausen, who extended the range of de Wette's forgers to cover practically all Scripture. The Torah of Moses, in particular, Wellhausen argued, was a multilayered fake from the first word to the last.

Wellhausen originated little, and he gave due credit to his predecessors. The general idea of the Wellhausen theory, derived for the most part from Astruc, de Wette, and Graf, was that the

Old Testament had been in large measure doctored, phonied, or badly counterfeited by the priestly canonizers under Ezra in the time of the Second Temple. They pretended to fix a canon of Israel's existing sacred books. They really performed a work of massive manufacture with one end in view: to shore up their own claims to power and money. Their main aim was to perpetuate a single falsehood: that Moses had legislated, and Solomon had put in effect, central worship at one sanctuary: the Tabernacle, and later the First Temple. Wellhausen said there had never been a tabernacle. The description in Leviticus, full of antique words and details, was a forgery like the pseudo-antique poems of Chatterton and Ossian. The account of central worship at Solomon's temple in the history book was also a mass of priests' inventions.

Starting from this premise, Wellhausen reared a new evolutionary vision of Israel's history. There had been no revelation at Sinai. Moses was not the fountainhead of the faith. The Hebrew religion grew out of a crude anthropomorphic polytheism. Moses, if he existed at all, thought himself the votary of a local thunder god or mountain god, possibly a real piece of sacred stone ("Our Rock whose ways are perfect"). Gradually in Canaan the Prophets evolved a more purified faith; but this was hopelessly distorted and falsified by the forgers.

To maintain this novel view, Wellhausen in 1875 published his *Prolegomena to the History of Ancient Israel,* a panoramic work in almost five hundred pages of close print, with perhaps five thousand textual references to the Old Testament. He traversed the Hebrew Scriptures from the first word of Genesis to the last word of Chronicles, expounding his thesis by chapter and verse. For a generation and more the *Prolegomena* took the field of Bible criticism and held it. Most Bible critics went down before it like ninepins.

I have read Wellhausen's *Prolegomena,* and I have checked all his textual references in the Old Testament in Hebrew. It may well be that I am the last man on earth who will ever accomplish this feat. The book is a museum piece now, and even young Bible scholars are not required to plow through it. But I thought

I owed it to the readers of this discussion to perform the task. I will try to describe the book, which was for a while a sort of inside-out Bible for non-believers.

Wellhausen starts by announcing his grand theme: the forging priests, the non-existent tabernacle, and the phony doctrine of central worship. Then he plunges into his main task: getting the Bible to retell its story according to Wellhausen, in its own words.

His method is simple, but the working out in detail is grandiose. Whatever passages of Scripture support his thesis, or at least do not oppose it, are authentic. Wherever the text contradicts him, the verses are spurious. His attack on each verse that does not support him is violent. He shows bad grammar, or internal inconsistency, or corrupt vocabulary, or jerkiness of continuity, every time. There is no passage he cannot explain away or annihilate. If he has to change the plain meaning of Hebrew words he does that too. He calls this "conjectural emendation."

Early in the game he seems to realize that he will not quite be able to shout down one haunting question: how is it after all that hundreds and hundreds of Bible verses refute his theory in plain words? Wellhausen answers this challenge by unveiling an extraordinary hypothetical figure, the Interpolater, a sort of master forger. Seeing across a span of twenty-three centuries, this man (or men) obviously anticipated the Wellhausen theory, and went through all of Holy Scripture carefully inserting passages that refuted it!

With the discovery of the Interpolater, Wellhausen's difficulties were at an end. As a tool of controversial logic this figure is wonderful. Sections of the Bible that appear to contradict Wellhausen are not only shorn of their genuineness, they turn around to become arguments in his favor. Wellhausen, of course, does not name the Interpolater. He does not even personify him as a single figure. He merely summons an interpolater, perhaps once on every other page, to do his duty. When all else fails Wellhausen — grammar, continuity, divine names, or outright falsifying of the plain sense of the Hebrew — he works an interpolater.

This odd spook in priest's clothing is really the key to the *Prolegomena*. It is of course quite possible that over thousands of years interpolations crept into the Hebrew holy books. But when a historian finds in a long-stable text dozens and scores and hundreds of verses that directly contradict his pet theory about the text, and reaches the conclusion that this state of things proves a clairvoyant interpolater's hand, his work seems to cross the red line into the curious literature of systemized delusion.

The puzzle today is how such a work ever captured, even for a few decades, a serious scholastic field. But the history of science shows that any vigorously asserted hypothesis can have a good run, in the absence of solid facts. The main thing, probably, was that in 1875 evolution was in the air. The battles over Darwin were still being fought, but it was obvious who was going to win. A theory that imposed evolution on Old Testament religion radiated chic and excitement, even though it stood the Bible on its head. Wellhausen's job of documentation, shrill and twisted though it was, lacking any scientific precision, nevertheless was overpowering in its sheer mass of minute scholarly detail. His construction lasted, with increasing shakiness, until the 1930s. It still lingers to some extent in popular culture, which does not turn on a dime. Serious Bible scholarship has dropped it.

A three-way attack put the forgery theory in the discard. The first assault came from archaeology, which really began to show its first important results around 1890. Wellhausen's imagined state of early Hebrew culture turned out to be moonshine, once archaeology replaced his speculations with some facts. It was one of his major premises, for instance, that the art of writing was virtually unknown in Mosaic times. The archaeologists found whole mounds of evidence to the contrary. Mosaic tabernacle ceremony he had identified as very late practice, mostly post-exilic. Archaeology uncovered so many parallels in the surrounding cultures of Mosaic date that the Hebrew rites obviously fell in the same distant antiquity. The tabernacle itself was the kingpin of the Wellhausen theory. He had declared it an absolute fiction, wholly unsuited to desert life or to ancient times. Again, archaeology discovered the opposite to be true (details of this reverse are in W. F. Albright's *From the Stone Age to Christianity*).

While archaeology battered the theory from without, Wellhausen's own disciples weakened it by a sort of scholarly termite-eating from within. They continued to analyze the Bible by his methods, and began uncovering still more hypothetical documents within the professor's old J, E, P, and D. About thirty different documents, editors, and interpolaters at last piled up. Wellhausen disciples were finding traces of half a dozen documents in a single verse of the Torah. At this point the most rabid adherents of the theory began to see that it was dissolving in absurdity.

But there was no way to backtrack. It would have been like trying to unscramble an egg. At every point the advocates of the new documents had done what Wellhausen had done, and they had come up with these clear results. Arguments from jerkiness of continuity, shifts in style, variation of divine names, and curiosities in vocabulary led to this atomized end, or they led nowhere.

What the scholars had found out at long last, of course, was that literary analysis is not a scientific method. Literary style is a fluid, shifting thing, at best a palimpsest or a potpourri. The hand of Shakespeare is in the pages of Dickens; Scott wrote chapters of Mark Twain; Spinoza is full of Hobbes and Descartes. Shakespeare was the greatest echoer of all, and the greatest stylist of all. Literary analysis has been used for generations by obsessive men to prove that everybody but Shakespeare wrote Shakespeare. I believe literary analysis could be used to prove that I wrote both *David Copperfield* and *A Farewell to Arms*. I wish it were sound.

In the 1930s a new school of formidable Scandinavian critics officially rejected the Wellhausen scheme from start to finish. They have never been refuted, and modern criticism has moved far along new paths. Ivan Engnell of this school dealt the death blow to the *Prolegomena* by analyzing Wellhausen's villainous ghost, the Interpolater, and driving it from the field with a polite scholarly horse laugh. His ironic name for it was *interpretatio europeica moderna*. Examining the web of supposed interpolations, he found in them the self-portrait of a European desk scholar, moiling patiently through Scripture to construct a nineteenth-century hypothesis, and then projecting his own image backward into the environment of the fifth century before Jesus. Once he had demonstrated this, there was not much left of the Wellhausen theory.

I beg the reader not to imagine that Higher Criticism has thrown in the towel to tradition, and acknowledged the verbal infallibility of the Hebrew Scriptures. The fresh note in Bible criticism today is its humility and its frank uncertainty, following on the ruin of the Wellhausen scheme. This body of scholars is emerging from a collective nightmare. They are not eager to enter another one. There are graybeard Prolegomanes who fiercely propose to go to their graves believing in Wellhausen. It is a hard thing for men who have given their lives to a theory, and taught it to younger men, to see it fall apart. The main body of criticism, however, has left behind the whole method of literary analysis.

At the moment the tendency is to go slow, to absorb the vast and still flooding disclosures of archaeology, to expand the study of ancient languages, and to question modern guesses at least as much as old traditions. The Scandinavian scholars lean toward dismissing the documentary theory entirely, and toward the idea of long oral tradition of very high reliability. The notion of priestly fraud in Scripture is rejected on all sides. The usage of divine names as a clue to parallel documents is under strong critical attack. It never did hold up, because the names repeatedly cross over from "document" to "document." This was once supposed to be the work of interpolaters, but those busy ghosts have by and large heard the cock crow and retired. No former certainty of the Wellhausen days is safe from challenge, not even the dating of the Book of Deuteronomy. In this wholly open state of things, it is hard to describe a consensus, but I will try.

The Torah is now taken as certainly Mosaic in origin and in content. Critics clash as to how the law of Moses has come down to us, and how reliable the text is. It is becoming clear that there have been two major developments in Bible study: text analysis and archaeology. Text analysis came first. Uncontrolled by external evidence, it flew into fantasy and came a cropper. Archaeology has swung back toward tradition. With the facts of archaeology, and of the crucial study of ancient languages, in hand, criticism hopes in time to construct a sober picture — but one which will always have large elements of guesswork — of the composition of the books of the Bible.

The reader who wishes to pursue this topic can have a lifetime of reading. If he can spare the time and energy, he ought to try the *Prolegomena,* out of curiosity if nothing more. It should be read Bible in hand, so that one can watch the professor at work making his crazy-quilt scriptures. Without knowing Hebrew, one cannot see the liberties he takes with the ancient tongue, but the chopping and changing are plain for the most part in English.

For an up-to-date and gracefully written picture of critical Bible scholarship, I know of no book that equals W. F. Albright's *From the Stone Age to Christianity*. There is some murderous demolition of Wellhausen's "idiot forgers" in Walter Kaufmann's *Critique of Religion and Philosophy,* but the work will be of small comfort to pietists. It is a serious, often very witty, statement of a non-religious man, the best of its kind I have read since Bertrand Russell's books in that field.

For a more technical survey, including a detailed account of the Scandinavian school, there is *The Old Testament and Modern Study* (Oxford 1951), edited by H. H. Rowley, a symposium by the leading scholars of the day, including Albright. Here one will find defense of Wellhausen by old-time disciples, as well as the radical new criticism. Naturally such a text is hard going, but solid.

Beyond such general contemporary works, there are whole libraries of Higher Criticism stretching back to Spinoza. The interested reader can pursue the indicated paths *ad libitum*.

"Higher" Criticism, by the way, means the attempt to discover dates, authorship, and documentary origins by speculating on the text; as opposed to "Lower" Criticism, which seeks to recover the most exact and reliable version of the text, word for word.

CHAPTER 15. THE TALMUD

p. 173. *the Talmud is a sealed book . . .*

A few Christian scholars like Danby, Moore, and Herford have achieved remarkable knowledge of the Talmud. The feat can be appreciated only by a Jew who has studied it from boyhood. Aside from the gnarled, terribly compressed style itself, there is the pervasive survival of oral learning in the abbreviations. Some columns of the Talmud, and nearly all of the commentaries, look like algebra: strings of initial letters in baffling little groups, not words but first letters of phrases presumed to be so familiar to the reader that the printer need not spell them out. There are no effective glossaries of these initial letters; to compile one would be to compose a new Hebrew legal dictionary. You have to join up with the chain of oral learning to unravel the phrases. I got them, or most of them, from my grandfather, and I am still thrown by unfamiliar ones. How Danby, Moore, and Herford did it I cannot imagine; they must have spent years working with expert Talmudists.

p. 174. *The narrow columns are commentaries . . .*

RASHI

What makes it possible for a man like myself to study the Talmud is the column that flanks the heavy text along the inner margin of each page. This is the commentary of Rashi, a French Jew who lived about a thousand years ago.

Rashi is the great teacher of Judaism. It is perhaps not too much to say that he kept the Talmud alive, and made it a subject of study for all the Jewish people, instead of an esoteric work. He was master of an enviable prose style — clear as spring water, brief, alive, exact; and like all the very greatest styles, warm and almost conversational. Rashi leads you through the Talmud by the hand. He assumes that you know little Aramaic, that your grasp of Hebrew is probably not too good, that you lack a general knowledge of Talmudic law, and that you have trouble following an argument. He never patronizes you, he makes no parade of his learning, and he is not interested in moralizing. He wants you to know what the Talmud means. If you study it with Rashi, you usually find out.

The column on the other side of the main text is called *Tosephos,* or additions. These are subtle and arresting technical comments worked up over several generations by a school of analysts, many of whom were disciples or descendants of Rashi. The ability to unravel a Tosephos comment marks a working Talmud scholar. The tiny sub-columns around the margins refer you to Torah verses, or the legal codes; or they give variant readings.

The great commentators are almost always known by their initials. Rashi, for example, is *Ra*bbi *Sh*elomo *I*zaki.

Rashi also wrote a commentary on the Torah which is as much a part of childhood study as the text of Moses itself. This is in the main a compilation of classic exegesis, put in Rashi's spare clear words, with occasional explanations of hard Torah idioms. His work on the Talmud is of another order; it is the logical analysis of the common law *par excellence.* Serious study of Hebrew jurisprudence starts with Rashi's comments on the Talmud, and Rashi remains one of the final authorities.

p. 175. . . . I wrestled with Aramaic.

Aramaic was the prevalent Semitic tongue in Mesopotamia and Palestine from Bible times onward. There are passages of Aramaic in the later prophetic books. During the Talmud period it was the everyday tongue of the Jews. The sacred books were translated into *Targums,* Aramaic versions, and Aramaic prayers entered the liturgy. It is about as close to Hebrew as French is to Spanish, or perhaps a bit closer. If one knows Hebrew one can stumble through an Aramaic passage and get the gist of it, with occasional reaching for a dictionary. Students of the Talmud pick up Aramaic because there is so much of it. Rashi helps one over the rough spots. There is little question that Jesus of Nazareth spoke this tongue. He lived midway in the Tanna era. Paul of Tarsus was a pupil, according to his own statement, of the Tanna Rabbi Gamaliel.

p. 179. This, then, in the briefest skimming outline, is the Talmud. The Babylonian or Bavli Talmud has been the subject here. Another recension exists, the Jerusalem Talmud, which is the province, even in Jewish learning, of but a few specialists. Its Gemara is fragmentary, and the Aramaic more difficult; and it lacks the stream of brilliant commentators who through the centuries have lit up the dark corners of the Bavli. Yet the Jerusalem Talmud does help unravel difficult and corrupted passages of the Bavli, and legal minds in each generation who have to solve crises of religious law consult both. It is almost the mark of a Hebrew sage, I would say, that he is at home in the Jerusalem Talmud.

It is perhaps not accidental that the authoritative common law was worked out in the academies of the exile, rather than in the schools of the smaller community which remained in the Holy Land. The focus of Jewish life had shifted to exile. The great problem was survival in exile. This situation continued from the year 70, when the Romans broke Jerusalem and the ancient Jewish commonwealth, to the birth of a new state of Israel in 1948. The possibility now exists, for the first time in two millennia, that the center of Jewish life can shift back to the Holy Land. But most of the Jews in the world are still outside Israel; and the confrontation of an exile Judaism with a swiftly developing Israeli outlook is the most exciting part of modern Jewish life.

The Talmud is not the only surviving work of the era of the sages. There are many compilations of law like Tosefta, Sifra, and Sifri, and of hagada, like the Great Midrash. A modern legal authority is expected to be at home in all this literature.

p. 181. . . . the Jews' mystery book.

THE CABALA

Many people loosely link the Talmud with the Cabala, since both books are Hebrew lore, mysterious and recondite even to the educated person. But the books have no relation whatever to each other.

The Talmud, as I have indicated, is our main source of common law. Its difficulty arises from its compression and — in the legal debates — its frequent abstruseness. But it is a wholly hard and declarative book. Its light is the light of day. It yields all its contents to the trained and sharply questioning legal mind. Its tools are learning, facts, logic, and inquiry, the classic tools of intelligence.

The Cabala, on the other hand, dwells in the moonlit landscape of mysticism, and its light is the phosphorescence of occult imagination. It is a separate and arcane study for the few. Its status is outside the main line of authoritative tradition, and it has no bearing on our law, though for its followers it has had, in recurring mystic sects, a marked influence on thought and conduct. There is a luxuriant body of cabalistic writing, some of it bearing the names of famous rabbis. All these mystic compositions cluster around one strange, very controversial book, the *Zohar,* or Radiance. This is the work that the gossip of centuries has referred to, usually in whispers, as "The Cabala." There is no need to whisper anymore. A full translation in English exists, and anybody can read it who wants to. Everyday light is not kind to the text. I am certain that cabalists would declare all translation hopeless and worthless.

The Zohar is written in difficult Aramaic and presents an opaque surface even to a person who can read the Talmud. In form it is a running commentary on the Pentateuch, but the Scripture words are only the launching platforms, one might say, from which the rockets of esoteric fancy soar. Hidden meanings, worlds beyond worlds, angelic and demonic hosts, supernaturally powerful numbers and names abound. I know learned men who study this work with delight, and others equally learned who put it aside as confusing and destructive.

The important writers on Jewish literature divide over the Cabala. Some attack it freely. An importation of Zoroastrian angelology and black magic into a rational faith, they call it; a sterile, exhausting diversion of the intelligence. Others find, under the puzzling language and dark parabolic allegories, great poetry and vision. It has a dynamic charge of inspirational energy, without a doubt; the Zohar is the source of the Hasidic movement, a powerful outburst of Jewish religious vigor in recent times.

Its origin is as obscure as its diction. Its devotees attribute it to an early Tanna, Simon ben Yokhai. Scholars report that it is a thirteenth-century compilation of older material. My grandfather did not study the Zohar, and recommended that I put my time into Talmudic studies; and the occasional amateur sallies I have made into Cabala have, inevitably, left me puzzled. Though the study is not part of general learning but an esoteric art, scholars of note, including some among the living, have called it a main Jewish source of strength and light. If it be so, it is certainly not available to the ordinary intelligence as the Scriptures and the Talmud are; and that is all, in my present ignorance, that I can report.*

Martin Buber's *For the Sake of Heaven* is a vivid and pathetic picture of the attempts of nineteenth-century cabalists to influence the course of the Napoleonic wars with occult incantations. One can find wry irony and humor in the account, but there was nothing comic in the great surge of cabalism called the Sabbatian movement, a century earlier. Thousands of Jews become hypnotically convinced that a strange young dreamer from Smyrna named Sabbatai Zvi was the Messiah. He drew all his followers at first from the cabalists, but his movement grew to a mass hysteria. Its end was anarchy in the ghetto, much loss of life and treasure, and horrible disillusionment. The "messiah" converted

* See my further comment in *References,* at the end of these notes, on the works of Gershom Scholem.— HW (1987)

to Islam to save his life and became a menial in the Turkish court. Even yet the remembrance of this tragic movement has not died out. There are obscure pockets of Sabbatians who still believe. The reader will find in a recent book by the former President of Israel, Itzhak ben Zevi, *The Exiled and the Redeemed,* an amazing account of a certain crypto-Jewish sect in Turkey whose liturgy calls yet on the unlucky name of Sabbatai Zvi. The President's book contains absorbing accounts of other strange sects of Jewry coming to light in the return to Israel.

CHAPTER 16. JEWISH COMMON LAW

p. 183. The Torah, for instance, allowed slavery; Jewish law no longer does.

THE TORAH AND SLAVERY

It is often asked why the Torah did not abolish slavery.

The Torah reports the great intervention of God in human history as a deliverance of slaves. Its civil legislation begins (Exodus 21) by limiting the power of indenture, hedging the ownership of slaves with difficulties, and prescribing freedom for slaves as recompense for certain injuries. The common law made slave ownership so difficult that the Talmud says, "He who buys a slave, buys a master." This was especially true of a Hebrew servant; no power could keep him longer than seven years, unless he formally asked a court to make his status permanent, and even then he was forcibly freed at the jubilee.

The universal economics of ancient times rested on bonded labor. Jews captured in war automatically became bondmen, and they made bondmen of their captives. The Torah could not have changed this without a miraculous springing into existence of the industrial advances which made bonded labor an anachronism. The development of machinery is a historic process, not a matter of inspired or wise legislation. Three thousand years ago slavery could not be abolished, but the teaching that slavery was an evil, and the start toward its abolition, were possible. Moses described his law as immediately practicable — "it is not in the heavens, or beyond the seas." It had to take effect and start operating in 1200 B.C. The economic laws of the Torah changed with changing times, by the amending process described in this chapter, provided for by Moses.

p. 185. undertakings like Sadduceeism and Karaism.

We know little about the Sadducees. They were a sect in Talmudic times, apparently associated with the Hellenist element in the priesthood. They are quoted as opponents of the Talmudists in debate. They vanished long ago without a trace, except for the Talmudic record and some references in the New Testament and in Josephus.

The Karaites made the only serious bid in Jewish history to reject the common law, the body of tradition coming down through the Talmud, and to live only by the law of Moses as written in the Torah. Their movement began in the eighth century as a political move against the Gaonate. Their main contention — not unfamiliar to modern ears — was that the rabbis had imposed a man-made superstructure on Mosaic law, and that their teachings had no binding force. The history of the movement is informative and melancholy.

The Torah, like any statutory law, is too brief to cover instances. One needs common law to relate it to the broad span and multiple detail of everyday life. Reject the common law that descends from prophetic times, and you are forced to improvise a common law of your own. That is what the Karaites did. Within a couple of generations they had a sort of Karaite Talmud and code law in some details more liberal and in many others far more harsh than traditional Judaism. The movement drifted into grotesqueness in the effort to avoid following the customs and practices of the main tradition. Karaism once had considerable vigor, and produced notable scholars. It is now virtually extinct. A few families survive in Asia Minor, and they are mostly moving to Israel.

In the Yale Judaica series there is an excellent book on Karaism, *Karaite Anthology*. The name derives from the Hebrew root *kara,* meaning the written word in the Torah.

p. 188. Certain teachers of this oral law were foremost in intellectual and moral prestige . . .

I wonder if any other nation or religion has a group in its past just like the Jewish Talmudists, affectionately called "the Hazal" — initial letters in Hebrew for the *Wise, may their memory be a blessing*. Their sayings, their ideas, their conduct burn in the Jewish mind as a steady light. "Our Hazal said . . . The Hazal decided . . . As the Hazal put it . . ." They were not saints, but everyday men, many of them menial laborers, a few of them vastly wealthy. The period of the Pharisees was one of an unusual intellectual democracy. Only three things counted for eminence: learning, piety, and brains. These values carried through all the ghetto generations. Up to the twentieth century a rich merchant family whose daughter married a penniless but brilliant scholar was acknowledged to have scored a great match, a link with the elite. In our own time this value system has paled, whether for the moment or for ever nobody can say. But the Jewish regard for learning, if generalized now to the arts and sciences, remains an obvious trait of our people. It comes from the influence and the example of the Hazal.

CHAPTER 17. FROM THE TALMUD TO THE PRESENT

This chapter will, of all I have written, perhaps most offend and shock any scholar who reads this far, with its staggering omissions and compressions. What, to discuss the Rishonim without mentioning Rabbenu Gershom, the Ramban, the Rashbo, and a dozen other great luminaries; to put them together in one meager chapter with the Akharonim, and to gloss completely over this last huge stratum of jurists, the source of most of our present-day rulings; to pass by Jewish medieval poetry and philosophy, with not a word of Judah Halevi, Ibn Gabirol, and the master liturgists; to keep silence about tremendous figures like Radak and Ibn Ezra; to mention the Vilna Gaon, in passing, instead of giving him a chapter; does such compression leave any information worthy of the name?

It is precisely here that I have cut thousands and thousands of words that I wrote with pleasure and with care. I was told — I am sure correctly — that I could not hope to carry the general reader through a detailed review of a thousand years of a complicated and many-sided legal literature. For all I know, the reader finds even the material that remains an academic tale.

If I were to give myself back some of that lost space, I would dwell on Ibn Ezra, I think, and the M'iri of Perpignan, two teachers who have helped me as none have save Rashi. If this account proves of any value, I may someday tell of these men in another book. Here I have tried to give the reader the main line of Jewish law. A bird's-eye view takes in a lot of ground, but with great loss of detail.

p. 193. The Gaonim were university presidents . . .

Saadya, son of Joseph, one of the last of the Gaonim, is the best known. It is a mark of the westward drift of the Jewish people at this time that he was born in Egypt. Summoned to Sura, one of the two great Babylonian schools, to assume the Gaonate in his thirties, he brought to Babylon the new spirit of the dispersion, an inquiring turn of mind caught by the challenge of Western culture. His writings, the sunset burst of the Gaonate, prefigure the era about to dawn. The questions that trouble the modern mind troubled Saadya. His *Book of Beliefs and Reasons* is in essence the kind of work that Jewish thinkers have been writing ever since, a confronting of the Mosaic heritage with the ideas of the West. It is wholly medieval in spirit, but not the less full of wisdom and sense.

p. 197. He had been brazen enough to lay down the law of Judaism without citing his authorities . . .

Maimonides' "armor-bearers," the commentators, have long since supplied the Mishna Torah's deficiency in source references; we know where he derived all his rulings, and we know which rulings are original with him.

p. 198. "Guide for the Perplexed."

GENERAL NOTE

The second great work of Maimonides, his *Guide for the Perplexed,* threw oil on the blaze of opposition, for in it he dealt wholly with what we could call the conflict of science and religion. As if to underline its modern nature, he composed it in Arabic, the English of his time and place. Setting Judaism against Aristotelian and Mohammedan philosophy, he made out a case for our faith, which in an evolved vocabulary still holds the field. He took on all the big questions of moral inquiry: the problem of evil, free will versus fatalism, the nature of God, the difficulties of Scripture, the possibility of revelation. A good grounding in Greek philosophy and at least an elementary grasp of medieval Christian and Mohammedan thought are needed if one is to cope with the Guide. Aquinas and the later Catholic scholastics, as well as Mohammedan philosophers, are said to be in debt to the Rambam. The rabbinic judgment is that the Guide, probably understood, stands as the supreme effort of a Talmudic master in the essentially external field of speculative metaphysics; in parts most brilliant but in parts most disturbing.

What my grandfather would think if he knew that the awesome *Guide for the Perplexed* was available in a paper-bound English translation for less than two dollars, and that American college boys skimmed it in a weekend and wrote confident twenty-page themes on it, I cannot imagine. My grandfather always retained the impression that America, at least the Jewish part he knew, was more or less mad.

Maimonides wrote a number of other works. The one I know best is his commentary on the Mishna, originally composed in Arabic, a marvel of clear thinking and clear writing. It makes no sense to attack any treatise of the Talmud without first reading the Rambam's discussion of the Mishna; he saves you weeks of time, by diagramming the theme and structure of the law discussion. It is interesting that the fine commentators, men like Rambam, Rashi, Ibn Ezra, Malbim, are all first-rate writers.

p. 198. the standing of Maimonides . . .

Perhaps the final irony in the story of this irony-haunted great career is the form in which the Mishna Torah appears today. A main intent of Rambam's, you recall, was to avoid the conflict of authorities by giving the reader clear halakha and nothing else. One of his more violent opponents, a French Talmudist named Abraham ben David, wrote a scathing chapter-by-chapter polemic against the Mishna Torah; and this commentary (the Ravad) is printed in all editions of the Rambam's work — in smaller type, to be sure — thrust like a thorn into the smooth side of the Maimon text, making jagged lines where the author planned clean straight ones. The armor-bearers, naturally, come to the Rambam's defense. Dispute rages, sometimes three- or four-cornered, often acrid, on almost every page of the book that was written to end dispute.

Nor is there malice or adverse judgment in this practice of the printers. They are following the old Jewish instinct for preserving diversity of opinion and arriving at law through the clash of minds. There is only one last word, the Torah. The rest of the tradition comes down to us balanced in debate. It was no accident that the Mishna reported dissenting opinions throughout, or that the Gemara took the very form of continuous dispute. Talmudic learning is the review of old battles. One comes to the heart of a matter by studying what two sides thought of it; and in the yeshiva, the student must be able to show the logic in the rejected views of Shammai, as well as in the Hillel ruling. Maimonides offered Jewry the one gift it will never accept from anybody, except possibly the Messiah: an end to controversy.

p. 199. another great code-maker, the Tur . . .

"The Tur" is so called because he divided his code into four sections or rows (turim) corresponding to the four rows of gems on the breastplate of the high priest. His name was Rabbi Jacob ben Asher, and he lived in Germany in the fourteenth century. Germanic Hebrew learning, which forms an immense library, is exhaustive and exact. German Jewry for centuries was noted for piety; only after the enlightenment did the term "a deutsch" in Yiddish come to mean a westernized agnostic.

p. 201. *As Caro returned to the Holy Land, so his handbook returned to the plain law . . .*

Living in Spanish and then Palestinian circles, Caro wrote the law according to Sefard or Mediterranean tradition. There was already a well-formed second branch of exile learning, the Ashkenaz or German tradition, centered in Teutonic lands; the word "Ashkenaz" is a Scriptural name for one of the Noah families spreading through the earth after the deluge, and Jewish learning has always identified it with Germany. Writers like to say that the Ashkenaz practice is more austere, and the tone of its learning more heavy and stern, than that of its Southern counterpart. One recalls the general contrast of the Latin and Northern temperaments, and a temptation rises to draw conclusions about the influence of climate on thought and law. I doubt that a serious analysis would sustain this simple notion as applied to Jewish literature. Both traditions have their points of severity and leniency. The codes of the Southerners, Maimonides and Caro, will be found rigorous enough, I should think, for the most stringent taste.

Nevertheless, to bring Caro's code into the Northern learning, it was necessary to amend it step by step on Ashkenaz lines. Rabbi Moses Isserles (the Ramo) of Cracow, Poland, executed this task in a running gloss on The Ready Table called the Tablecloth. His writing is not an attack on Caro's, but a respectful dissent, and a statement of Ashkenaz practice, at all points where the two traditions differ. Today his gloss appears in all editions of the Table, as a series of parentheses in the Caro text itself. So Isserles achieved a dependent but permanent place in the main line of law writing.

p. 201. *My grandfather's personal law library . . .*

My grandfather's books are now a separate collection in the master library of the Chief Rabbi of Israel, housed in the imposing edifice in Jerusalem called Hechal Shlomo, the central religious court. His collection contains, of course, all the main codes and authorities as well as the specialists' volumes which distinguish it. But works like the Talmud, the Rambam, and the Shulkhan Arukh have been reprinted so often, in so many editions, that they are readily available, new and secondhand. He had dozens of books that are virtually irreplaceable.

p. 203. The candidates undergo a bar examination in Hebrew law — the semikha test . . .

The title "rabbi" is conferred in the dissenting denominations as well as in orthodoxy. Reform Judaism does not recognize the force of Mosaic ordinances or the common law, and so does not confer semikha. Its seminarists study the law as part of history. Conservative Judaism does not require semikha for the title of "rabbi"; it grants the title to divinity students who pass less extensive tests as teachers and preachers. It also gives some students semikha. All orthodox rabbis must have semikha. There is the general degree, and there are advanced degrees for scholars who master special fields.

p. 204. With the fall of the Jewish State in the year 70, the Mosaic civil and criminal law, by the edict of its own jurists, gave place to the . . . laws of lands where the Jews lived.

(1987) While this statement may be strictly true, it does not quite reflect the course of civil and criminal Halakha after the year 70. In later periods, in some lands, Jewish diaspora communities achieved a large measure of autonomy, and the Halakha continued as a general rule of law. But the Jewish administrators functioned by the sufferance of overlords; and they often earned their autonomy by facilitating the collection of taxes from the Jews.

Readers interested in the post-Talmudic history of Halakha should consult two outstanding articles in the *Encyclopaedia Judaica: Codification of Law* and *Mishpat Ivri,* written by a Supreme Court Justice of Israel, Professor Menachem Elon. Justice Elon is a master of the recondite field called *Responsa* — written opinions of Torah sages down the centuries to the present day — in which Halakhic precedents have developed to meet changing conditions.

The Enlightenment disrupted this vitalizing process. Elon astutely points out that as emancipated Jewry more and more turned to secular courts, the rabbinic authorities found their scope narrowing, their power dwindling. The reach of the Halakha, once a binding force of dispersed Jewry, contracted toward purely religious areas, such as problems of personal status and questions of ritual, with a concomitant splintering in Judaism. In Israel these separated streams of civil and religious law once again converge, with sometimes turbulent effect. But as the center of gravity of Jewry shifts to Israel, scholars of Menachem Elon's stature are lighting the long, difficult way to reconciliation and understanding.

CHAPTER 20. ORTHODOXY

p. 216. The base of primary teaching is in the all-day or day schools.

DAY SCHOOLS

Day schools oppose the democratic idea, some critics say, by segregating children because of religion. Jewish parents who share this view express their opposition by not enrolling their children. The purpose here is not to settle the question, which remains in active debate. Some points are clear. No workable way of keeping the Mosaic law alive in modern times has been found, except the new learning. The old separatist learning is gone. The Talmud Torah was a stopgap, and it still gives a useful elementary training to many children. The Sunday school offers a sort of bare orientation, but the imparting of a culture like Judaism in an hour or two a week is not possible. It is to be the new learning or nothing, evidently. There are many Jews to whom a knowledge of Judaism in depth seems superfluous, and to them the day schools have no value. For the orthodox they are becoming a standard instruction instrument.

One might say that all private schools segregate children for one purpose or another. *Segregate* is the bad word; *select* is the good word. One's bias makes one's vocabulary. Judaism has always revolved around a deep and broad intellectual discipline.

The day school is an effort to keep it alive in modern life. Whether one thinks this aim attainable or desirable is another matter. Certainly for a great number of parents and children the curriculum is too demanding, and the Hebrew learning too intensive; and public schools, or non-religious private schools, suit their tastes better.

CHAPTER 21. DISSENT

p. 222. the two religious structures in Jewry outside orthodoxy.

There are smaller movements of dissent, like Reconstruction and Jewish Science. But there are no serious rivals to Conservatism and Reform, which have followings all through the United States, and some congregations in Europe and Africa. Outside America orthodoxy is the almost uncontested main communion.

Reconstruction, which stresses a sociological and cultural approach, centers on one distinguished preacher and writer, Dr. Mordecai Kaplan. In practice Reconstruction is like Conservatism. Dr. Kaplan had a brilliant associate, Rabbi Milton Steinberg, who unfortunately died very young.

p. 223. Traditional rabbis fought Reform hard . . .

At the height of the Reform drive in Germany, there were strong counterattacks by enlightened advocates of orthodoxy, men like Moses Mendelssohn and Samson Raphael Hirsch. But they were speaking against the storm. Today the ideas of Hirsch are an important part of the orthodox revival. His *Nineteen Letters of Ben Uzziel* is still a readable and forceful book.

CHAPTER 22. ISRAEL

p. 236. After Titus razed Jerusalem, the Jews . . persisted in looking toward Zion . . .

Zionism itself begins in the prehistoric past, on the day that Abraham left his home in Mesopotamia to come to Palestine. The Exodus from Egypt under Moses was the first national act of Zionism. Hebrew Scripture in all its books narrates the bond between the Jewish people and Zion, the Holy Land. When a child first begins to study the Torah he finds Rashi saying — in the first note on the first verse — that the account of creation sets the moral basis for the Hebrew inheritance of Zion. Zion is a commanding mount in Jerusalem, the old capital city of the Holy Land; but the name since Bible times has stood for the mystic soil itself.

p. 243. The socialism of Israel today seems to me a far from crusading ideology.

In the farm communes, the remarkable *kibbutzim,* the socialist ideal lives as a flame still — there, I believe, as nowhere in all the vast lands behind the iron curtain. "From each according to his ability, to each according to his need" is no slogan there, but the law of daily life. Some young people leave the communes; the demand on human nature is too hard. But others found new communes, deliberately selecting danger areas at the borders to farm, so as to create strong military points with their work, as well as productive fields. But I believe the spring of this idealistic movement is the instinct to build and defend the land, not the abstractions of socialism, though socialism writes the slogans. There are religious and irreligious communes. No visitor should miss seeing them; they are wonders.

EPILOGUE

p. 250. I was gambling my whole existence on one hunch . . .

The decision to experiment with one's life by taking up the laws of Jewry does not even now seem to me a steep or wild gamble. At worst one undertakes a challenging scheme of study and action while giving up certain foods, some freedom of movement on sacred days, and random ease of manners, for a chance at rejoining a great mainstream of ideas and — this is the real stake — a hope for finding God. I have gone into wilder ventures with no comparable stake to be gained. I see no "leap to an absurdity" such as the existentialists prescribe for the modern religionist. What is absurd in Judaism? The Torah is there. Its heroes are human. Its history is accurate. Its religious imagery is immortal. Its disciplines are understandable. Moses is as persuasive a lawgiver as any that ever lived. The Prophets are apostles of the social justice that the whole world seeks today. Is it absurd to look for God? It is just as absurd not to look for him, life today being what it is. No man can make the decision except out of the impulse of his heart, but he can make it without taking leave of his senses or his critical intelligence. It may be, quite the other way, that his critical intelligence will force the decision.

p. 258. Hitler saw himself as the apostle in action of . . . Nietzsche. . . .

NIETZSCHE AND THE NAZIS

During the Hitler era there was a widespread tendency, carefully promoted by the Nazis themselves, to equate the thought of Nietzsche with the doctrines of Nazism. This was an injustice to one of the most extraordinary minds of recent centuries. Nietzsche was no more a Nazi than he was a Holy Roller. He wrote a savage critique of European society which proved in some respects alarmingly prophetic. His style was romantic, wild, often obscure, yet on balance perhaps no philosopher since Plato has written more vividly and electrically.

His books are full of anti-Semitic sentences and paragraphs. But they equally heap scorn on the anti-Semitic movement, which he considered evil and moronic. Nietzsche's opposition to the Jews came from his insight into their place in the world. He deeply respected the Hebrew Bible, and accepted it as the true origin of the Christian civilization, which he thought was sick to death. The Jew was for him the figure of a "life-denying" morality which it was the Nietzschean mission to destroy. He was, in his own words, the first immoralist. But his abuse of the Jews was philosophical polemic, not a cry to raise the mob.

This being clear, it remains to be said that — at least to my mind — Nietzsche's grave has blood on it; that his intemperate (and I believe often unbalanced) use of his great pen helped open the floodgates of twentieth-century barbarism. Here are his own words in *Ecce Homo,* his valedictory work before his mind broke:

> I am a joyful herald, unparalleled in history; I am acquainted with tasks of a grandeur formerly inconceivable. Hope is reborn with me. Thus, I am necessarily a Man of Destiny. For when Truth engages in struggle with the falsehood of ages, we must expect shocks and a series of earthquakes, with a rearrangement of hills and valleys, such as has never yet been dreamed of. The concept of "politics" is thus raised bodily into the realm of spiritual warfare. All the mighty forms of the old society are blown into space — for they all rest on falsehood: there will be wars, whose like have never been seen on earth before. Politics on a grand scale will date from me. . . .
>
> I am by far the most terrible man that has ever existed; but this does not negate the fact that I shall be the most beneficent. I know the joy of *annihilation* to a degree commensurate with my power to annihilate. In both cases I obey my Dionysian nature, which cannot separate the negative deed from yea-saying. I am the first immoralist, and thus I am the essential destroyer.

Anyone who has read the main work of Nietzsche will agree, I think, that this is not a passage wrenched from context, but a representative statement.

It is impossible to imagine that Hitler was not influenced by this destroying-angel vein of Nietzsche. It sounds through *Mein Kampf,* at times tinny and squeaky, at times howling and booming, always off-key and discordant, but the same tune. One can picture Hitler taking this very passage as his daily devotion, reciting it in the morning and at night as the pious man says his prayers. A man who would do so could order the slaughters at Auschwitz and Belsen, or even inspect the piles of dead women and children, and still sleep a sound eight hours that night.

If Nietzsche's first crop of dancing, laughing, sunlit supermen, the clear-eyed glad-hearted yea-sayers, the hard immoralist worshippers of Dionysos, turned out to be the scum of the German psychotic wards, that fact does not prove or disprove Nietzsche's critique of Europe. It is a historic comment that men of intelligence are still digesting.

Thinkers like Albert Camus and Walter Kaufmann, dedicated to the proposition that man must find his integrity in a world without God, are rightly at the greatest pains to dissociate Nietzsche from the Nazis. The case for godlessness has never been stated more vigorously than Nietzsche put it, nor is it likely to be soon; and the godless men of good will in our time (such men have existed ever since Epicurus) cannot abide the calculated perversion of this master statement into a mere anticipation of the ravings of Goebbels. In Kaufmann's excellent book on Nietzsche there is a final refutation, fully documented, of this error.

The Nazis vulgarized Nietzsche, misconstrued him, used him falsely. But that he was wide open to this misuse, that his influence on mediocre minds was gravely and massively pernicious, and that he unwittingly gave murdering nihilists a respectable and coruscating vocabulary of ideas and party cries — these things remain to my mind, with all deference to Nietzsche's formidable defenders, plain facts of the recent past. These facts do not render Nietzsche's masterpieces any the less worth serious study.

References

SINCE 1959, when *This Is My God* first appeared, there has been a publishing explosion of books in English on Judaic themes. The appearance in 1972 of the *Encyclopaedia Judaica* has transformed the scene. Keter Publishing House, Jerusalem, produced it in the phenomenal time of five years, employing a galaxy of scholars and authorities. All encyclopedias are uneven in readability and quality, and all require frequent updating. A second edition of the *Encyclopaedia* will be very welcome. But as it stands, it offers a broad survey of Judaism, Jewry, and Jewish history, beyond compare for grandeur, completeness, readability, and sheer fascination; and for each important entry it provides a bibliography. A home library in Judaism should start with the *Encyclopaedia,* and no library in a synagogue, temple, or Hebrew school should be without this masterly reference work in sixteen volumes.

Among the books referred to in my text and notes, *The Lonely Crowd* may have fallen out of fashion; but *The Theory of the Leisure Class* and *Democracy in America* hold their own as classics. Existentialism is no longer the *dernier cri* it was in 1959, though its leading authors like Kierkegaard and Sartre still speak to the thoughtful mind.

I have made no attempt to list the many hundreds of books on Jewish themes, scholarly and popular, which have appeared in recent decades. The *Encyclopaedia* is a good guide to these, and no university library is without its Judaica section. I recommend a very few works herewith; not as excluding others of comparable value, but as a personal choice, for the way these books have helped my own thinking.

First and foremost there is *The Destruction of the European Jews* by Professor Raul Hilberg of the University of Vermont. In the course of writing my novels *The Winds of War* and *War and Remembrance,* I must have read or examined nearly all the serious literature on the German massacre that then existed. Significant books have since appeared, but Hilberg's monumental work — reticent in tone, somberly ironic in style, epic in scope — still stands alone, in my judgment, for completeness and grasp. It is one of the masterpieces of the century. Recently it has been reprinted in a revised three-volume edition; the whole stunning tragic story, as well as it will ever be told.

On the development and realization of the idea of the Jewish State, I recommend two linked volumes by David Vital of Tel Aviv University, *The Origins of Zionism* and *Zionism, the Formative Years.* The Irish historian Conor Cruise O'Brien, in his book *The Siege,* offers a swift insightful panorama of the hundred-year history of Israel, beginning with the pogroms in Eastern Europe which generated the seminal Lovers of Zion movement, and sweeping through all the wars to the present day. The writings of the British historian Martin Gilbert on Jewish subjects are especially informative and moving.

For readers interested in Cabala and Jewish mysticism, the writings of Gershom Scholem have opened up that long-sealed garden of the Jewish spirit. In 1959 I remarked, in my sparse note on the Cabala, pp. 317–319, "that is all, in my present ignorance, that I can report." Gershom Scholem's books, and his voluminous articles in the *Encyclopaedia Judaica,* have been an education for me, and I have since done some study in the original Aramaic classics. They remain difficult writings for the western-trained mind; but Scholem has shown beyond question their consequence in our heritage.

— HW (1987)

GLOSSARY

Glossary

PRONUNCIATION of Hebrew differs regionally. And certain terms in familiar usage, especially if they have been adopted into Yiddish, take on a sound often very remote from classic Hebrew. A couple of letters in Hebrew do not exist in English and cannot be duplicated. These facts make transliteration an approximate and unsatisfying business. I have tried to invent transliterations, or to use those already existing, which the reader will naturally pronounce in a way close to familiar Hebrew.*

In classic and Israeli Hebrew the stress is almost always on the last syllable of a word. Popular usage in the United States, derived mostly from East Europe, often stresses the next to last. Thus, the word *menorah,* meaning candelabra: Israeli, mĕ-noh-*rah;* American, usually mĕ-*noe*-ruh; not to mention the extensive group that says m'*nay*-reh, the Lithuanian variation.

Pronunciations are indicated only where mispronunciation is likely to occur.

Hebrew has two throat letters, the *hes* and the *khaf,* both of which are spoken something like the *gh* in ugh, or the German *ch* in *macht.* I have seen many attempts to reproduce this sound

* NOTE: Readers fluent in modern Israeli Hebrew — as I have become myself — will be jarred by the usage here of the Ashkenazic, or Northern European, soft *taf* when it lacks the *dagesh* — *s* instead of *t,* as in Atzeres [*t*]. This usage, natural to me thirty years ago and still widespread in America, reflects my upbringing by Russian-born parents, and I leave it as I wrote it. — HW, 1987.

in English lettering, none successful. For want of a better way, I use either kh or h, depending on the euphony of the word.

Ad'lo Yoda — "Until he cannot tell the difference." The name of the Israeli street pageant on the Purim holiday, derived from a Talmud saying that a man may drink on this holiday until he cannot tell the difference between the hero and the villain of the Purim story.

Akeda — ă-kay-da. "Binding." The great event in Genesis when Abraham met a supreme test of his faith and bound his son on an altar, prepared to sacrifice him at God's command. God forbade him to do so, and a ram was sacrificed instead.

Akharonim — ă-kha-roe-nim. "The Later Ones." Jewish jurists and commentators from about the seventeenth century to the present day.

aliya — ă-lee-â. "Going up." A call to the reading stand to pronounce a blessing over a portion of the Torah. Also, immigration to Palestine.

Amora'im — "The Commentators." The stratum of jurists who produced the Gemara, the report of legal debates making up the bulk of the Talmud. They flourished in Babylon and Palestine in the third, fourth, and fifth centuries.

Atzeres — ă-tseh-ress. A final assembly day. Talmudic name for Pentecost (Shavuos), also the name of the day that closes the Sukos autumn festival.

Av or *Ab* — Eleventh month in the Hebrew calendar, falling in midsummer.

bar-mitzva — "Son of the commandment." The ceremony marking a boy's thirteenth birthday, when he takes on religious responsibility for his own conduct, and begins to pray as an adult and to count in a quorum for worship.

bas-mitzva — A modern ceremony for girls instituted in the Reform and Conservative movements to parallel the bar-mitzva.

bris — "Covenant." A circumcision ceremony.

Cabala — "Tradition." The esoteric body of mystic literature centered in the Zohar, especially important in Hasidic thought and practice.

dino d'malkuto dino — dee-noh d'mal-khoo-toh dee-noh. "The law of the government is binding law." This famous Talmudic ruling, made in the Babylonian exile by the Amora Samuel (third century), became the basis for the civic loyalty of Jews outside the Holy Land. It gives to the law of the lands where they dwell the full force of religious law.

dreidl — dray-dl. A four-sided top used in a children's put-and-take game on Hanuka.

esrog — The lemon-like fruit, native to Palestine, used in the harvest ceremonies of the Sukos (Tabernacles) holiday.

Gaonim — "Eminences." Presidents of the two major Babylonian academies at Sura and Pumpeditha, the ruling legal authorities in Jewry from the fifth to the tenth century.

Gehenna — "Valley of Hinnom." In parable, the place of retribution after death. The Valley of Hinnom in Jerusalem is by tradition the place where human sacrifices were burned in Canaanite idolatry.

Gemara — "Completion." Record of the debates on the common law in the academies of Babylon and Palestine, third to fifth century, forming with the Mishna (see p. 341) the text of the Talmud.

gezera — ge-zay-ra. "Decree." The rulings of ordained sages in the traditional line of legal competence, by which the common law has met changing social and economic conditions.

gilgul — "Rolling." The concept of reincarnation, an important feature of cabalism.

glat kosher — "Flawlessly fit." Meat guaranteed by high religious authority to have been slaughtered according to law, and to have been found free of doubtful symptoms.

hagada — "Telling," or story. The second side of Jewish literature and tradition, the first side of which is *halakha*, the law. Hagada embraces all the varieties of ethical, poetic, historic, scientific, and imaginative discourse found in classic Judaism. "*The* Hagada" is the retelling of the Exodus tale, an ancient book read in chorus at the Passover feast, the *seder*.

halakha — "The way, or the going." The Jewish law, originating in the statutory Torah of Moses, and spelled out in detail in the oral law (*lex non scripta*) and thereafter in the codes, decisions, rulings, and digests of the recorded common law, down to the present day.

Hanuka — "Dedication." The feast of lights, celebrating the rededication of the Second Temple after the military victory of the Maccabees over the Seleucid Greeks.

Haskala — "Enlightenment." The introduction of modern Western culture into the European ghettos, a matter of crucial controversy in the nineteenth century.

heder — khay-der. "Room." The schoolroom of the ghetto, briefly used by American immigrants in the early twentieth century, replaced by the Talmud Torah and day-school systems.

kaddish — "Sanctification." An ancient Aramaic and Hebrew prose-poem in the liturgy which closes various sections of a congregational service, recited by the prayer leader when a quorum of ten is present. The last *kaddish* in a service is recited in unison by mourners.

Karaites — Devotees of the written law, from *kara,* the reading, which means the Torah. A movement arising in the eighth century which denied the authenticity and therefore the force of the common law in the Talmud and its subsequent lines of rabbinic jurists. Karaism in time evolved its own common law, with bizarre variations from the main tradition. It lasted with dwindling energy and adherents until the nineteenth century, and is now virtually extinct.

keenos — "Lamentations." Medieval poems of mourning for the fall of Zion, in the Ninth of Av liturgy.

kibbutzim — kee-boo-tzim. Communal settlements in Israel, mainly agricultural.

Kol Nidre — "All the vows." A prayer in Aramaic sung at the start of the evening service of Yom Kippur, cancelling ill-considered religious vows or vows made under duress, as in times of religious persecution.

Lag B'Omer — "Thirty-third day in the omer." See *omer* and *Sefira,* p. 342. On Lag B'Omer the mourning customs of the *Sefira* period are suspended.

latka — A pancake, usually of potato batter.

lulav — The palm branch used with the *esrog* in the liturgical harvest rites of Sukos (Tabernacles).

maftir — "He who concludes." The last call to the reading of the Torah on Sabbaths and holy days, which includes a reading of a selection from the prophets, the *haftorah*.

maggid — "Teller." A popular preacher.

maikil — may-kil. "One who lightens." A jurist known for liberal construction of the law. Opposed to *makhmir*, "one who is severe," a strict constructionist.

mashgiah — mash-gee-ah. "Overseer." An inspector who assures ritual fitness of food; also a headmaster in a yeshiva.

matzo — Unleavened bread, eaten during the Passover.

Megillah — "Roll," or scroll. Five books of the Bible are called scrolls in tradition: the Song of Songs, Ruth, Ecclesiastes, Lamentations, and Esther; the last is the one popularly referred to by this term.

melamed — "One who teaches." Elementary Hebrew instructor in former times, especially in Eastern European Jewry, and in immigrant communities of such origin.

menorah — Candelabra, used on Hanuka. It was one of the sacred vessels in the desert sanctuary and in the two Temples.

meturgeman — A translator. The meturgeman in Talmudic times translated the Hebrew lectures of the sages into Aramaic as they spoke.

mezuza — A doorpost; by extension the boxed scroll containing the Sh'ma with other Bible passages fastened on the doorposts of Jewish homes.

Midrash — "Interpretation." The enormous body of parables, tales, and homilies in classic Judaism, based on exegesis of Scriptural passages.

mikva — "A gathering [of waters]." Ritual pool for immersions of purification and dedication.

minyan — "Counting, or quorum." Ten male worshippers over the age of thirteen, the quorum for reciting certain congregational prayers like the *kaddish* (see p. 340).

Mishna — "The Teaching." A systematic digest of the oral common law, compiled and recorded by Rabbi Judah the Prince of Palestine at the end of the second century. Universally accepted, it became the core of the Talmud.

Mishna Torah, or *Mishneh Torah* — "Second Torah." The great medieval code of Jewish law written by Maimonides in the twelfth century.

mohel — A circumciser.

Musaf — The additional service on Sabbath and holidays, recited after the morning service.

Neturai Karta — "Guardians of the City." A small sect of ultra-zealous Jews living in Jerusalem.

nigun — "Melody." The traditional chanting of the services; the melodies change according to the holy seasons and the time of day.

Nisan — The seventh month of the Hebrew calendar, the spring month in which the Passover falls at full moon.

omer — A Hebrew dry measure, probably between three and four quarts. An omer of barley was brought to the Temple as an offering on the second day of Passover, at the start of the barley harvest. See *Sefira*.

Pesakh — pay-sokh. The Passover holy days.

Purim — The Feast of Esther.

Rishonim — ree-show-nim. "The First Ones." The group of Hebrew jurists and commentators, living mostly in Europe and in the Mediterranean littoral, who carried forward the common law from the tenth to the seventeenth century.

Rosh Hashana — "Start of the year." The Hebrew New Year, falling in the autumn on the new moon near the autumnal equinox.

Savora'im — "Reasoners" or reflecters. Post-Talmudic editors and jurists, about the sixth to eighth century.

seder — say-der. "Order." The Passover banquet, so called because it follows a traditional order of ceremonies, symbols, chants, and prayers, found in the *Hagada* (see p. 339).

Sefira — "Counting." The period of seven weeks counted off day by day from the second day of Passover to Pentecost (*Shavuos*). Also called the counting of the omer, because it commenced with the bringing of the measure of barley to the Temple. In our times a period of national semi-mourning. See the chapter on "The Nature Festivals."

semikha — "Bringing near, or laying on." The ceremony of ordination of a Hebrew jurist, also the academic degree thereby conferred, equivalent to Doctor of Laws. Required in the orthodox rabbinate.

Shabbat — The Sabbath.

shaila — shy-loh. "Question." A query about religious practice. The answer is called a *t'shuva*. The literature of shailas and t'shuvas of eminent jurists forms an important part of Hebrew law study.

Shalakh Manos — "The sending of gifts." One of the ceremonies of Purim.

shamas, properly *shamash* — "One who serves." The sexton of a synagogue, generally responsible for the sacred properties and the smooth running of the services.

shatnaze — A mixture of linen and wool in clothing, banned by Mosaic law.

Shavuos — "Weeks." The feast of Pentecost, the conclusion of the seven weeks of *Sefira* (see p. 342), fifty days after the second day of Passover. Also called the holiday of the Giving of the Law, since the time coincides with the revelation at Sinai.

sheitel — shy-tell. The wig worn by women in the ghetto, adopted by some devout women of the present day in modish transformations.

Shiva — "Seven." The first week of mourning after a death.

Shloshim — sh'loe-shim. "Thirty." The first month of mourning after a death, which includes *Shiva*.

Sh'ma — "Hear." The creed of Judaism, Deuteronomy 6:4: "Hear O Israel, the Lord our God, the Lord is One."

Sh'mini Atzeres — "Eighth Day, Final Assembly." The concluding holy day of the Sukos harvest feast, in which the rites of hut, palm branch, and fruit are not observed.

Shmone Esrai — sh'moe-neh ess-ray. "The Eighteen." The central service of the Jewish liturgy, recited three times daily, four times on Sabbaths and holy days, five times on Yom Kippur. Also called the *Amidah,* or Standing Prayer, because one recites it on one's feet, and *Tefilah,* or "The Prayer" par excellence.

shofar — A ram's horn, blown in the synagogue as part of the High Holy Day ritual.

shohet — A trained ritual slaughter of fowl and cattle.

Shulkhan Arukh — "The Ready Table." The authoritative code (with its many commentaries) of present-day Hebrew law, composed by Joseph Caro (see pp. 199–200).

Simkhas Torah — "Rejoicing Over the Law." A jubilant observance that marks the conclusion of the annual reading of the Torah, and the commencement at once at the beginning. In the diaspora a separate day, the second day of *Sh'mini Atzeres* (see above). In Israel part of *Sh'mini Atzeres.*

Suda — seu-da. "Banquet." Specifically, the feast that is part of Purim day; also any festive meal marking a religious occasion.

suko — A hut or booth — the archaic word is tabernacle — in which Jews observe the autumn feast of Tabernacles.

Sukos — The harvest feast of Tabernacles, commencing on the full moon of autumn and running eight days (nine outside Israel).

tallis — A prayer shawl with the fringes (*tzitzis*) prescribed by Mosaic law.

Tammuz — Tenth month of the Hebrew calendar, falling in summertime.

Tanna'im — "Teachers." The jurists whose decisions are recorded in the Mishna and associated legal literature of the four centuries from 200 B.C.E. to A.D. 200.

Targum — "Translation." Specifically, translations in Aramaic of the Scriptures, the most famous being the Targum on the Pentateuch written by the convert Onkelos.

tefillin — "Phylacteries" (see p. 121).

Tisha B'Av — The ninth day of the month Av, Judaism's national day of mourning, marking the destruction of the two Temples.

Tosephos — "Additions." A running commentary on the Talmud composed mainly by *Rishonim* (see p. 342) of France, Spain, and Germany.

trefe — trayf. "Torn." Meat inedible under Jewish law, the opposite of *kosher.* By extension, any flaw in religious preparation or practice.

t'shuva — "Return." Repentance; also the answer of an authority to a religious query.

Vilna Gaon — Elijah ben Solomon Zalman, 1720–1797, also known as Elijah or Eliahu of Vilna, and in learned circles as *"Ha'Gra."* He was the preeminent Gaon of the vanished Polish-Lithuanian-Russian Jewry known as *Litvaks,* destroyed by the German massacres of 1939–1945. The Vilna Gaon mastered the secular sciences as well as the Cabala, and raised Talmudic studies to a level of subtle excellence which remains the standard to this day. The term "Gaon" means genius.

yahrzeit — Yiddish "year time," from the German. Anniversary of a death, when *kaddish* (see p. 340) is recited.

yarmulka — Skullcap worn by observant Jews.

Yiddishkeit — from the German and Yiddish, "Jewishness." A term covering the traditional culture of observant European Jewry.